Dear Reader:

The book you are about to read is the latest bestseller from the St. Martin's True Crime Library, the imprint the *New York Times* calls "the leader in true crime!" Each month, we offer you a fascinating account of the latest, most sensational crime that has captured the national attention. St. Martin's is the publisher of bestselling true crime author and crime journalist Kieran Crowley, who explores the dark, deadly links between a prominent Manhattan surgeon and the disappearance of his wife fifteen years earlier in THE SURGEON'S WIFE. Suzy Spencer's BREAKING POINT guides readers through the tortuous twists and turns in the case of Andrea Yates, the Houston mother who drowned her five young children in the family's bathtub. In Edgar Award-nominated DARK DREAMS, legendary FBI profiler Roy Hazelwood and bestselling crime author Stephen G. Michaud shine light on the inner workings of America's most violent and depraved muderers. In the book you now hold, THE PALM BEACH MURDER, Marion Collins looks at a world of money, privilege, murder—and a search for justice that goes halfway around the globe.

St. Martin's True Crime Library gives you the stories behind the headlines. Our authors take you right to the scene of the crime and into the minds of the most notorious murderers to show you what really makes them tick. St. Martin's True Crime Library paperbacks are better than the most terrifying thriller, because it's all true! The next time you want a crackling good read, make sure it's got the St. Martin's True Crime Library logo on the spine—you'll be up all night!

Charles E. Spicer, Jr.
Executive Editor, St. Martin's True Crime Library

At 8:15 A.M. the doorbell on the Buckhead townhouse rang. Lita opened an upstairs window. She peered down on a scruffy-looking individual with thinning hair and a flower box under his left arm. "What is it?" she asked.

"Flower delivery, ma'am," he called back.

"Okay, I'll be right down," she told him. When she unlocked the door, he thrust the box at her. "You need to sign for them," he said. Lita told him, "Come in, I'll find a pen." He followed her into the foyer, the door partly closing behind him. Seconds later, three shots rang out.

TITLES BY MARION COLLINS

Without a Trace

The Palm Beach Murder

FROM THE TRUE CRIME LIBRARY
OF ST. MARTIN'S PAPERBACKS

The Palm Beach
MURDER

MARION COLLINS

St. Martin's Paperbacks

THE PALM BEACH MURDER

Copyright © 2004 by Marion Collins.

Cover photograph of Palm Beach courtesy Corbis Royalty Free. Photograph of James Sullivan courtesy AP/Wide World Photos.

ISBN: 0-312-99086-3
EAN: 80312-99086-2

Printed in the United States of America

St. Martin's Paperbacks edition / July 2004

10 9 8 7 6 5 4 3 2 1

Acknowledgments

Thanks to Malcolm Balfour and Cliff Linedecker for generously handing over their copious files, to Brad Moores, Pat McKenna and David Ritchie for their practical help, to John Connolly for revisiting his groundbreaking article in "Spy," to Jane Podd for her letters from Thailand, and to everyone who shared their memories of Lita McClinton and Jim Sullivan, most especially, JoAnn and Valencia McClinton.

ONE
Dateline: Thailand

In just two days it would be July Fourth and no American was savoring his liberty more than James Sullivan, the Massachusetts-born millionaire whose face currently decorated walls in post offices from Maine to California. Was he chuckling to himself as he lit a fat stogie and shifted his feet onto the railing of the balcony of his luxurious seaside digs? Did the dumb cops and the flat-footed Feds who had been chasing him really think he would ever spend another hour behind bars? Heck, he had been in court more times than they'd had sex with the missus. A man picks up a thing or two about the wheels of justice that way.

From the day his beautiful and politically connected black wife was shot fifteen years before, ending an ultimately socially inconvenient marriage seemingly motivated by his desire and the thrill of flouting convention, they had been trying to nail him, and he had cheated them of their ounce of flesh at every turn. Sometimes he had gotten lucky, like when the judge in Atlanta, wringing his hands at the unfairness of it all, had reluctantly thrown out charges that he had paid $25,000 to a bunch of goons to kill her; other times he had just plain outsmarted the posse of police and FBI agents who had been on his tail since the murder warrant was finally issued in 1998. And when they began to close in on him, he had dug into his deep pockets and bought his way out.

The indictment announcement had been made on the steps of the Fulton County Courthouse in Atlanta by a district attorney, puffed up with his own power and relishing his fifteen minutes of fame in the glare of press cameras and TV lights. Well, he was a day late and way more than a dollar short, Sullivan probably thought as he idly amused himself by flicking ash onto an insect crawling up the leg of his chair. By the time the lawman was banging on about "bringing him to trial," Sullivan was thousands of miles away, hunkered down in a posh little resort in Thailand, where even a killer could easily disappear.

Not that his wanted status was anything new. Since 1987, he had been the prime suspect in the assassination of 35-year-old Lita, who had skipped down the stairs of her expensive Atlanta townhouse on a damp January morning expecting an armful of roses, and was blown away by a cold-blooded killer.

Right from the start, the cops were convinced that Jim Sullivan was their man. Lita's death was just too damned convenient. They were embroiled in a bitter divorce; she was murdered just hours before crucial financial details were to be thrashed out in court resulting in what everyone—including Jim Sullivan—expected to be a generous settlement for Lita. With her out of the picture, not only was he free to marry his exotic young lover, he would hang on to every last cent of his $5 million fortune and the spectacular Palm Beach mansion that was the launching pad for his social ambitions.

But thoughts of his long-dead wife were a million miles away from Sullivan that balmy July day. At 61, he had chiseled features, piercing hazel eyes and a shock of wavy hair that had faded from auburn to peppery gray. He was still in good shape, thanks to a strict regimen of daily workouts and a healthy diet. There was not a spare ounce of flesh on his toned frame and he was, his wealth notwithstanding, still attractive to the ladies.

Life had been good in his sunlit paradise during the four years since he'd gone into hiding, one step ahead of the Feds. He had already weathered a trial on a lesser charge, then lost, won and lost again two years later in a civil case brought by Emory and JoAnn McClinton, his unrelenting former in-laws. But now the thug who'd pulled the trigger was in an Atlanta jail, singing like a canary to save his own miserable skin, and the song he was warbling fingered Sullivan; the lethal injection once reserved for the gunman had Jim's name on it.

Sullivan had foiled every attempt to track him down. Every time the cops came close, he had slipped through the net and turned up in another country. In 1998, his continent-hopping spree—which had bounced him to South America, then Europe and Asia—had ended in his easy anonymity in Thailand. Even his love life had survived the chase. At his side was his chic Thai-born fiancée, Chongwattana Sricharoenmuang, the former Palm Beach divorcée Chongwattana (Nana) Reynolds, who had been married to a local basketball coach when Sullivan had stolen her away with promises to make her his fourth wife. His new digs in the Springfield Resort cost four million bahts (US $128,000). A three-hour, air-conditioned coach trip from the capital of Bangkok, it was domestic bliss.

While the pathetic cops went home to their dull wives, struggling to pay their mortgages and worrying about how they would put the kids through school, he was lord and master of a luxurious 1,453-square-foot condominium overlooking the sparkling turquoise Gulf of Thailand, his bank accounts bulging. Honest to God, it must have made him laugh himself silly just to think about it.

Sullivan had landed in paradise. Cha-am is a short ride from Khao Sam Roi Yot (Mountain of 300 Peaks) National Park, a veritable wonderland of forested hills, deep valleys, gushing waterfalls, caves, white sandy beaches, dense mangrove swamps and peaceful coves; its sister town, Hua Hin, is Thailand's oldest beach resort, where Thai royalty spend their vacations. A little farther south is the province's capital, Prachuap Khiri Khan, and the Mirror Mount Beach where a troop of playful monkeys capers around their own pagoda. Forty miles to the north is the old town of Phetchaburi with its superb ancient temples, and Phra Nakhon Khiri, the 19th century hilltop palace of King Mongkut.

He whiled away the days of his self-imposed exile contemplating the ocean from his frond-fringed terrace, strolling along the pristine shore, grocery shopping in his snappy metallic blue 525i series BMW and keeping his rigid lunchtime appointment at the hotel gym. He was also careful to adopt a low profile, rarely venturing far from the peach-colored complex protected by security gates and uniformed guards who patrolled its boundaries to assure the privacy and safety of the affluent residents. He and Nana occupied a spacious two-bedroom unit behind a row of swaying palms that provided welcome shade from the hot Asian sun, and fluttered in the cooling sea breezes that fanned him in the evenings as he lay sprawled in a lounger, puffing contentedly on a cigar.

The only times he was in danger of blowing his cover was when his short fuse was lit. On weekends and holidays the resort would fill with crowds partying late into the night accompanied by loud music, exploding fireworks and revving car engines. This rude invasion of his tranquil solitude would propel him from bed, to rage red-faced, at the revelers.

But on this particular Tuesday, as he prepared to join in America's annual celebration of shucking the colonial yoke with his lover, hot dogs and a few beers, he had no idea that his own freedom was about to end. A few weeks before, the FBI agents who had dogged his trail since he went on the lam had received a tip that had them rubbing their hands in glee.

One of his new neighbors was a fan of *America's Most Wanted*, the weekly TV series that has helped put hundreds of felons behind bars. On May 4, 2002, the show profiled the unsolved case of Lita Sullivan and her millionaire husband, who had fled the country taking his fortune with him. Sullivan's neighbor stared at the mug shot on his screen. "That's him!" he yelled. "That's the guy who lives here at the Springfield Resort." He picked up the phone and dialed the number on the screen. In minutes he was talking to the United States Embassy in Bangkok.

The Embassy called the FBI. Back in December, the bureau had posted Sullivan's mug on their "Most Wanted" Web site and had just received another tip, also from Thailand, from someone who was trolling the Internet and thought they recognized his picture.

Agents immediately started extradition negotiations with the Thai authorities, who agreed to put him under surveillance. At first, the young cops watching him were not sure they had the right guy; he looked much too old to be the man in the FBI photo. For nearly two months they clocked his every movement and reported back to the Americans. Despite their early doubts, they had found James Sullivan.

On July 2, word came from Bangkok authorities to pick him up. Heavily armed Thai police surrounded the building. Sullivan and his fiancée had just returned from a leisurely evening stroll and were in the kitchen preparing dinner when there was a sharp rap at the door. Forty-four-year old Chongwattana reached for the knob just as the door was kicked open and five stony-faced cops burst in. "James Sullivan? You are under arrest. We have a court order to search your apartment," Captain Noui-pin, the officer in charge of the raid, barked at him in flawless English.

Stunned, Sullivan sank down on his bed where he sat in silent disbelief as they swarmed all over the apartment, emptying drawers and rifling through closets. "He was caught completely off-guard," said Noui-pin. "He didn't resist, but he began to sweat all over." Jim had been so sure he was home free in Thailand that he had even printed "Nana and James Sullivan" on a scrap of white paper and stuck it on the front door. Now he watched helplessly as they piled his meticulously kept financial records and journals into boxes—he knew their contents would tell those damn McClintons where he had hidden his wealth.

Chongwattana swore she'd had no idea that her lover was wanted for the murder of his wife. She reportedly told Noui-pin that they had lived secretively because she did not want her former husband to find out she was living with Sullivan. She collapsed in tears as he was led away in handcuffs and stuffed unceremoniously into a police van. They had planned to spend the rest of their days in their seaside heaven.

Sullivan's long run was over. In the years since Lita was so callously slain, he had steadfastly maintained he had nothing to do with her death. When the cops dug up crucial evidence in the shape of an accomplice who ratted him out to save his own neck, Sullivan had used his millions to flee. He had led the police and the FBI on a chase across the globe, but here, in Thailand, it had all come crashing down. With his arrest, James Vincent Sullivan became the 715th suspect tracked down by *America's Most Wanted*.

Back in Atlanta, Lita's parents clung together and cried with relief. Their ex–son-in-law was locked up in a Thai jail and the American authorities vowed to bring him home to face justice. "Jolly good," Lita's father, Emory McClinton, said in a massive understatement. Lita's sister Valencia describes their exhilaration: "We had champagne. I told my parents, 'We are going to enjoy every day he is incarcerated.'"

While the McClintons rejoiced, Sullivan spent his first night in a very uncomfortable cell. He had been required to swap his dapper khakis and freshly-pressed shirt for stained orange and rust-colored prison scrubs that consisted of a baggy pullover top and even baggier shorts. The other inmates had bare feet and sandals. Sullivan, the only Caucasian in the holding cell built for twenty prisoners but currently crammed with fifty other luckless alleged felons, was an incongruous misfit with his pale freckled legs peeping out between the end of the pants and his long black dress socks. On his feet were a sorry-looking pair of scuffed brown shoes.

As word of Sullivan's arrest hit the airwaves, Thai police Colonel Somchai Yoklek met with reporters. "James Sullivan's arrest was requested by the FBI, and today he was arrested in Cha-am," he confirmed. "The next day, Major General Surasit Sangkhaphong, who heads the Crime Suppression Division in Bangkok, said that Sullivan would be held in custody while the Foreign Ministry organized extradition proceedings to return him to the United States to face trial for the contract murder of Lita McClinton Sullivan.

When Sullivan's first wife Catherine, thousands of miles away at her home in Cape Cod, heard that her former husband was in a Thai jail, she heaved a sigh of relief. For thirty years, she had lived in fear of what she knew about him, and of what he might do to her and their children if she ever got in his way. "I didn't think he would ever get caught," she told *The Atlanta Journal-Constitution.* "I thought he was way too smart."

TWO
A Match Made In Hell

Sullivan may have been enjoying the lifestyle of the idle rich when he was nabbed by Thai police, but his first steps were taken in the harsher world of Dorchester, the working class suburb on the south side of Boston.

His father, James Sullivan, Sr., worked as a typesetter for the Hearst-owned newspaper the Boston *Record American*, which later morphed into the tabloid *Boston Herald* in 1981. Caroline, his homemaker mother, who ruled over her family in their modest home on Morton Street, was a God-fearing pillar of St. Gregory's parish. Jim, the oldest of the three Sullivan children, arrived on April 5, 1941, and was followed by his brother, Francis, two years later; the baby of the brood, Rosemary, was born in 1950.

Determined that the rougher element in their hardscrabble blue-collar neighborhood would not interfere with her ambitions for her youngsters, Caroline turned to religion for help in keeping them on the right path. Her uncle, Edward Murray, was a rising star in the Church and had studied at the Vatican. As a devout Catholic, she entrusted the children's early education to St. Gregory's parochial school.

In 1954, Jim passed the entrance exam for acceptance to the academically tough Boston Latin School, where all the cleverest kids in the area vied for a coveted place. Admission to the school provided the first rung on the ladder to a professional career and, if you hit the books and kept out of trouble, it was a ticket across the tracks to a better life. Despite the school's high scholastic standards and rigorous discipline, Sullivan sailed through high school, graduating in 1958. In the yearbook, beside the picture that showed him as a freckle-faced youth with a mop of Titian curls, the accompanying tagline signaled young Jim Sullivan's intention of being noticed: "May his future be as glorious as his past," it read.

An amiable kid with an irrepressible grin, "Sully," as he was known to his classmates, was a hall monitor, a golf team and weightlifting club member and was on the staff of both the school magazine and the yearbook. He played in the school orchestra and sang in the choir.

"He was a redheaded, nice-looking kid, a classic Latin School kid. He came from a decent family without much money—we are not talking real poor or anything," says Fred Markey, the former executive director of the Boston Latin School Alumni Association. "It is a tough place. You had to study two or three hours a night, so it was a discipline thing. But if you get through there, you can pretty much go on to any college you want. I remember Jim was in the gun club." Young Jim was also bright enough to cope with the exacting academics. "Two thirds of the kids that got into the school flunked out."

Mike Kelly was one of his classmates. "He seemed normal, neat and nice-looking. I'd say he was a more obvious striver than other kids. But he thought he deserved some special recognition because, according to him, his uncle was a bishop." It seems Sully "adopted" Bishop John Wright of Worcester into his family. Wright, to all accounts, was a brilliant and charismatic preacher with links to the school, but he was no relation. This was possibly the first of what would become a long list of the lies and exaggerations that Sullivan trotted out throughout his adult life.

Like most working-class families, the Sullivans were frequently strapped for cash, but when it came time for college, young Jim was able to help himself, qualifying for a scholarship to the Jesuit College of the Holy Cross in Worcester to study economics. Although he was still a good student, keeping his grade point average up was not always his first priority; like all teenagers, he was a mess of raging hormones.

Catherine Murray, known to her family and friends as "Cappy," was 16 when she met Jim. They were introduced by her Uncle Edward, who was then a parish priest at the church in Roslindale where Jim was an altar boy. He was already honing the charm that would later prove so compelling to women, and the smitten Catherine had no defenses. She found him irresistible. "What did I see in him? What does any 16-year-old see in anyone? Jim is very charming," she once said.

Before long their puppy love blossomed into a full-fledged teen romance. They spent summers at her family's vacation cottage in Nantusket Beach, the pretty little seaside town that was the first playground of the Kennedys. It endured through the seemingly endless semesters apart when he went back to Holy Cross and she was at Boston College School of Nursing. Ann Mulligan met the lovebirds when they were all in high school.

"My best friend was Cappy's older sister, Joyce, and Cappy was a couple of years behind me in college. She was a very bright girl, but Jim, he was never a guy I was fond of. He was like Eddie Haskell in *Leave It to Beaver*, very personable, very nice and he was always rubbing you the wrong way," she remembers.

Cappy's family life was far from a happy TV sitcom scenario, says Fred Markey. "Her father John [Jack] Murray had terrible booze problems which kind of descended on to his girls. I don't know if Cappy was a boozer, but Joyce drank and the other sister drank too. Their father was a very, very smart guy, but he was screwed up with alcohol. I always remember him being down in Center Street in Roxbury getting the paper in his pajamas."

Jim graduated Holy Cross in 1962 and was met with a rude awakening. Despite his respectable academic record, he found that a degree in economics was not an automatic pass to the good life. His first job was in the comptroller's office at the Boston department store Jordan March, and while he was thankful to be earning a steady wage, he found the work tedious. Setting his sights higher, he applied for a position with the accounting firm of Peat Marwick and enrolled in night classes at Boston University to study for a master's degree in finance. He completed a year of graduate school before dropping out.

He was just 24 when he and Catherine married in 1965. Ann Mulligan and her husband Joseph, who had been a year ahead of Jim at Holy Cross, were invited to the large family wedding at the Sacred Heart Church in Roslindale. "They had the whole works and Cappy was a beautiful white bride," she says.

The newlyweds quickly settled into a life of domesticity in a quiet part of Boston. Four children, Dierdre,

James, Jr., Laura and Marcus, arrived in almost as many years, and although the details of Jim's work were a mystery to Catherine, she had few complaints. Jim was a good enough provider and they lived in comparative comfort. His mother's efforts to raise him according to her faith had paid off; he had become a hardworking family man with a large and lively brood to support. Uncle Edward kept a fatherly eye on his young protégé.

But Catherine doubted that the role of a solid Christian husband and dad would be enough for Jim. Preoccupied though she was with raising her children, she sensed the restless ambition that stirred within her husband. She also began to suspect that whatever plans he was making for his future, she and the kids were not going to be included in the grand scheme. Her only role in his life was as the mother of his kids; he did not confide in her or ask for her opinion. "I knew he needed me to bring up our four children, and he knew that I knew," she later said.

Who knows how long their increasingly uneasy truce might have lasted had their lives not changed overnight? In 1974, Sullivan's wealthy uncle made him an offer so appealing, he would have been a fool to turn it down. Frank Bienert owned Crown Beverages, Inc., a distribution link in the massive Seagram's liquor empire in Macon, Georgia. Business was flourishing, but at 64, Frank was getting tired of the daily grind and wanted to retire. He had a wife, two brothers and two sisters, but no children. With no sons (or daughters, for that matter) to follow him into the family firm, he had been keeping an eye on his bright young nephew, and in him, he saw the solution to his problems.

Jim was a go-getter with a good education in finance behind him and had a personable manner that could only help when dealing with customers. He seemed to be a stable sort of guy—at 33 he had been married for nine years to a sensible wife, and he had a small tribe of youngsters to feed, which alone should have ensured that he turned up on time every day, Frank reasoned. Jim would surely be grateful for the opportunity Frank was dangling before him. The plan was for Jim to do the heavy lifting for a couple of years so Frank could take it easy, then, if the lad made a success of the job, his uncle would leave the whole kit and caboodle to him.

Jim jumped at the offer. His potential earnings with Crown Beverages made the $24,000 a year that Peat Marwick was paying him seen like chump change. But he was not the pushover Uncle Frank might have expected. In exchange for relocating to Georgia and learning the beer distributorship business from the ground up, he demanded a minority share in the company and insisted on being named as Bienert's sole heir from the outset.

At first Frank balked at his nephew's demands, but there really was no one else on the horizon, and he admired Jim's tenacity; his hard-nosed approach would stand him in good stead as future owner. After months of wrangling, they shook hands on a deal. Jim was to get a 10 percent share of the company on moving to Macon, and that figure would increase, over time, to 48 percent. On Frank's death, Jim would inherit the business outright.

Catherine was a harder sell. She had no desire to uproot her young children from the only home they had ever known and move so far away from her family and friends to a state where she knew no one. But as the negotiations between Jim and his uncle picked up steam, she knew that if she wanted to keep him, she had little choice in the matter. "Our money will go further in Macon," he had said. "We will be able to afford a bigger house." Despite her misgivings, she reluctantly gave in. True to his word, Jim found them a spacious home, and while she looked for schools for the youngsters, her husband set about learning how to be a boss.

Sherri Davis was the office manager. She was just 19 when she was hired and Sullivan was already beginning to flex his managerial muscles. "He was there when I started," she says. "I went to work at Crown Beverages in 1974 and was there for ten years; for nine of those I worked for Jim." Sherri says she liked working for the younger man, he was friendly and flirtatious with her, whereas his elderly uncle had struck her as somewhat cold and offhanded. "Frank Bienert was intimidating, he never talked to me and it was much easier after Jim arrived. He was very charming, very intelligent and real good with statistics. He knew a little about lots of things."

But if Sherri enjoyed the more relaxed attitude around the office, Frank was less happy about the transition. His aggressively ambitious nephew soon made it plain he had scant respect for the way the company was run. Worse, as the designated owner, he ran roughshod over some of the longtime employees who bitterly resented the interloper from the north. He may have had the same accent and the same easy Irish charm as the legendary Kennedys, but this Bostonian had a nasty side which he unleashed increasingly often on the help. He treated them like dimwitted Southern hicks and unsurprisingly, many of them grew to loathe him.

Catherine, too, was growing increasingly unhappy. She hated Macon, rarely saw her husband and suspected him of cheating on her. As the year wore on, Bienert had soured on his arrogant nephew and, according to some of Bienert's former employees, openly lamented his decision to leave his business to him. It was clear everyone needed a break.

Just before Christmas, Jim and Catherine and the kids took off for Boston to spend the holidays with their families back east. While Jim was gone, Frank reportedly came to a decision: Jim was just not working out. Frank had grown to heartily dislike him; he knew there would have to be a showdown, however unpleasant the consequences, when Jim returned. According to published reports, Frank's plan was to tell him that, unless there were some radical overnight changes, he should start looking for another job.

On January 3, Jim flew back to Macon. Later that day, Frank was downtown in the warehouse when he was stricken by a seemingly mysterious illness. Overwhelmed by sudden gut-wrenching cramps, he collapsed on top of some crates of liquor where he was found by a couple of stockmen. Luckily for him, they discovered him before they closed up for the night. The building was in an industrial zone and largely uninhabited after the end of the working day. He could have lain there for hours, maybe until the next morning, and nobody would have heard his cries for help.

The poor man spent a miserable night flitting between his bed and the bathroom, racked with pain, nausea and vomiting. The next morning he was no better. Unfortunately for Frank, his wife, Agnes, was a committed Christian Scientist with an unshakable conviction that whatever ailed him, only God in His infinite mercy could save him.

For five days, he suffered stoically until he could bear it no more. When he could no longer deny that Agnes' hours of prayer had gone unnoticed by the Lord, he managed to drag himself to a phone and call for help. Jim met the ambulance at the hospital. A few hours later, Frank Bienert, who hitherto had enjoyed the constitution of an ox, expired at age 65. The attending doctor noted the cause of death as cardiac arrest. Without further ado, Jim signed for the body and had it shipped back to Boston, where it was reportedly cremated the following day.

Why Jim was in such a rush to dispose of Uncle Frank's remains, and why there was no investigation into the puzzling death, have never been fully explained. Bienert was a strong, healthy man, whom had never taken a sick day in his life. Yet no autopsy was performed and no one at the coroner's office seemed to think it suspicious that his nephew, who inherited a multimillion-dollar business as soon as the old man stopped breathing, was in charge of the funeral arrangements, given that his widow was still in the picture.

Also evident to all concerned was Jim's lack of grief over the tragic death of a man who had not only been his uncle, but his benefactor. Recounting the tale to writer John Connolly, Jim said: "After I was there [at Crown Beverages] only ten months, the fat old bastard keeled over from a heart attack, right onto a pallet of vodka."

Anyone sniffing around the plant would have found out what Connolly readily discovered years later: that as early as December 1974, everyone knew Jim was going to be fired. Frank Bienert had even put his decision in writing and had planned to confront him on January 10, when Jim returned from his Christmas vacation. The letter of dismissal, which Connolly says ran several pages long and included several drafts, was a damning indictment of his ungrateful nephew's shortcomings and obnoxious attitude. In it, he characterized Jim's business management practices as "the worst I have ever experienced, and [ones that] are leading to chaos."

According to Connolly, the statement went on: "You have not carried your weight, earned your keep or made our lives easier, better or happier for your coming here. On the contrary, you have made things harder for just about everyone and have put a serious and undue strain upon me and my family's well-being. Further, you have shown little reciprocity, appreciation or constructive response and action. You have made our relationship a one-way street—your direction only. In short, you haven't been a good relation. We expected much more." And while Bienert had not gotten around to firing him outright, Connolly says, he had told his attorney, Ellsworth Hall, Jr., to write his nephew out of his will. Uncle Frank died before the revision was made.

The lack of an official inquiry did not stamp out the rumors that were rife at Crown Beverages, according to Sherri Davis. "When Frank died, we all suspected Jim from the beginning. Frank's friend Joe Cohen asked about an autopsy and found that Frank had been shipped back to Boston or wherever he came from. Everyone suspected Jim killed his uncle, but there was no police investigation at the time," she says.

The insinuation that somehow Frank had not died from natural causes filtered back to Massachusetts. "I always wondered, was there an errant gene and here's the opportunity? You don't care what you do," says Fred Markey. But either the buzz that he had helped his uncle through the Pearly Gates never reached Jim's ears, or he just ignored it. With no cops hanging around asking awkward questions, why should he care? He was now king of all he surveyed—not only did the lucrative Crown Beverages, Inc., belong to him, he also stood to inherit Frank's lavish 12-acre Macon estate on the death of Agnes. All he had to do was pay her rent for the company building, as per the instructions in his uncle's will.

When the initial rumblings died down, the old man's death should have signaled better times for Jim's marriage; his financial future was now secured and as the new owner, he could afford to hire a manager and spend with his wife and children. Yet as soon as she was in the position to enjoy a life of comparative ease as the boss's wife, Catherine made a seemingly inexplicable move of her own. Ten days after her husband came into his fortune, she moved out. He could keep Macon, she told him, she was going back to Boston. "Money doesn't make you happy," she warned him as she headed out the door.

As soon as she returned to Massachusetts, she filed for divorce and found a home for herself and the kids in Hingham. She also got a taste of what was to become her husband's tight-fisted approach to ex-wives. In what was a truly woeful settlement, she received the sum of $10,293, the three-year-old family Chevy Chenille station wagon and custody of the children. Their father, who had just inherited a multimillion-dollar business, claimed he earned just $24,000 a year. He was ordered to pay the paltry sum of $1,000 a month in child support. Then he told Catherine she had better pull Dierdre out of private school because he had no intention of footing the bill.

Cappy's acceptance of the situation is barely comprehensible. If she had gone back to court and spilled the beans about her ex-husband's new status as a millionaire, no judge in the land would have denied her a hefty increase in child support, and would probably have thrown in some alimony for her while he was at it.

"As far as I know, he did nothing for his children," says Markey, "yet she never went after him."

Ann Mulligan remembers that for years, Catherine could barely make ends meet. "The kids were in private school and then all of a sudden, she had nothing from him whatsoever. We were outraged [by his callousness towards his children]. I remember Joyce saying, 'He is just a mean guy. You just got to look at his business, yet what did he send up to the kids for birthday presents? One of those things that are handed out as ads, like a coke bottle balloon or something.'"

If Sullivan was at all upset at the breakup of his marriage to Catherine and the virtual loss of his children, he kept it to himself. Anyway, he had already set his sights on the lovely young woman who was to become his next wife.

Lita LaVaughn McClinton was just 23 when Jim Sullivan first hit on her. Fresh from Spelman College, where she'd made the dean's list, the sweet-natured beauty with a model-girl figure was working as an assistant buyer at T. Edwards, a fancy boutique in Atlanta's Lenox Square Mall, and had moved into her own apartment. If her politically connected parents had any regret that she did not want to follow them into public service, they kept it to themselves. Lita was resolved to make a career for herself in fashion, and they were not about to stymie her dreams by lecturing her about social responsibility. "I don't know whether my parents thought it was frivolous or arty. Probably both, knowing them," says Valenica. "But she loved her job and she was very good at it, and they'd be like, it's frivolous unless you pursue it to the ultimate level and become a buyer."

Marriage was the last thing on Lita's mind when Jim Sullivan walked into the store to buy a coat for a girlfriend. Spotting the pretty black girl behind the counter, he sidled over. "I'm looking for a gift," he told her. As she looked for outfits he might like, he watched her appreciatively. Newly single at 33, he was definitely interested, and turned on his considerable, if oily, charm for her benefit. Lita was not unflattered. To her unworldly eyes, he was quite handsome in his own way. Slim and fit at 5'9", his Irish-pale face was topped by the worst haircut she had ever seen; his dress sense was nil, though there was definite room for improvement, she thought. But what struck her most forcibly were his intense hazel eyes. They were mesmerizing; they seemed to stare into her very soul.

"She came home one night and told me she had met someone in the store, he was very nice and polite," says her mother. "He came back and asked her to go to an [Atlanta] Hawks game with him. She didn't know anything about the Hawks, so she took a family friend along."

That first date turned into a second, and a third, and soon they were a serious item. The McClintons, who were accustomed to vetting their daughters' boyfriends, suggested she bring him home. "When we first met him he had a broken leg, from a skiing accident, I think," says JoAnn. He chose loud red polyester pants for the occasion and ugly black horn-rimmed glasses obscured his eyes. But if their daughter was enraptured by the urbane wit and banter of her sophisticated new boyfriend, her parents were unmoved. "He had a way of bowling you over," says her mother. "He wined and dined her and knew how to turn a young girl's head." They pretty much hated him.

For a start, they were convinced that, just shy of 34, he was way too mature for her. Secondly, after his initial attempts to ingratiate himself, he came across as a phony, a supercilious know-it-all who could not resist blowing his own trumpet, maintains Emory, who saw through his transparently obvious future son-in-law from the get-go. "It was always 'I did this, I did that.'"

To JoAnn, Jim was simply devoid of manners. "Usually when parents walk into a room, most young men stand up. Jim did not respond as quickly as we thought he should have. Maybe he didn't think it was necessary—he was nearer our age than Lita's," she says. He was also maniacally competitive. He took up tennis to challenge Emory, who was a good player, and tried in vain to beat him; because Emory drove a red Rolls-Royce, Jim had to have one too.

Despite her parents' foreboding, the romance went full steam ahead. Jim showered Lita with expensive gifts and took her on lavish dates. JoAnn and Emory kept silent about their true feelings, hoping their daughter would grow tired of Jim. Not only did they not like him, they were not totally comfortable with the fact that he was white and their daughter was black. They knew that, even with the best will in the world, an interracial marriage in the heart of Dixie would be paved with difficulties, and they fretted over the prejudice their daughter was bound to face if the relationship became permanent.

If Jim sensed their misgivings, he ignored them. His pursuit of Lita was relentless, says JoAnn. "It was as if she was a prize and he was determined to get her. She knew we didn't particularly care for him; he was from Macon and Macon did not have a good reputation in dealing with an integrated situation." His reticence about his own family history prompted Emory to mutter, "We don't even know him."

But a year after he first swept into her life, it was plain that Lita was crazy about the man she spent every free moment commuting the ninety miles between Macon and Atlanta to see. One night, she turned up wanting to talk to her mother. "I can't remember whether she told me, 'I want to marry Jim,' or 'Jim wants to marry me,' but anyway, I didn't react immediately, I waited a day or two and then discussed it with her father," says JoAnn.

"All hell broke loose. Emory said, 'No, and that's it!' For the next week, Lita was in tears. My husband and son were steadfast in their opposition to any wedding. There were arguments, there was screaming—my husband did the screaming, Lita never screamed at her father. I remember one awful breakfast where I was in tears, Lita was in tears and Valencia's nose was red, she was so upset for Lita."

"My parents were immediately, 'Oh, he's way too old.' I didn't think that. Parents think differently from siblings," says Valencia. "He was very nice around me. I just figured he was in love with her and she was in love with him."

The standoff went on for a week or longer, JoAnn says, before she tackled Emory again. " 'She's an adult, she's living on her own and doing well,' I told him. I urged him to think of her happiness, to imagine how unhappy would I have been if my parents had interfered between us. I just wanted Lita to be happy. Emory was never convinced, but eventually he caved in. While all this was going on, we did not see Jim. I think Lita advised him to stay away."

Faced with her steely determination, they relented; after all, the happiness of their daughter was paramount. If she truly loved him, well, they would just have to accept him, welcome him into the family with open arms and pray that he truly loved her, too. But their hearts grew heavy with misgivings. They were still mightily offended by the way their daughter's prospective groom had handled the impending marriage: where they came from, a young girl was not left to tell her parents she was engaged; Jim Sullivan should have come to them like a true gentleman would have done.

She was the apple of their eyes. The oldest of their three children, Lita was beautiful and clever. "She was very bright and pretty and liked dressing up, loved fashion and clothes," says Valencia who now owns a successful vintage clothing store, Aisle 5, on North Decatur Road. "I was the exact opposite. I was a slob, I wore blue jeans all the time, or a mini skirt that I was only allowed to wear with thick black tights. My father was always saying, 'You are not going out in that!' The only time I was dressed up is when mom was buying our clothes. She used to take us to this great store called Snooty Hooty to get outfits for special occasions like Thanksgiving or Christmas when jeans were definitely not allowed. Lita was always the center of attention because she had a real bubbly personality. We were very different, I had one close friend in elementary school and one in high school; Lita had five, six, seven girls around her."

Lita had excelled at the parochial schools she attended, graduating from St. Pius X High School in 1970. She attended Spelman College, where her best friend was Poppy Findley, and left four years later with a bachelor's degree in political science, a course that made perfect sense for a girl who had grown up in a socially active family and thought of becoming a lawyer. Andrew Young, President Jimmy Carter's U.S. Ambassador to the United Nations and later president of the National Council of Churches, was a visitor to the

McClinton home, as was Congressman Charles Weltner, who later became Chief Justice of the Georgia Supreme court.

Emory was then head of the regional civil rights office of the U.S. Department of Transportation, and JoAnn was active in the local Democratic Party, the NAACP, the Urban League and the Urban League Guild. Since 1992, she has represented DeKalb County in the Georgia House of Representatives, serving on committees dealing with child welfare, health and ecology issues, state planning, community affairs, and education. They made sure that their children knew their history. Lita talked of being taken with her brother, Emory, Jr., and Valencia to see *Gone With the Wind*. To their parents it was important that they understood the progress that had been made since the days of the old South.

The McClinton children grew up light years away from the oppression depicted in the film. Home was a brick, split-level ranch at 3422 Lynfield Drive, in affluent Cascade Heights. Braves baseball legend Hank Aaron lived down the street. JoAnn was such a textbook mom that her neighbors dubbed her youngsters "the golden guinea kids." "It was a slap at me, but I didn't care," she says.

"I took them to Mass every Sunday at St. Paul of the Cross. I felt it was my responsibility to give them some understanding of organized religion until they were of an age where they could decide for themselves. They were confirmed, we did everything Catholics do." JoAnn and Emory, who have been married since they were teenagers, agreed that she would raise the kids while he supported them. Every morning she was up early to drive him to work before taking the kids to school in the family car.

They viewed the evening meal as an opportunity to influence their children to become caring individuals. "We taught our kids from an early age that you must give something back. That's why dinner was so important," says JoAnn. "At the dinner table you get some idea of what your children are thinking and you can imbue them with the notion that you have to give something from being here on this earth."

They also raised them to be at ease in any company. When would-be beaux came buzzing around the girls, they soon learned that three was very definitely a crowd, because Emory went along on their dates.

If Lita's choice of a husband was upsetting to her parents, in retrospect, they suspect she may have fallen for Jim Sullivan on the rebound, and for all the wrong reasons. He was exactly the opposite of the young men who had been beating a path to her door. JoAnn believes that Lita would not have been so susceptible to his overtures if she had not just emerged from a failed college romance with the son of a former mayor, an experience that had left her feeling humiliated and confused.

With her wedding just around the corner, Lita went to work sprucing up her fiancé. She found a stylist to tame his reddish mane, which was beginning to be speckled by silver strands at the temples, and showed him how to whip the unruly mop into a fashionable do with mousse. She picked through his dated closet, replacing his ill-fitting suits with expensive Italian tailoring, and she persuaded him to try contact lenses. Under her expert eye, Sullivan emerged restyled, suave and presentable. She thought he was debonair and wonderful, and even her skeptical friends admitted he was now serious husband material.

By Christmas 1975, she had picked out her dress and

quit her job so she could be free to be with him whenever he beckoned. Her parents resigned themselves to the inevitable and tried to share her excitement. Then their future son-in-law dropped a bombshell. They say the night before the wedding, he casually mentioned that he had been married before and that his divorce had become final less than a year before. He also had four children, none of whom were invited to the ceremony, he added in an afterthought.

Emory and JoAnn were staying in a suite at a hotel in Macon when the phone rang. "Lita called me from Jim's house; she was calm, but I knew that she was very upset," recalls JoAnn. "She told me that Jim was divorced, he had just told her. 'He's what?' I said and handed the phone to Emory. He talked to her, then Jim came on the line. There were some harsh words said. I was in tears and ready to call it off, but Lita said, 'No.'

"All that she knew about him was that he was from Boston and he had a business in Macon. She was not aware then that Jim got the company because his uncle had died. I had thought it very odd that no one from his family was coming to the wedding—we had been told they were all in Boston. He told me he had a sister and brother, but was out of touch with them," she says. Embarrassed and heartsick, JoAnn, who had been determined to banish her doubts and relish her role as mother of the bride, called her friends, "I didn't explain, I just told them not to come."

With Lita refusing to entertain second thoughts, the wedding went ahead on December 29, 1976, at the 12-acre Macon estate that Jim had inherited on Uncle Fred Bienert's unfortunate demise, with Lita's great-uncle, the Reverend John Robert Smith of the African Methodist Episcopal Church, officiating. Lita wore a gorgeous champagne-colored dress with spaghetti straps from Neiman Marcus. Poppy, the friend who was with her the morning she died, was her maid of honor. Around her neck were the pearls given to her by her groom.

"Why did she marry him? I've been wondering about that for sixteen years," admits Valencia. "You wonder about the choices we make, but she was in love and she had my parents as role models. She thought it would last forever."

The wedding party's smiles hid a second drama that had erupted just hours before when Sullivan suddenly produced a prenuptial agreement and talked Lita into signing it. It was stunningly uncomplicated: she was to have no claim on any assets he had amassed before their marriage. "He didn't want her to have anything, not anything," says her mother. "The wedding was one of the most miserable and disappointing days of my life. I tried not to show it, Emory and I went through the act. Later I found a photograph of myself sitting at a window looking so dejected, so bad, that I tore it up. I saw all of the pain on my face and I just couldn't keep it."

That their new son-in-law would neglect to tell his bride and her family about his secret past appalled the straightforward McClintons, but it did not surprise them. They lumped this latest revelation with the parcel of lies he had thrown at them over the previous months when he was chasing their daughter, including one that he had graduated from Harvard and another about his father being an editor at one of the Hearst newspapers in California.

And so it was full of foreboding that JoAnn watched Lita take her solemn vows to love and cherish her new husband until death would part them. Ever since her oldest child started to blossom into a lovely young woman, she had dreamed of arranging a fairy-tale wedding for her. This reality fell far short of her plans. "It was not the wedding I had imagined for my girl," she says. "But she thought she could make it work, and I thought she would make it work, too. We would help her make it work."

THREE
Married in Macon

But while Sullivan was happy enough to walk down the aisle, his new bride quickly found out that he would not be tied down. For the first year of their marriage, he managed to persuade Lita that he was so busy kicking the Macon business into shape that he would have little time for home decoration, furniture shopping or any other normal pursuit of newlyweds, and urged her to stay in Atlanta where she would have at least the company of family and friends. He seems to have had no intentions of being a faithful husband—if anything, being married seemed to add spice to his philandering. She took a job as an assistant buyer in the fur department at Rich's, driving up from Macon on Monday mornings and returning back to Jim on Fridays.

According to one of his employees, Jim Sullivan refused to admit for months that he had wed for a second time. "He was so secretive. At first he denied that he had married Lita," says Sherri Davis. "We had heard about it and we would ask him, 'Are you married?' and he would say, 'No, I'm not.' I asked him, 'Would you lie to me about it?' and he said, 'No, I wouldn't.' But he did. He wouldn't admit it to his children either. His first wife, Catherine, hated it down here, and after they were divorced, he had visitation rights with the kids. They came down in the summer vacation. I heard that they went back home and told their mom that their father was sleeping with the maid."

"When Lita got married, she instantly became a stepmom, she absolutely loved it, and the kids loved her," says Valencia.

"She was so anxious the first time they came," remembers JoAnn. "They were so young, all under ten, the baby was just about three, but she tried to entertain them. The day before they arrived, she prepared all sorts of different dishes she thought they would like. But they wanted fast food and she got it for them, understanding that [she was] another lady in their lives. What she didn't know [was that] the children were not used to their father and so they were not comfortable around Lita or Jim."

Thinking it would be easier for the kids, tired of being a part-time wife and wanting to have a place of their own—Uncle Frank's widow was still living at the estate—in 1977 Lita urged Jim to buy a property on Nottingham Drive in the upscale Shirley Hills section of town for $350,000. She quit her job in Atlanta and started work at Davison's department store in Macon (it later became Macy's), leaving after a few months at Sullivan's insistence to happily throw herself into decorating her posh new surroundings. It was an impressive "starter" home with columns straddling the front door, 15 acres of woodland and a swimming pool. She had exquisite taste and settled for nothing but the best. Their guests, mostly friends of Lita's from Atlanta, gathered around a table groaning with Wedgwood china and Baccarat crystal, vases of freshly cut flowers brightened every room. A part-time maid helped her with the housework. They had two Irish wolfhounds they named Seamus and Adrienne. Sherri Davis looked after the dogs when they went on vacation.

In the first few years of their marriage, how his young wife was coping with her new life was not at the top of Sullivan's list of major concerns. She was a gracious hostess and kept a home he could be proud of. He would brag of her talents, gleefully telling the tale of one memorable dinner party she'd given. Lita had decided to serve roast suckling pig and, according to her husband, was not about to settle for any old porker from a butcher's store. In what was another exaggeration, the way he told it, she took herself off to a pig farm, where she picked out a chubby little creature she judged would fit nicely into a serving dish, then chased and caught the unfortunate animal herself.

Dr. Clyde Marlow and his wife lived about half a mile down the street. Jan Marlow had bumped into Jim at a barbecue a few months before and met Lita at a Christmas cocktail party in 1978. Clyde was an oral maxillofacial surgeon with a practice in town. Jan helped out at her husband's office, but mostly was a stay-at-home mom. The two women hit it off immediately and soon were dropping by each other's homes. Lita enjoyed going over to her friend's house, which was usually awash with children—Clyde's four boys from a previous marriage, and Jan's daughter from her first trip down the aisle—and the happy chaos reminded Lita of her own carefree childhood.

The Sullivans also became friendly with neighbors

Ed and Fran Wheeler. Ed was an administrative law judge with the Department of Social Security and a twenty-year veteran of the U.S. Air Force. "My wife and I thought the world of both of them," says Ed. "I met Jim in 1979 through an attorney friend and invited him and his wife to dinner the next week. I remember at the time he acted kind of surprised that I had asked them over, but I had not met Lita at that time—and it would not have made any difference if I had—but I thought about that afterwards.

"Jim was very Irish and I liked that part of him, I really like the Irish combativeness—he had it, and I had it, too," Ed says. "Right after I met him, someone told me the most ridiculous story about him—I don't know how it came up, I think I said that Jim and Lita were coming to dinner—but anyway, this man told me this lavish story about how he thought that Jim had murdered his uncle. That's exactly the kind of story that roiled around in Macon. I was very suspicious about the stories I heard about Jim, but apparently the ones about his womanizing did hold water."

Despite the friendships they had forged with the Marlows and the Wheelers, the arrival of an interracial couple in their midst did not sit well with all of the neighbors, and some soon made their feelings known. Jim and Lita would wake up to find garbage strewn all over their front lawn, and crates of watermelons were delivered to Sullivan's office at Crown Beverages in a clear message to his young bride: You do not belong here.

At first, Lita tried to ignore the slurs. Although she lived in an enviable home, went on splendid vacations to Europe and the Caribbean, and had good friends in the neighborhood, it was hard for her to brush off these overt acts of racial hatred. Oddly enough, the harassment washed right over her husband. Sullivan almost appeared to revel in the abuse, and never seemed to mind that his marriage made him an object of interest and contempt to many of his new acquaintances. He made no secret of the fact that he considered anyone born below the Mason-Dixon line to be less worldly and less smart than himself. "It was hubris," he boasted to John Connolly when the writer commiserated with him over being singled out for such ignorant treatment. "I wanted to show them I could get away with anything."

Ed Wheeler says Lita and Jim talked to him and Fran about the racism they encountered, and tried to laugh it off. "You probably couldn't pick a much worse town than Macon to have a black wife," he says. "They both had a wonderful sense of humor. I guess they talked about it superficially to cover their hurt, but they were effective in the way they talked about their experiences . . .

"I remember one story Jim told. He said he had this vision of owning a home in the South and pulling up in his yard and having the little black boy come out and park the car for him and all that. Then he said, 'Little did I know that the black boy might be my son.' And Lita roared with laughter; we all did. . . . They put on a brave face."

When the first throes of marital passion wore off, Lita's Prince Charming, who had showered her with gifts before their wedding and in their first months together as man and wife, began to display some frugal tendencies. He put her on a budget of $50 a week, from which she was supposed to run the house. The ungenerous sum was also supposed to cover dining out, trips to the beauty salon, entertaining and clothes.

If Lita had asked her, Sherri could have told her that

Jim Sullivan, although capable of dropping large sums on occasional luxuries, for the most part avoided parting with money.

"When he first started at Crown Beverages, he drove an old Ford T-Bird. After he inherited the business, he bought two 450 SL Mercedes Benzes. And his clothes were awful. He wouldn't spend money on clothes. We were always on at him about it," Sherri Davis says. "He'd wear white shirts until they began to turn yellow. He'd wear dress pants and a dingy shirt around the office, and if he had a meeting he'd wear a suit. But all of his suits were really old.

"He had a maid, Minnie Lou, who worked for him at home and also cleaned the office. She told me that he made her save used paper towels," she remembers. "Every time he bought Lita a piece of jewelry, he wouldn't let her keep it. He'd put it in a vault in the basement and she only got to put it on when he wanted her to wear it." According to Sherri, he was also too much of a skinflint to keep the place cool during the baking heat of Georgia summers. "We all were so hot working there. As soon as he would go out, I'd put on the air conditioning. It wasn't that he didn't like it, he just hated paying for it."

Lita also found out that Sullivan could be controlling and vindictive, and later, she would testify during their divorce proceedings that he would withhold her limited allowance if she displeased him. Crown Beverages employees remember her turning up looking for money to pay her hairdresser on more than one occasion. She claimed that she had no say in how their joint assets were managed. Her only glimpse at any accounting was when their tax returns were thrust under her nose and she was to sign.

Worse than his stinginess was his infidelity. "He cheated on Lita all the time," says Sherri. "I heard the name Tanya, and there was a woman who was married. One husband punched Jim out. He broke a tooth and had to go to the dentist. He never wanted any of his women to know he had money, so he would borrow my car—I had a Pontiac Grand Prix then—to go meet with them, and give me his Mercedes."

Sullivan even had the chutzpah to sometimes take Lita's sporty silver Mercedes on those afternoon romps. When he returned, he would throw the keys down and tell her she was out of gas. Sherri felt bad that her boss made her an accomplice in his deception. "Lita used to come into the office. She was nice, a real sweet person. She was suspicious of him and with good reason. I kept a log of all his phone calls and I remember her sitting there going through the book and checking out all his calls."

Lita called her mother every day. "One time she said, 'I am coming up to Atlanta, I have something to tell you,'" says JoAnn. "When she arrived, she told me she had found a blond hair in the sink in her bedroom. Naturally I asked her, 'Are you sure? Is this the first time? What are you going to do about it?' She told me she had confronted him and he had denied it. She wanted him to talk to a marriage counselor. She called her friends and went out to dinner and a movie. Then she went back home. I didn't tell her father, not the first time, but the second time I did. There were other occasions [when] she talked about leaving him."

With her threat to walk out the door hanging over him, Jim agreed to counseling and, like many errant husbands, time and time again he would apologize and swear he would change. He would try to win her over with gifts and after one major row, he slunk home with a

$28,000 diamond ring. "He cheated on her from the get-go," says Valencia. "He would cheat and she would end up with something nice. He had the Kobe Bryant syndrome [the Lakers star bought his wife a $5 million ring a few days after admitting to having had sex with a hotel worker in Colorado]. Once he bought this fabulous full-length mink. Another time he bought diamonds."

But any trust had gone, and so had Lita's desire to have him in her bed. She could not bring herself to welcome him back into her arms every time he strayed. "Over time Lita changed completely, beginning from the day she found that first strand of blond hair," says JoAnn. "You wouldn't know it if you didn't know her, but she was filled with mistrust and disillusion." Years later, after her murder, Sullivan told John Connolly he had never loved Lita. "It wasn't love, just lust," he said.

Despite his assurances, he carried on with his flings, and Lita knew it. She began snooping around his office again, and this time she she got unwitting help from her anal spouse, whose habit was to jot down every appointment, both business and carnal, in a diary. As she pored over the journal, one name in particular kept cropping up: Tonya Tuggle Tanksley, a woman who turned out to play a major role in Jim's secret life.

By 1981, Sullivan had grown tired of the novelty of being in an interracial couple in white-dominated Shirley Hills. He was also chafing at the constraints of marriage and heartily sick of running the liquor business. Even though it made plenty of money and afforded him a comfortable lifestyle, he began thinking about cashing in his chips. If he hung on to the company, it would keep paying him a handsome salary for the rest of his working life; if he unloaded it, he would get his hands on the millions of dollars it was worth. In the end, running the family firm was too confining for the quicksilver Sullivan. He put out word that he was looking for a buyer.

Sullivan also decided to sell because his finances were stretched to the limit. In July 1981, he began negotiating to buy an eighteen-room landmarked oceanside mansion in Palm Beach, Florida. The house was co-owned by Joe Johnson of Lexington, Kentucky, and his former wife, Palm Beach resident Joyce Edwards. They had bought it for $985,000 in 1980 with the idea of turning it over and making a quick buck. They lived in it occasionally, but mostly, it was left in the care of a housekeeper. Five months later, their investment paid off handsomely.

Years later Johnson recalled the sale in court. "Donna, I don't even know her last name, called me in Lexington and said a gentleman had dropped by the house, told her it was his dream home and that he had to have it. He wanted to talk to the owner. She gave me his telephone number, said his name was James Sullivan and he lived in Macon. I rang the number and asked for Sullivan. 'I have to have this house,' he said. 'I want to buy it as a present for my new wife.' 'How bad do you want it?' I asked him. 'Tell me what you'll pay for it.' His first offer was two million dollars. I told him, 'If you have two million dollars, you've just bought yourself a house.'"

By November, it was his. Johnson had gotten the impression that Sullivan would pay cash, and was surprised to discover that he wanted financing. It was a complicated deal, since the house was, literally, being sold in two halves. "We had a different tax situation," said Johnson. "Ms. Edwards didn't really want to sell because back in that era, taxes were very high on ordinary income and lower on capital gains. But I had lost money in the coal business very severely, and I wanted to sell my half before it got to be a capital gain. I wanted the income. She didn't sell until she had owned the house for a year."

In the first transaction, Sullivan agreed to pay Johnson $950,000 and another $50,000 in interest. The pair never met; the business, concluded on July 27, 1981, was conducted by lawyers. Johnson got a check for over $500,000 and a promissory note for $450,000. Sullivan agreed to pay the interest on the unpaid principal by November 15, 1982, and to make a principal payment of $375,000 by November 15, 1986, with the balance of $75,000 due a year later.

The second closing later that year was brokered by Palm Beach real estate attorney Jonathan Commander. "Joyce Edwards' former husband financed the deal. He lent her the money and she held the mortgage. I represented Joyce when she sold her half to to Sullivan," he says. "He bought it for $980,000, I think it was half a million down and half a million mortgage."

Again Sullivan signed a promissory note in which he agreed to make regular interest payments and was given until November 15, 1987, to pay it off in full. To come up with the cash for the down payment, he "loaned" himself $713,000 from the Crown Beverages employees' pension fund. When he inked the bottom line on November 10, his was the only name on the deed.

Sullivan visited his house twice while Joyce Edwards was still living in it. At his trial she said she thought it odd that Mrs. Sullivan never showed up to inspect her new home. "He called and asked me if he could come down and would it be convenient for him to stay at the house? He wanted to do some interviewing with people to work there and I said that would be fine, he could have the north wing and I would probably never see him while he was there. He asked me if I would sit in on a couple of the interviews.

"I was surprised, you know, a wife not seeing a big house, as big as that, but he said she was busy in politics and things. I asked why she wouldn't see the house, to make sure she wanted that type of house, and he said she would love it, he wanted to give it to her." Sullivan also arranged to lease some of the furnishings from Edwards for $10,000 a year. While the negotiating was going on, he kept his plans secret, not only from his wife, but from his workers. Sherri Davis says she found out her boss was about to move to Florida when she saw the papers concerning the house on his desk.

The Casa Eleda was undoubtedly her husband's pride and joy, but Lita hated it from the moment she first clapped eyes on the sprawling manse. According to her, Jim had made up his mind and was uninterested in her opinion. He did not want her in Palm Beach until the deal was signed and sealed. Just how deeply she felt became evident later in her divorce deposition. "When my husband purchased the Palm Beach home, he did so over my objections," she said.

Keeping Lita behind the scenes had always been a part of his plan; he was afraid that the sellers would renege under local pressure if word got about that the next occupant of the historic estate had a black wife. The Civil Rights struggle may have been over in the sixties, but the Palm Beach of 1981 was not interested in integration. More importantly, with Lita back in Georgia, Jim was free to fornicate without having to pay the usual penance of begging forgiveness, promising it would never happen again and placating her with expensive gifts.

According to Lita's divorce testimony, in December

1982, while she was decorating her Macon home for the holidays, she stumbled on evidence that her husband was still playing around. Opening a pile of Christmas cards, she ripped into an envelope addressed to him. "Missing your kisses at Christmas," it read.

It had come from Tonya Tanksley. Incensed that the woman had the gall to flaunt the relationship in her face by sending a card to her home, Lita reportedly jumped into her car and headed for Tanksley's house. Angrily, she demanded a confession from her husband's lover, and she got it.

When she got home, she called her friend Jan Marlow, who came right over. Pacing up and down her kitchen, Lita vented her pent-up hurt. His stinginess and the adulterous behavior that made her the laughing stock of the town. Well, she had been humiliated for the last time, she said, as she ran upstairs to her bedroom and started ripping her clothes from the closets and stuffing them into bags.

She tossed her belongings into the back of the Mercedes and drove to her parents' home in Atlanta. Before she slammed the front door, she stripped the Macon house of everything that would fit in the car, according to Sullivan. "She took every single valuable object that she could lift out of the house."

Furious upon arriving home and realizing what had happened, Sullivan called the McClintons demanding to speak to Lita. He insisted she come back and return his property, but she refused. He served her with divorce papers which included a detailed list of the possessions he wanted back. The wrangling went back and forth for nearly a month until it became clear that neither really wanted to go through with the divorce. Although he cheated on her horribly, Lita had left to shock him into showing her some respect, not to embark on a new life. He begged her to reconsider; he told her he would do anything to patch up their marriage. Lita agreed to reconcile, but only if he promised to make some major changes.

"She said that she didn't want to have to come groveling to me every week for an allowance. That was a very big issue for Lita," he admitted. On the advice of his lawyer, he agreed to her demands. He would tear up the prenuptial agreement that she'd signed on her wedding day and replace it with a new post-nuptial agreement that would guarantee her $15,000 a year during the marriage and $30,000 a year if they divorced. The first installment of the annual $15,000 settlement was to kick in on April 1, 1983, and it was to cover their food, her clothes and her car expenses, nights out and Christmas gifts.

She was still excluded from claiming a share of Sullivan's assets in the event of a divorce, but he agreed to take out a $300,000 life insurance policy naming her as the beneficiary. What she did not discover until much later was that he paid the premium for just two months, then let the policy lapse.

Although Lita agreed to the new terms, she was not entirely happy with the outcome of the negotiations. She had wanted more, but, she later told the divorce court, "My husband kept telling me he could simply not afford it." It was a stance from which he never deviated. "We were cash-poor," he claimed. "We basically had assets of which the major one, obviously, was the corporation. But on a personal living situation, it was very tight." Somehow, the sugar-tongued Sullivan managed to talk Lita into going home, and despite her qualms, she agreed to give the marriage another go. "We signed the post-nuptial agreement in bed back in the Macon house," he said.

But Lita never really trusted him again. She may have come out of the spat feeling a little more financially secure, but the rows had taken their toll. She was no longer an infatuated 23-year-old swept off her feet by a sophisticated older man. The reality was that she was stuck with a tight-fisted, vengeful tomcat of a husband. But she had sworn, in front of her family and in the sight of God, that she would love and honor this man, and that's what she had to do. And she did love him, in spite of everything.

What she could not do was disguise her resentment of being betrayed and humiliated by him, so she turned a cold shoulder to him in bed. Baffled and angered by her rejection, Sullivan convinced himself that she must be having flings of her own, and began spying on her, noting down her every move in his minuscule handwriting.

Although Jim was still in the marital doghouse, his financial situation was looking up. On October 3, 1983, he accepted an offer for $5 million for Crown Beverages from a Florida-based outfit, Standard Distributing Co. of Pensacola. It was a sweet deal. He would retain control of the pension fund and receive a monthly payment of $20,883 for signing a non-competition clause, not that he ever wanted to see another bottle of liquor unless it was on a table in front of him. For Sullivan, desperate to leave Georgia for the good life in Palm Beach, the decision to sell was a no-brainer.

Just before the deal went through, he had an ugly scene with his young office manager. Sherri had some serious reservations about his handling of the employees' retirement fund. "I questioned him several times about the statements. We got them once a year and I said we ought to have them more often. Jim would be a little vague and say, 'The accountants are working on it.' Then I found out he was leaving. I started reading up all my information and I learned that I had the right to question him about how the fund was run. When I asked him about repaying the loan he'd given himself to finance the purchase of the Casa Eleda, he went red in the face and started shaking with anger and spat out that he would get me the information. I'd never seen him like that before and I wasn't exactly frightened, but concerned enough to seek legal advice. The lawyers were real positive, and said I had a good case." They also agreed to work on a contingency basis, and Sullivan found himself being sued by a 25-year-old woman. "I don't know whether I opened a can of worms, but suddenly people started getting their money," she says. "People who had left years before began saying they had gotten paid.

"Jim threatened to countersue. That's when my lawyers told me to settle the case out of court. I'd got the money I was due and there were to be no punitive damages handed out, and I didn't have a lot of money to carry on with it." But their relationship never recovered. "After I questioned him about the money, it was all downhill," she says.

With his marriage teetering on the brink, the acrimonious lawsuit with his employee over and his bank account bulging, Sullivan decided to reinvent himself in Palm Beach. The decision was to have a devastating effect on both his and Lita's lives.

FOUR
No Paradise in Palm Beach

The same month that Sullivan pocketed the $5 million from the sale of his company, he and Lita moved into the 22,253-square-foot Florida mansion. There was no doubt it was a home that would automatically confer prestige on its new occupants. Situated on the best mile of town, the house had been built in the twenties by Palm Beach's then-favorite architect, Swiss-born Maurice Fatio, and it had been designated a historical landmark by the Palm Beach Landmarks Commission. Locals dubbed it "the ham and cheese house" because it was built of alternating layers of pink brick and white coquina (coral).

Although it had seen better days, the Casa Eleda was the home of Sullivan's dreams. Its twenty-four rooms enclosed a white coquina courtyard with a swimming pool in the middle, and the property included a four-room apartment above the three-car garage, and a wine cellar. The imposing east wing afforded sweeping views out over the Atlantic. Across the two-lane highway that separated it from the ocean was 165 feet of private beach, complete with a cabana built like a miniature version of the house. It was reached by a tunnel that ran underneath the roadway. He immediately launched into a series of expensive renovations, installing new windows and repairing the roof.

Jim was like a kid with a new toy, anxiously hovering around the workmen to make sure that the construction was completed before the beginning of the Palm Beach season when, in compliance with the town's laws, all tradespeople had to pack up their shovels and clear out to leave the pampered year-round residents and vacationing northern nabobs, to be disturbed by nothing louder than ice cubes clinking in a glass of gin.

Jim had to pinch himself sometimes to make sure he was not dreaming. In his imagination, he would throw fabulous parties that would be the talk of the town. With the money he had made from the Crown Beverages sale, he would jump into the stock market, and with the profits that would surely come rolling in, he would savor the leisurely life.

Lita did not quite see it that way. Although she had grown sick of the prejudiced racist neighbors in Shirley Hills, she had a loving family nearby, good friends, and a position of prestige in the black community, which held her parents in high regard. She enjoyed her charity work, was a sponsor of the Miss Macon competition and loved her comfortable Nottingham Drive home. She did not know anyone in Palm Beach, and had not even helped choose the house. Despite its prestigious address, she could see the rambling mansion was a "fixer-upper." While Jim decided it reeked of class, to her, it was a dingy pile of bricks, and besides, she was pretty sure that if the folks in Georgia objected to living next to an interracial couple, the wealthy snobs of Palm Beach were hardly likely to be any more welcoming. Jim assured her that they would keep the Macon property and she could make frequent visits home.

Lita's misgivings proved horribly right. Palm Beach was full of cliques—there were all sorts of exclusive clubs and societies that accepted only people from old money, only those with new money, Jews only, or anyone as long as they weren't Jewish—but nobody was rolling out the welcome mat for a black woman. Although on the surface the people she met were excruciatingly polite, they were no less racist than the bigots in Macon; the only difference was that they slammed the door in her face with a ruthlessness refined over generations. One of the couple's new neighbors, Lois Terry, admitted that the area was rife with prejudice and that most people on South Ocean Drive avoided the newcomers. "There still is a feeling here that it's all right if your gardener is black, but you are not going to have him over for cocktails," she told *Atlanta Journal-Constitution* reporter Bill Montgomery.

One of the ways to isolate themselves from the local apartheid was to import their own social life. Lita's parents, as well as the Wheelers and the Marlows, were frequent visitors. "We went dancing with them, we saw a different social life there than we did in Macon," says Ed. "It was kind of platinum-plated, but we enjoyed it. I thought the Palm Beach newspaper—*The Shiny Sheet*—was well named. We spent New Year's Eve 1981 with them at the Breakers [the poshest hotel on the waterfront]. Jim's real estate attorney was there, and the Marlows. Another couple, the Willinghams, were also staying at that time. Broadus Willingham was a stockbroker and he set up a trust for Sullivan's children."

The Wheelers also met a Roman Catholic cleric,

whom they knew only as Edso, at the Casa Eleda. Sullivan introduced him as his mentor. Ed remembers an evening he spent with Sullivan and the priest, who he recalls being told was related to Sullivan's first wife. Of course Edso was Catherine's uncle, Monsignor Murray, who had not only introduced Sullivan to his niece, but had stayed in his corner even after they were divorced, despite his miserly treatment of his former wife and children.

"It was one of the best evenings I have spent in my entire life. Jim said, 'Come over, I am going to open special bottle of wine.'

" 'What are you opening?' I asked.

" 'I am going to open up a 1928 bottle of Joquim,' he said. That's not only the best sauterne in the world, 1928 is arguably the vintage of the century. We all had a grand time sitting around talking about wine and smoking cigars—that was typical of an evening at Jim's house. We'd talk about a wide range of things, philosophy, politics, whatever; we'd smoke cigars, drink cognac and wine. It was relief from the humdrum existence in Macon, I'll say that."

It was a charmed life. Apart from the opulence of their new digs, neither of the Sullivans seemed to do any work. They went to bed late and rose just before lunch. Clyde Marlow remembers weekends in Palm Beach sitting around the pool in the courtyard while Jim plied them with drinks. He was a good host, mixing cocktails and splurging on expensive dinners and fine wines at local restaurants for his guests. When the Marlows' own marriage began to fracture, Jan became an even more frequent visitor, staying for weeks at a time.

When Jan was with her, life was more fun for Lita. The two women would go out after dinner, leaving Jim, and Clyde when he was there, puffing on cigars and nursing vintage brandies. That the two striking women were out on the town on their own did not go unnoticed by unattached local men, who swarmed to their side. One in particular, a soccer player named Stephen Brumley, was especially taken with Lita.

"Emory and I visited a few times," says JoAnn. "I remember one night sitting in the parlor at the front of the house overlooking the ocean and we were sitting talking after dinner. Jim told me that as a child, when his family came to Florida on vacation, they had driven by the Casa Eleda. 'This is the house I always wanted,' he said, puffing on a cigar and drinking. I found out later that the family never went to Florida on vacation. He had some imagination. I don't know whether he thought some of the things he said were true, he told so many lies about his experiences in life. One night he told my mother about having dinner with a cardinal in Rome, dining on a balcony off gold plates and looking down on the poor people below; my mother was in awe. But it was a lie. Jim was very good at making things up."

The one person he could never fool with his fanciful tales was his father-in-law. "Emory developed this habit of ignoring Jim and saying very little in his presence. He rarely responded to Jim unless Jim spoke to him directly. It was the easiest route to keep the peace and not make a scene," says JoAnn.

Broker Jeff Weiner, whom Valencia had married in 1979, also couldn't stand him. "Jim was charming to me, but I was female. My ex-husband had interactions with him that I never knew, and so did my father," she says. "He was very competitive and arrogant around them. But, I was not aware of that at the time. He was nice around me."

But he wasn't nice enough to have her visit Florida. "I never made it to Palm Beach, I was never invited," she says. "I didn't have any power. I had married a Jew, and no Jews were allowed in Palm Beach, [the town] was created for that reason. It was obvious to me Jim didn't like Jews. He was sick. We saw Lita when she came to Atlanta and we just laughed about it. It was bizarre and insane, but we laughed."

When her friends went home, Lita was overcome with loneliness. She doted on Ashley Wilkes, the pampered little terrier she had named after a character in *Gone With the Wind*, and threw herself into good works, joining the board of the Planned Parenthood Society and volunteering at a program for teenage girls run by a Catholic church in West Palm Beach. Sullivan persuaded her to take flying lessons, but she soon lost interest; he went on to obtain his pilot's license. As his wife's feelings of isolation grew, he encouraged her to spend more time back in Georgia. With Lita out of town he could cut a swathe through the local ladies, picking them up at his favorite hangout, Charlie's Crab House, a few hundred yards along the road from his door.

Before long, Lita persuaded Jim to buy a place she had found in Atlanta. He paid $440,000 for number 4, The Coaches, at 3085 Slaton Avenue in the tony Buckhaven section of the city. The exclusive little community of nine luxury townhouses, built in a cul de sac, was made up of successful lawyers and doctors. Once again, her name was not listed on the deed of the property, but Lita viewed it as her main home and began distancing herself from her unhappy life in Palm Beach. That suited her husband just fine.

The Wheelers were on the move too. They had tired

of Macon after a stressful year during which Ed lost his father, his mother and a race for Congress. When he was offered a teaching post at Emory University, he jumped at it. "We moved to Atlanta in early 1983, and from then on we saw a lot more of Lita than we saw of Jim. . . . It was immediately apparent to me that this was to be Lita's home," he says.

No matter how elegant the new home in Atlanta was, Jim Sullivan had no intention of giving up his luxurious life in the Florida sunshine to follow his wife back to Georgia. The way he apparently saw it, without his inconvenient wife, he was more sociably acceptable to the Palm Beach natives. He set about ingratiating himself with the very people who had cold-shouldered Lita, and spread it around that he was an heir to the Hearst newspaper fortune—a variation on the lie he had spun for the McClintons years before.

In 1984, he registered to vote, joined the Palm Beach Tennis Association, attended the ballet and openings of art exhibitions and was a fixture at all the black-tie social functions. He forged a friendship with an heir to to the Schmidt beer fortune, George Bissell, who introduced Sullivan to his wealthy pals at the Everglades Club. He showed up at charity balls at The Breakers, occasionally with Lita on his arm when she was in town, but more often, reportedly, he left her at home alone, dwarfed by the empty vastness of the gloomy mansion. Neighbors say they were rarely, if ever, visitors at the house when Lita was living there. They remember her as friendly; she would wave to them from her front door as they jogged past and chatted to them from the doorstep when they were out walking their dogs. Jim was much more garrulous, freely popping in and out of the other homes on the street.

For the next two years, she shuttled back and forth to Florida, but Lita was spending more time in Atlanta where she picked up her old friendships, volunteered with the Cystic Fibrosis Foundation and hired a decorator to furbish her new home. "I enjoyed having her around. I think by then, everything she had felt for Jim had completely gone—she did not trust him at all, for anything," says JoAnn.

With Lita often out of the picture, Sullivan found another way to fast-track himself up the social ladder. He quickly grasped that becoming involved in local politics could buy him some clout. He threw his support and some money behind the campaign of Palm Beach Mayor Yvelyne (Deedy) Marix, who was running for a second term in office. He threw a fund-raising dinner for her at Casa Eleda and actively touted her cause in the run-up to the February 1985 election.

Although Marix now plays down her association with Sullivan, for a while they were very close. She was already a pillar of the community, having been on the council for eight years before becoming the first-ever woman mayor of Palm Beach. With her former pilot husband Nigel, she ran a successful travel business.

When Marix was safely voted back in for another term, she rewarded her new backer by appointing him to the Landmarks Preservation Committee, citing the improvements he had made to the Casa Eleda. The committee vetted homeowners' plans to renovate or add to their properties, then doled out permissions, or refusals, depending on its opinion of the proposed changes. It was a voluntary position, but it carried with it considerable influence. Every Palm Beacher bent on making some additions or improvements to his home had to suck up to Jim—not a bad return for his meager $460 donation to the mayor's war chest.

But if her husband was relishing his new position as arbiter of community good taste, Lita was getting increasingly fed up with his tight-fistedness towards her. Despite their revised financial arrangement, she found it nearly impossible to make her allowance of $15,000 a year stretch to cover all their food, entertaining and other miscellaneous expenses. Despite the outward trappings of wealth, the mansion and the expensive cars—by this time Sullivan had also acquired a classic 1957 Ford Thunderbird in immaculate condition—and the thousands of dollars he was shelling out in renovations, he continued to keep strict tabs on every penny she spent. When she complained that she simply could not manage, he trotted out the poverty plea: "The house costs $20,000 a month, with mortgage payments, taxes and upkeep."

At Sullivan's first trial, Jan Marlow described Sullivan's schizophrenic attitude towards cash.

"Lita had a list he had given her," Jan Marlow testified. "She was on a weekly allowance and if he, during the course of the week, bought anything he considered to be household items, grocery store items, he would deduct what he had spent from her next monthly allowance. In Macon, that allowance was one hundred dollars a week, in Palm Beach it was three hundred dollars. She was responsible for her personal items, when she had her hair done, all the groceries that were bought for the house, anything that she wanted personally, anything she bought, her clothes, her dental appointments. If they entertained, if there was a big event, like New Year's, Jim would pay for the dinner, but she was still responsible for entertaining the group through the weekend. She showed me a list one time, it had ginger ale, fifty-nine cents, dental appointment, sixteen dollars, dog food—it was a long list. When she wanted eight-hundred-dollar speakers for her car, he bought them and deducted two hundred dollars from her allowance until she had paid him back."

What made his stinginess especially galling was that the philandering that had surfaced in Macon no sooner than the ink was dry on her marriage license, had grown more urgent in the Florida sunshine. On one occasion, she came back from a trip to Atlanta, to find a bra in her bed. With a wife's instinct for such betrayals, she knew he was squandering money he denied her on other women. The only time she felt the benefit of his fortune was when she actually caught him cheating on her with some new infatuation, and he would try to mollify her with an extravagant gift.

Lita told her friends back in Georgia that she felt ostracized in Palm Beach. She knew that no matter how hard she tried to be an excellent hostess, how much time she put in to raise money for worthy causes, no matter how much money she had in the bank, she was always going to be viewed as a second-class citizen. Her husband did little to assuage her. At one party they attended in 1985, he abandoned her in a corner while he worked the room. Her unease was noted by Suki Rogers, the beautiful young wife of investment consultant Leonard Rogers. Sullivan was drawn like a magnet to the exotic Korean-born beauty and waltzed over to introduce himself to her. A few moments later, a shy-looking woman came over and stood at his side. "Oh, this is Lita Sullivan," he said offhandedly. Suki remarked later that the only hint that they were man and wife was the last name.

Ed and Fran knew that Lita was encountering overt racism that her husband did not challenge. There was no joking about it as there had been in the early days of the marriage in Macon. During one weekend visit, they were shocked by one example, one of many they suspected Lita kept to herself.

"Jim and I were going to play tennis at the Bath and Tennis Club which was just down the road from their house, and I suggested that we all make an outing of it, that Lita and Fran would come and we'd all play tennis," recalls Ed. It became very clear to him that Lita was not welcome. I asked him, 'Is there a problem?' 'Yeah,' he said, 'there is a problem.'

"That was the only incident I saw, and she did not complain about discrimination, but it bothered her," says Ed. "She was sad about it, rather than bitter. Looking back on it, and I have looked back on it many times, she came from a socially prominent black family and she was not used to being shunned. That hurt her. But I think in a way, she was prepared for it, after having gotten the watermelon rinds thrown at their door in Macon."

Still, Lita was reluctant to turn her back on a marriage that had survived for nearly ten years despite the odds and the cultural difference in their backgrounds. And to strangers, she kept up a good front. Auto repair dealer Bruce Forman, whose Forman Motors, Inc., specialized in fixing ailing high-end autos, and his wife were pals of the Sullivans, yet they had no inkling that their marriage was on the rocks. "Whatever their squabbles in private, they hid their differences behind a smile. They were two very nice people who were fun to be with," he told *The Palm Beach Post*.

One night Ed and Fran were staying at the mansion when they were awakened by pounding on their bedroom door. "I heard the dog bark—they had a large wolfhound which slept in their bedroom—and a few minutes later there was a knock on the door." When Ed opened it, he was faced with Lita, sobbing that Jim had beaten her. "She was upset and crying. She said Jim had hit her, or beaten her up, and the way she said it, she kind of wanted me to do something about it. And I said, 'Lita, I'm sorry, I'm a guest in Jim's house, I really can't get into this.'

"She had what looked like drops of blood on her white satin bathrobe, but I couldn't tell whose blood it was. She wasn't bleeding and she did not look like she had been beaten up. The next morning I saw Jim's ear was grazed, and I am completely convinced that she got the better of that scrap," he says. "He always treated Lita well in my company. I never saw any abuse."

In mid-1985, Lita took stock of her life. She had been married for nine years, she was 35 years old, childless, lonely and alienated. What was the point of having an eighteen-room mansion and ten bathrooms if you had no kids to fill it with laughter? There had been a time when she had desperately tried to have a baby. She had turned 30 and her clock was ticking. "She wanted kids of her own, but she couldn't have them," says Valencia. "She came up to Emory University to have tests done. It wasn't as easy as it is now, this was before *in vitro* fertilization. I don't think Jim wanted any more kids, but he went along with it to humor her." Lita ended up having a hysterectomy.

Jim certainly showed no interest in the four children he already had. "I was never around him and the kids. If the kids were in Atlanta, Jim wasn't there," Valencia says. "Lita loved having them. They would come down from Boston and she would give them attention. Jim never gave them any. He was so stingy with them and that bothered her. One of the girls was born legally blind and he didn't want to pay for her glasses. Lita had the hardest time getting money for them. When they were in Palm Beach, she wanted them to have bathing suits and he wouldn't buy them. He buys himself a Rolls-Royce Corniche, but he'd buy them nothing. Come to think of it, I don't know why Catherine even sent them," adds Valencia. "I guess she had no choice. He certainly didn't want the kids. I guess it was control."

By now, even without the hysterectomy there would have been little chance of a baby. Their sex life was nearly non-existent. His infidelities were becoming more blatant, so in-her-face, that she could no longer look the other way. The marriage had deteriorated into one of convenience; it was as if, having taken the huge gamble of an interracial marriage, neither was willing to admit it was a failure.

Lita was never allowed to forget that she had signed the agreement, which stipulated that everything belonged to Jim. All three of their homes were in his name. Even the Mercedes, the car he "allowed" her to drive, was his. When she threatened to leave, his answer was, "Go if you want, but you're getting nothing from me." As he had made it clear in the papers she signed just before her wedding, he spelled it out again just in case there was any doubt: "Everything is mine, the food you eat, the roof over your head, your clothes, your car—without me, you are penniless."

By late summer Lita heard gossip that Jim had become involved with the wife of one of his friends. This was the last straw; she had endured enough. One night in August, when he was out of town, allegedly on a business jaunt, she called her mother. "I am coming home, for good," she said. JoAnn was uneasy at the thought of her driving alone through the night. "Let your father come for you," she urged. "No," Lita told her, "I'm on my way." Without further ado she rented a U-Haul trailer, packed her belongings, hitched it to the back of her Mercedes and headed north.

She would never set foot in that dingy Florida fortress again, she told herself as she drove. The white-painted Buckhead house was so much nicer; it was furnished with things she had chosen, and decorated in lively colors that reflected her sunny personality. The spacious ground floor, with two sets of French windows leading out to the garden, was perfect for entertaining. Even the entrance was welcoming with its pale marble floors and the two gold statues she loved, and lit by crystal chandelier; it was a wonderful setting from which to relaunch Lita McClinton.

In her purse was one of Sullivan's monthly $20,833 checks from Crown Beverages. She cashed it as soon as she arrived in Atlanta, then cleaned out their joint checking account. Two days after she had walked out on him, she rang Jim and told him she would not be coming back. She added that she had retained an attorney and was suing him for divorce.

On the advice of JoAnn, who knew him through Democratic Party contacts, Lita hired Richard Schiffman. "She came to see me in either August or September of 1985. Lita had moved back to Atlanta by that time," he says. "She was very charming, a striking-looking woman. You did a double-take and noticed her because she was attractive, with a kind of an exotic look. She was always very nicely dressed and she was just very, very sweet. Anybody who came into contact with her in my office liked her. The courthouse staff liked her a great deal because she was just a very pleasant person to be around.

"They had the two houses, the townhouse in Atlanta and obviously, the home in Palm Beach. Because she had been back and forth between the two places, there was some argument about her actual residence, but our position was that she had moved back. She was accusing her husband of being unfaithful and of treating her very poorly.

"In the beginning of any divorce case you are looking for temporary support to try and maintain the status quo, and at that stage we were looking for temporary alimony and permission to stay at the house in Atlanta," he says. "That was something I know she insisted on, the town-house. She wanted a place in Atlanta. She didn't like Palm Beach, her family was here and she was very close to her parents. Although it was an amazing house, Palm Beach clearly wasn't where she wanted to be. . . . We asked for $7,000 a month and that's what we got."

FIVE
Separate Lives

Sullivan immediately cut off the electric power to the Buckhead townhouse and stopped paying the insurance on her Mercedes. While Lita huddled with her divorce attorney in Atlanta, Sullivan licked his wounds for no more than a few minutes before calling in his own legal team and filing papers that countercharged: "Lita Sullivan has abandoned the marriage. Furthermore, she has taken with her virtually everything of value in the residence, property which was not hers to take." Okay, Lita replied, he could keep his precious Casa Eleda and all its dismal contents in Palm Beach. She would settle for the townhouse, alimony, plus dental, medical and life insurance policies in her name.

Whether or not he did care about his estranged wife at this point, as he said he did, scarcely matters, especially since he had embarrassed her so often with his other women; but the one thing he did love, unreservedly, was his money. And if keeping his fortune intact meant patching things up with his wife, then that is what he

would do; there was no way he was going to hand over
the house in Atlanta. He called Lita: "Why don't you
come back to Palm Beach? We will put the Buckhead
home up for sale and we'll make a fresh start," he suggested. Lita thought it over: "All right," she answered,
"if you are serious, then put some of the property in my
name."

He replied through his attorney. "Mr. Sullivan has
worked hard all his life to acquire everything that he
has, and to be quite blunt, he does not feel that Mrs.
Sullivan is entitled to anything in the event of a divorce." Moreover, he wanted Lita back in Florida, not
because he was fooling himself that she would never
leave him again, but so any future divorce proceedings
would come under that state's jurisdiction. "He was terrified the divorce would be heard in Atlanta," says
lawyer Brad Moores, who represents JoAnn and Emory
McClinton. "He would have had a jury trial in Atlanta
and the McClintons were very politically connected in
that city."

Sullivan's resolve to cut Lita off with only the pit-
tance he had guaranteed her in the post-nuptial agreement was deeply shocking to the Wheelers. "The
meanness about money was new to me," admits Ed. "I
thought I knew these people. I never knew about this attitude towards money. It seemed to me that Lita always
had plenty of things, I never knew she had a tight budget. I knew she had very good jewelry. Jim gave her
wonderful jewels. He gave her a huge seven-carat
emerald-cut diamond ring, he gave her the most stunning diamond bracelet I have ever seen; it was also
emerald-cut, and at one point I heard Lita say it was in-
sured for $20,000 and it was undervalued. That was lost
at some point and there was some question about it

later—was it really lost or did Jim give it to someone else? Lita suspected that's what happened to it."

While he may have been upset by the selfishness of his pal, as a practicing attorney himself, Wheeler was hardly shocked by a marital split turning nasty. "It seemed her life was pretty easy here [in Atlanta], she didn't have to work, and I thought Jim was still providing for her. But I knew that money was going to be an issue—you didn't have to be a rocket scientist to work that one out. I also knew intuitively when they announced they were going to have a divorce that there would be a big spat about domicile, because domicile decides everything."

A month after she sued for divorce, Sullivan lost his bid to have Lita declared a Florida resident and was ordered by a Georgia court to fork over the $7,000 a month her lawyer had requested in temporary alimony. It was a major victory for Lita in what was shaping up to be a protracted and messy war.

After having to answer for every single cent and having to keep detailed accounts of everything she bought, from toilet paper to tea-bags, she was almost giddy with having so much cash at her disposal. Her spending alarmed Jan Marlow, who cautioned her to put some aside. Lita told her: "You are right, but it's so hard, I have been living in such a life of deprivation for that long that I feel I deserve to order a magazine if I want to."

Her lawyers put Sullivan on notice that they fully expected the judge to throw out the post-nup and would seek a 50/50 split of everything he owned. Sullivan was not only furious at being challenged by Lita, but he had another reason for wanting to hang on to his wealth; he had already picked out her successor. He had lit on Suki

Rogers, who was married to one of his new friends in
Palm Beach, Leonard Rogers. The patrician Rogers had
raised eyebrows all over town when he divorced the
first Mrs. Rogers and married the beautiful, and much
younger, Hyo-Sook (Suki) Choi. In fact, he had married her twice.

They were a handsome couple: he was slim and fit,
with rakish good looks and silver hair that showed off
his year-round tan to perfection; Korean-born Suki was
slender, petite and exquisite. With lustrous blue-black
tresses that fanned out over her slender shoulders and
swung to a stop halfway down her back, she exuded a
whiff of danger: her fractured English, which improved
or disintegrated depending on the situation, had every
red-blooded Palm Beach male begging for her phone
number.

She had blown into town with a husband in tow back
in 1979, having arrived in America four years earlier as a
21-year-old on a student visa and settled in Chicago with
family friends. What she did there to support herself is
murky, but on one topic at least—men—she was a quick
study. During her stay in the Windy City, she married financial consultant James Schnider. When they relocated
to North Palm Beach, Suki claims she took a job at the
Palm Beach Mall working as a counter clerk at R. Kauf-
man Jewelers. How often she actually showed up for
work is also questionable. The local paper has said she
never could remember the name of her boss.

But it did not take her long to notice that the stuffy,
moneyed resort was just teeming with older men who
appeared to be sex-starved and willing to share their
good fortune with lovely and attentive young girls. It
also took her no time to shed Schnider—there were a

lot more desirable pickings to be had in Palm Beach, and she was after a higher standard of living.

"She had this friend, a Japanese girl, and they hung out together for a long time," says writer Cliff Linedecker, whose Korean-born artist wife, Junko, knew Suki in those early days. "They came to Palm Beach looking for rich husbands. She was a beautiful girl with hair down to her waist, but somehow she never made it. It was Suki who landed the millionaire."

Suki hit the jackpot when she caught Leonard Rogers' eye at the Colony Club Hotel. Before long, she was wearing his ruby-and-diamond ring on the third finger of her left hand and they were married on December 15, 1980. She was 28, her new husband was 51. "She was pretty and thin—I hated her," jokes Chairman of the Lantana Nature Preserve, Ilona Balfour, who met her at several social functions. "There are plenty of young girls who throw themselves at old rich Palm Beach types."

After a tumultuous eighteen months they divorced, but Rogers could not live without her, and according to Suki, they continued living under the same roof even after they were legally split. They remarried on New Year's Eve 1982 and moved into a new house that Rogers bought on Tangier Avenue. Suki, with access to almost unlimited cash, hired an interior decorator and a landscape gardener to turn her new home into a palace.

She launched a short-lived course of self-improvement at Palm Beach Community College, dropping out because classes put a crimp on her active social calendar. For the next few years, she and Rogers were staples of *The Shiny Sheet*, the glossy rag that chronicles the party habits of the upper crust. She found it impossible to lever herself out of bed for 9:00 A.M. classes and, to make it even harder for her, the school's semesters were thoughtlessly scheduled in the winter months, just when the Palm Beach season was at the height of its social whirl. "I had to get up at 6:30 A.M.," she reportedly complained. "Classes were always during the season. We go out every night and we come home at midnight. It is very hard for me to go out and get up so early."

By the time Sullivan came under her spell she was 34 and as gorgeous as ever. She was also bored. There were croquet, golf and tennis lessons to keep her occupied, and took her on plenty of glamorous vacations to exotic locations. With an army of domestic staff at her beck and call, she had virtually nothing to do in the house. And there was only so much shopping a girl could stand—Worth Avenue is, after all, not even half a mile long. Her husband traveled out of town for weeks at a time, leaving her looking around for some extramarital entertainment.

She had met Jim Sullivan at several events with her husband, but now that his unhappy wife was out of the way, she was aware that Sullivan was seriously interested in her. Unlike Rogers, he did not seem to have any job to speak of and had plenty of time to pursue and amuse her. She enjoyed his attentions and flirted right back. To Sullivan, there was no doubt that Suki was a prize. Although he counted on Rogers as a pal, what better revenge on the snooty Palm Beach establishment than to steal away one of its wives, especially the most beautiful in town? For her part, Suki was flattered by Jim's unctuous charm and admired his flashy assets, especially the fire-engine-red Rolls-Royce convertible and his massive oceanside mansion.

But Leonard Rogers was no idiot. He began to suspect

that his wife was fooling around during his frequent trips out of town, and in January 1986, hired West Palm Beach private eye James Hegarty to tail her. Hegarty drove over to Tangier Avenue and parked down the street from the Rogers home and waited for Suki to emerge, with the intention of following Suki. Before the sun came up, he had evidence that she was embroiled in a raging, illicit affair.

"They came down the street that afternoon—Sullivan had the red Rolls-Royce, you couldn't really miss it," Hegarty says. "She hopped out, went into the garage, backed her husband's Mercedes out and parked it on the street. Then he drove the Rolls-Royce into the garage and closed the door. He stayed the night. It was simple. I sat outside the house all night long. In the morning one of the domestic staff arrived and wasn't allowed in while Sullivan was in the house. She paced up and down the street waiting for them to 'finish up,' so to speak. It was very funny, almost like watching a crazy comedy."

The investigator reported back to Leonard Rogers; there was no possibility that what he had seen could be misconstrued. Mrs. Rogers was definitely carrying on with James Sullivan. The cuckolded Rogers immediately called his lawyer and instructed him to start divorce proceedings, implicating his former friend.

Hegarty also got the job of handing Suki her divorce papers. "When Rogers saw the report he said, 'Go ahead and serve her.' She was still living at the house, and I handed them to her in the living room. She was caught by surprise—I don't think she knew it was coming. When she opened the envelope, she pretended that she really didn't understand what it was all about."

At the subsequent divorce trial, the Rogerses' maid, Sara Ann Ford, gave equally damaging testimony. She told the court that while she had not actually seen Sullivan in bed with Mrs. Rogers, she knew he had slept in the master bedroom. "His footprints are all over the carpet," she said. "The ashtrays were filled up by someone who smokes a cigar, liquor glasses and everything was all over the kitchen from more than one person." She added that when Mrs. Rogers' lover stayed over, madam changed the sheets herself.

The self-preserving Sullivan ungallantly left his paramour to defend herself. Although Rogers had him subpoenaed, Jim pleaded the Fifth Amendment. When Suki took the stand, she denied the whole affair. She even dismissed her sheet-washing flurry by explaining that it was blood, or maybe chocolate, on the bedding.

Her husband testified that the steamy romance had been going for at least a year. On October 1, 1986, Rogers got his divorce. Suki left the court with a lump sum of $120,000 in alimony, a portfolio of investments amounting to $135,000 and a three-year-old Cadillac El Dorado. Added to the proceeds of her marriage to Schnider, Suki's net worth now totaled $421,000. On the advice of her newly-ex husband, who obviously mistrusted Sullivan's intentions towards her, she bought herself a third-floor apartment in the Placido Mar Condominium building on North Flagler Drive in West Palm Beach. It was a only a short ride across the Royal Palm Bridge from her former home on Tangier Avenue, but light years away in luxury. Socially, her new address was unacceptable back then; nobody who was anybody lived in West Palm Beach.

With Suki's divorce out of the way, Sullivan turned his attention to the upcoming battle with Lita and stopping her walking away with a chunk of his fortune. Her lawyer was demanding the Buckhead home, then valued at $600,000, the furnishings of which were estimated at $200,000, $100,000 in jewelry, $200,000 in cash and an $18,000 car, totaling $1,118,000, or about one quarter of his wealth. That sent Sullivan into an apoplectic rage. He did not have that kind of money, he insisted. It was true that his real estate holdings were substantial, but he was cash-poor, he claimed. When Lita's lawyers demanded proof, they maintained his accounts were never available.

He tried to enlist the help of his buddy Ed Wheeler to discredit his estranged wife. "He called and asked me to be a witness on his behalf, arguing that the venue for the divorce trial should be Florida . . . and that when they moved to Palm Beach, they had intended to make Florida their home, notwithstanding that they had purchased a townhouse in Atlanta. That was to be a kind of second home," he recalls.

"I told him I really didn't want to get into it, I valued their friendship. I told him: 'You can ask for my right arm, but don't ask me to do this. I really don't want to testify in a way that would hurt Lita.' I figured I could only make enemies from this situation. I think he was disappointed, and our friendship cooled from that point."

While Sullivan was determined to make Suki the third Mrs. Sullivan, Lita was making the most of her new life in Atlanta. She had stuck her toe in the dating pool again, but was in no hurry for a long-term relationship. Despite keeping them at arm's length, she was never short of admirers. Stephen Brumley, the soccer player whom she had first met in Palm Beach, was still in the picture.

Another beau, businessman Bob Daniels, was also crazy about her, but sometimes, his possessiveness went too far. The previous November, after going on a drinking binge, he had rammed his blue Cadillac through her garage door. Alarmed, she had called the cops. According to later testimony, when they arrived, he had screamed that he was going to kill her. As he tried to kick his way out of the police car, he started yelling that he had spent a fortune on her and taken her on trips to Haiti and to the Super Bowl.

But since that ugly incident they had patched things up. He suffered from a serious heart problem that had resulted in major surgery, and Lita had been very solicitous of him during his illness and recovery. But he was married, and she never considered him a serious prospect.

She was feeling decidedly optimistic: her whole existence had dramatically improved since she had moved back to Atlanta. For one thing, she loved the house—although it was spacious, it wasn't a maze of unlit rooms like the Casa Eleda had been. Another obsession of her miserly husband had been to run around switching off all the lights while whining about the cost of the electric bill. The only time the place looked really welcoming was when he was throwing a bash to impress his snobby acquaintances, she thought bitterly.

"She had the Buckhead place for about a year before she died," says Valencia. "It took about a year to decorate it. It was beautiful, three stories, three bedrooms upstairs, two guest rooms and the master suite. Downstairs there was the dining room, living room, huge kitchen, breakfast room and patio, and a wine cellar in the basement. She had a decorator do the house. There were huge overstuffed sofas in the den, only it wasn't called the den, it was the *library*. When you walk through the front door, the library was to the right, the dining room to the left and the living room was at the back, overlooking the patio. I remember her drapes, they were a wonderful silk fabric held back with the biggest tassels and they puddled onto the floor. I don't know what happened to the furnishings. Jim moved the wine to Costa Rica."

One of the things Lita had salvaged from her years as a Palm Beach socialite was a closet full of gorgeous dresses. Now she was, for all intents and purposes, single again, and she had plenty of opportunities to wear them. Her closest friends, Poppy Finley (now Marable since her wedding to former New York State trooper Marvin Marable), whom she had known since school, and Jan Marlow, were also in the process of extricating themselves from crumbling marriages and, like Lita, were looking to pump up their social lives. She went with Jan on a double date to the Super Bowl and spent her last New Year's Eve with Poppy at a bash in Hilton Head, the upscale resort on the Carolina coast where the Marlows had a vacation home.

But most of her energies were consumed with helping her divorce attorney prepare her case. For months accusations and counterclaims passed between Schiffman and Sullivan's lawyers. One of the most unpleasant aspects of the split was having to answer intrusive questions about her private life in a pre-divorce trial deposition. Reminding her that she was under oath, John (Jack) Taylor, Schiffman's former partner and now Sullivan's attorney, asked if she had ever experimented with drugs; she took the Fifth Amendment. Later in the same proceedings she did admit to sampling cocaine on "five to eight occasions," and to letting party guests snort coke in her home.

She also confessed to sampling marijuana, thereby

giving her estranged husband a figurative hammer with which to hit her over the head at trial. He had pounced on her recreational drug consumption and fully intended to use it as his excuse for keeping her chronically short of cash—he would not condone her spending his hard-earned dough on dope. At the same hearing, she was asked if she had replaced diamonds in a necklace that Jim had accused her of stealing, and replacing the stones with virtually worthless zircons. Yes, she had said, she was forced to sell the original diamonds because Jim had reneged on alimony payments and she was struggling to pay her expenses. She had also taken the Fifth when asked about her sexual relations with other men.

After the grueling session, there was no doubt in her mind, or her lawyer's, that Sullivan was prepared to play dirty. In actual fact, his wife's transgressions were minor—she had experimented briefly with drugs at a time when it seemed everyone was doing the same, and she had sold her own jewelry to raise cash because Sullivan had welshed on his court-ordered payments. One of the things she had needed money for was to hire a private eye to keep tabs on him. As for dating other men—that was priceless coming from a man with the morals of an alley cat, who had cheated on her from the first days of their marriage and often in her bed. There was nothing that would be a serious problem in court, Schiffman told her.

Jim's strategy was to present himself as a generous, cuckolded husband, despite his own woeful record of marital infidelity. He paid the wages of the maid, the pool boy, and the mortgages; he had taken her on trips to Europe and on luxury cruises to the Caribbean where he indulged his passion for snorkelling and diving. He was in no frame of mind to settle the case out of court. Let her get a job, he told his lawyers when they floated the idea of a settlement, she was getting nothing from him.

Ed Wheeler recalled the last time he was in Lita's home. He was among the fifty guests she had invited to an elegant Christmas party. During the evening, Lita had drawn Ed aside to talk to him privately. She needed his help, she told him. "She asked me if I would be a character witness for her in the divorce proceeding. And I remember saying, 'You know, I don't want to say anything against Jim.' She said, 'No, it's not against Jim, it's for me.' And so I said, 'Well, I'll think about it,' meaning, of course, that I was going to talk to Jim about it. I would have testified to Lita's good character because I had no reason to testify otherwise.

"A few days later, I called Sullivan and told him: 'I have been asked by Lita to be a character witness. I see this as a little different from what you asked me to do. I thought you would be asking me to testify against Lita. I would not be testifying against you, I would only be testifying about Lita's good character, but I want to ask you what you think about this.'

"He told me that he would mind. He said something like, 'Anything you do to help her hurts me.' Then he added, kind of off the cuff, 'If you were to testify to her good character, you would show what a shallow character you are,' or words to that effect," Ed let the insult go unanswered. "I took the coward's way out," he says. I didn't even want to call Lita to tell her. I mean, it wasn't that I never wanted to talk to her again, it's just on this. I wrote a postcard saying, 'I talked to Jim and Jim does mind and I just can't get into it. I'm sorry. Please let me know if I can help you in any other way.' I never got the chance to talk to her again.

"On Christmas Eve afternoon, she came over to our house to deliver a small crystal bowl as a present to me and my wife."

Her last Christmas was spent with her family at JoAnn and Emory's East Lake Drive home. As they gathered around the tree, they talked excitedly about the upcoming addition to the McClinton clans. Valencia and Jeff were expecting their first baby.

A couple of weeks later, on January 13, Bob Christenson, who was then working at the law firm Fisher and Phillips, walked into his office to be greeted by a harried-looking receptionist. "This guy really wants to talk to you," she told him, handing him two messages written on pink Post-its. She had written down: "Jim Sullivan called at 8:58 A.M." and "Jim Sullivan called at 9:31 A.M. Please return his call." Bob was surprised, they had not been in touch for over a year, not since he had declined to take Jim's side against Lita at the upcoming trial. He took care of some pressing business before calling Sullivan's Palm Beach number at 10:38 A.M.

At Sullivan's trial he told the court: "I said, 'Hi, Jim, this is Bob, returning your call.' He wanted to know if I had seen anything unusual around The Coaches lately, around his house, specifically, a green car. I told him no, I didn't think I had ever seen a green car there." Christenson got the feeling that Sullivan was not really interested in the car, but sensed he was on some sort of fishing expedition. He later testified that Sullivan asked him for Lita's unlisted phone number. "I said to myself,

'Aha, that's what you really want.' I told him, 'I'm sorry, Jim, I can't give that to you. I can maybe give Lita a call if you want to talk to her, but I can't give you her unlisted phone number.' "

SIX
A Deadly Bunch of Roses

Lita was wakened in the early hours of January 13, 1987, by loud pounding at her door and Ashley Wilkes barking furiously. The insistent knocking, which had persisted for at least fifteen minutes, shattered the early morning quiet and disturbed her nearest neighbors. As suddenly as it had begun, it stopped. She eased herself up on one elbow to look at her alarm clock. It was 6:00 A.M. She waited for some moments to see if the racket would start up again, but all she could hear was the relentless chirping of birds outside her bedroom window. The dog had quieted. Deciding she must have been dreaming, she settled back onto her pillows.

Although she had meant to doze for another couple of hours, the early banging on the door had startled her and she could not go back to sleep. She reached for the phone and dialed Jan's number. Jan was surprised to hear her friend on the line at such an ungodly hour. "It was early, about 7:30 A.M. when she called," she said at Sullivan's trial five years later. "She told me that at six o'clock that morning a man had banged on her door for her to come and answer. 'Did you?' I asked. 'No one in Atlanta is going to open their door to strangers at six o'clock in the morning,' she replied. She said she had looked out of her bedroom window and he was standing on the doorstep. She said he had a cap on, not a baseball cap but a tweed kind of hat with a little brim, and she said a car had been pulled up to the front of the house. It was a small car, and she thought the windows were darkened."

The two women decided the mystery caller was probably a process server. Jim's attorney had been trying to serve Jan with a subpoena for weeks, to force her into a deposition. "Since this was two weeks before the trial, I had been advised to avoid it. That's the reason Lita called to tell me, she thought he was looking for me."

If she had reservations about how the divorce was proceeding, Lita never showed it, except to Jan and Poppy, to whom she would lament that Sullivan would rather squander thousands on the pricey attorneys he paid to fight and discredit her, than settle his obligations. He intended to walk out of the courtroom with his fortune intact.

But Lita's sunny smile was hiding real concern. Exactly how far would Jim Sullivan go to hang on to his money and his precious Casa Eleda? She was aware that he was in real danger of losing the house, he owed $1 million on it and needed her signature to secure a loan to pay it off. She had infuriated him when she'd refused to sign the refinancing application, and now the mortgage payment was already overdue by a couple of months. Withholding her signature gave her at least some leverage in the financial scuffle, she calculated. He must be getting desperate: she knew he was very nervous about facing a jury—a sympathetic one could give Lita at least half of his assets and if the decision went her way, she would walk out of there with the house, its contents and a very healthy bank account. She would also be driving a Mercedes and wearing some fine-looking jewelry.

Richard Schiffman says that Sullivan never had any intention of negotiating a fair settlement; every time they faced each other across a room, it was like trench warfare. "We met him at a number of depositions. Most of the time he was very rude, very combative," he says. "Lita never said she was frightened of him, not in a physical sense, but financially she was very wary. It wasn't his pride, or that he was hurt that Lita had left him; from my dealings with Sullivan, it was all about money."

Schiffman also says he saw another side to Sullivan when, early on in the proceedings, the couple was considering giving the marriage another go. "There was one point in time when they were talking about a possible reconciliation. I remember he was in our office and he became totally charming, a very different individual from the one we had been dealing with. But it was clear that he was going to make everything hard. It wasn't going to be done easily."

Ed and Fran Wheeler saw the couple during that futile last attempt to patch up their marriage. "After we moved to Atlanta, we saw Jim and Lita together maybe half a dozen times. Not long after they separated they called us and said they were going to get back together. We asked them over to our house for what we all joked was to be a reconciliation dinner and I opened a magnum of Grand Larose Bordeaux. Of course it went for naught. At some point during that evening, when Jim was out of earshot, Lita said she was already having doubts. I asked her why, and she didn't have a lot of time to answer because we heard Jim approaching, but she said, 'Well, I know he is never going to change his ways, and we've been here before several times.' "

Sullivan's lawyer later claimed it was Lita's ongoing relationship with Steve Brumley that had been the main obstacle to their reuniting. But Jan Marlow knew better. "Lita told me that Jim had come up [from Florida] and asked her to reconcile, and she had said, 'Okay, if you will put the townhouse in my name, I will,' and he said, 'No, we are going to sell the townhouse.' She told him, 'No, thank you.' "

With his mansion on the line, Sullivan kicked the smear campaign against his wife into top gear. He claimed that she had had numerous affairs, and threw out names of men he accused her of sleeping with. Schiffman says Sullivan failed to produce one iota of proof about the dates, times or places where these trysts were supposed to have occurred. He recalls the session where he grilled Sullivan about his allegations. "We asked him what evidence he had; there was basically nothing presented as anything. I don't remember it being any better than pure allegation. She wasn't seeing anyone at the time she was killed, not that I am aware of."

Sullivan also maintained that, far from being a very occasional recreational user, Lita was heavily into dope. Schiffman immediately demanded that he detail every incidence of this so-called drug abuse. "When we asked him how he knew that Lita used drugs, he answered, 'People told me.'

" 'Who told you?' we asked.

" 'I don't know,' he said.

" 'Well, what did they tell you?'

" 'I don't know.'

" 'Where were you when they told you?'

" 'I don't know.'

"And that was the extent of the conversation," says Schiffman. "That's what he did about a lot of stuff. . . . And we had Lita take a drug screen, which she certainly passed, in case the issue came up at trial and he raised it again."

Although as the hearing date approached, her time was consumed with meeting with her attorneys and trying to plan a future, Lita had not been raised by her hardworking parents to be idle. As soon as she returned to Atlanta, she had thrown herself in to charity work and become very involved with an organization that helped children suffering from cancer.

In the weeks before Christmas of 1986 she helped with a huge fund-raiser for the local chapter of the Cystic Fibrosis Association. The New Year's Eve Crescendo Ball was held at the Ritz-Carlton hotel in Buckhead and organizer Carol Knapp gave Lita all the credit for making the night a huge success. "We raised the $60,000 largely because of Lita," she told *The Atlanta Journal-Constitution*. "We could have spent every penny on arrangements and made very little money. She put it all together, handling tons of details, and she was like my right arm. If she said she was going to be somewhere, you could depend on it." To celebrate their triumph Lita invited all the people who had worked on the event to a party at her townhouse on January 17.

Lita had heard through the gossip grapevine that Sullivan was now openly being seen around Palm Beach with Suki Rogers. He had been unfaithful throughout their marriage, but this was beyond embarrassing. Everyone seemed to know about it and the salacious details

were the talk of every poolside bar in town after
Leonard Rogers filed for divorce. Lita had shaken her
head in disgust when she learned that a private eye had
uncovered compelling evidence that Jim spent nights
with Suki at the Rogerses' marital home when Leonard
was out of town on business.

What made the scandalous affair more galling to her
was that Suki was accepted in the very same circles that
had shunned Lita. There is no way that a black woman
would ever have been welcomed into the parlors of the
old-money mavens or aboard the yachts of the nouveau
riche. Her very presence would have been a reminder of
the roots they would like to forget.

Yet Suki suffered no such constraints. In the fall, Jim
had taken her to Massachusetts for his parents' fiftieth
wedding anniversary celebration. In a slinky dress and
sporting a diamond "like a headlight on a train," she
shone like a star in the roomful of pale-skinned New
Englanders whose fashion smarts began and ended with
the L.L. Bean catalog. James, Sr., and Caroline Sullivan
made their son's new girlfriend welcome. There was
no reason for the devout, churchgoing couple to fret
over the propriety of entertaining her: according to a
published report, they did not know he was still married. In fact, they did not know that Lita had ever been
his wife.

But even while he was in the throes of his passionate
romance with Suki, reveling in his status of bedding a
woman who reduced every man in sight to a drooling
schoolboy, Sullivan was not deterred from his goal of
stopping Lita from getting a dime of his precious
dough. The mental picture of his estranged wife spending her way through his fortune was burrowing into his

brain. He complained to Suki constantly about "the way she spends my money."

As the January 16 hearing loomed, Jim became almost paralyzed with anxiety over the outcome. He had been warned that he stood little chance of enforcing the mean-spirited post-nuptial document. And once they heard how she had stuck by him and tried to forgive his constant womanizing time and time again, the chances of her going home empty-handed were slim to none.

"Her parents have power in Atlanta," he grumbled to Suki. "And the laws are a lot more sympathetic to a woman there. If it goes to court, I could lose my property and my money." He had also whined to Ed Wheeler, who, as a lawyer and a friend, had advised him to bite the bullet. "Ed was a very nice man, who liked them both," says Brad Moores. "During the divorce he ended up picking up Sullivan from the airport. He told him that maybe he ought to think about resolving the divorce and being fair with Lita because he predicted that Sullivan was going to lose."

Ed recalls the conversation vividly. "I spoke very candidly to him. I said, 'I don't know what your lawyers are telling you, but Lita is going to get a representative share of your holdings, and she should.' . . . I said, 'If I was a member of the jury, I would probably vote in Lita's favor on this issue.' I had picked him up at the Ritz-Carlton in Buckhead and took him downtown and ran some errands while he met with his attorneys. On the way back to his hotel he mumbled something [about losing the case] and I asked him, 'Have you decided what you are going to do when this happens?' and he replied, 'Well, there will be scorched earth.' But I thought he meant money although I couldn't imagine he would scuttle his assets just to keep Lita from getting anything. I certainly had no idea he was thinking of that [killing her], and I am not even sure he was thinking that at the time."

Despite his friend's wise counsel, Sullivan refused to see reason. He had already lost the battle to have the case heard in Florida in November, and that whole month had been a nightmare for him financially. A few weeks before, he had received a letter from Bank One in Lexington, Kentucky, reminding him that the $735,000 payment on his mortgage was due on November 15. On top of that, he owed $49,000 in interest. By the end of the month, he was $900,000 in the hole, having missed the deadline. Now he risked losing the mansion; the bank and the other mortgage holder were entitled to foreclose on the property and evict him, although Jonathan Commander says, "I don't think there was any foreclosure action involved. Joyce Edwards was a nice person and she took the mortgage back on him."

What had him in a near panic was that the $5 million fortune he had inherited from Uncle Frank was fast diminishing. He had put nearly $1 million down on the house—most of which he had "borrowed" from the Crown Beverages Employees' Retirement Fund—spent another $1 million on renovations and had a further $1.6 million tied up in investments with business buddy George Bissell. The house itself was a drain; then there were the luxury cars and all the other trappings, the payments to Lita and fees to his divorce lawyers. Plus he still owed $250,000 on the Buckhead house, and $140,000 on the Macon property. Besides, courting the ex–Mrs. Rogers was proving to be very expensive.

There was nothing for it but to borrow his way out of trouble. In June, he had approached the Margaretten Mortgage Company to broker a $900,000 "jumbo" loan from the Bank of America in Boca Raton, no doubt wanting to hide his cash flow problem from his Palm Beach neighbors. On the form he listed himself as single, but when bank officials obtained his tax returns, they discovered the existence of a Mrs. Lita Sullivan.

Rhonda Paxton, the loan officer at Margaretten, explained to him that Florida law demanded that his wife's name and signature would also have to be on the application for any loan made on a marital property. Without it, no cash would be forthcoming. "We are getting divorced," he had assured her. She shook her head. "But she lives in Georgia now and anyway, the house is not in her name," he had protested. "Doesn't that make a difference?" Paxton told him, "No, as long as she is your wife, she still has to sign."

It was as if Lita had said "Checkmate." Without her signature, he could lose the mansion; if she won the divorce, it would have to be sold to pay her off, and the bank would take the rest. He was in a no-win position and his predicament gnawed at him over Christmas and New Year's.

On January 13, less than two hours after Lita had been rudely awakened by the banging at her door, the phone rang in the Casa Eleda. At 10:38 A.M., someone placed a call from Sullivan's house to a Howard Johnson Motor Lodge in Atlanta. That evening he threw a small dinner party; among those invited were George Bissell and his wife, Pilar. She later recalled thinking that Jim was not his usual hospitable self and he seemed to have something weighing on his mind.

While they were sipping cocktails in the study, the

phone rang. Sullivan excused himself and talked quietly
to the caller just out of earshot of his guests. A half-hour
later, the phone rang again. The oddness of the second
call stuck in her memory. "This time, he turned to the
wall and said in an exasperated whisper, 'Why not? You
let me know . . . keep me informed,' " she said. Around
10:30 P.M. the phone interrupted the end of dinner. Again
he sounded agitated. "Get flowers," she heard him bark,
before he replaced the receiver.

The next morning, Rhonda Paxton explained to him
again that her hands were tied without Lita's coopera-
tion. With neither his wife's signature, nor a divorce de-
cree, the loan was denied.

That evening, Jan drove up from Macon, meeting
Lita at Austrian Motors on 14th Street Northwest, where
she had arranged to drop off her car to be serviced. She
stayed the night, leaving the next day around 5:00 P.M.
when Lita drove her back to the garage to collect the
car. It was the last time she saw her friend alive.

On the 15th, a day after he had been turned down by
the bank, Jim had to hand over a court-ordered check
in the amount of $10,000 for alimony and attorney fees
to Lita. He did not make the payment.

That same morning he called George Pearl, a board-
certified evidence photographer who had been hired by
his divorce team to take pictures of the Atlanta house and
its furnishings to show that Lita was well provided for.
She had been notified of the arrangement and had agreed
to give him access on Friday the 16th.

"Sullivan said, 'There's been a change of plans, don't
go over to the house tomorrow,' " says Pearl. "I was to
make a video record of the contents of the house that
Friday morning. I was surprised when he called it off,
because he needed to demonstrate to the court that his

wife was living in luxury and didn't need his money. That is what the video was intended to do, to show her Mercedes, furs, jewelry and everything else.

"I talked to someone in his lawyer's office and was told just to forget it. I said, 'What, are you crazy? You want to cancel it?' And they said, 'Yeah, he doesn't want it.' I asked, 'What's the reason?' and they said, 'Don't know, he just doesn't want to do it.' Of course, on Friday morning I knew why he didn't want me there, because I would have been there videotaping who shot his wife."

That afternoon, Sullivan & Suki played tennis at the Palm Beach Tennis Club.

JoAnn and Valencia were passing Buckhead on the way back from shopping for the baby and dropped in to show Lita what they had bought. While they were there, the phone rang. "Lita answered it and said, 'That's strange, they've canceled the inventory,'" remembers JoAnn. "'What inventory?' I asked. 'They were coming to film the house and the furnishings,' she replied. Something made me uneasy and I said, 'Baby, why don't you come and spend the night with us?' She told me not to worry, that Poppy was coming over and she'd be fine."

Lita was looking forward to seeing Poppy and her two-and-a-half-year-old daughter, Ingrid. Poppy's marriage had fallen apart around the same time that Lita had split from Sullivan, and the two women shared not only their marital horror stories, but the same divorce lawyer.

"Lita and Poppy were joined at the hip," says Richard Schiffman. "We used to joke in our office that if you could find one, you'd find the other one, too. They came to the office together frequently. Lita had consulted us first and when Poppy discovered that her husband was wiretapping her phone calls, Lita brought her to the office, and so we represented her, too. But her case was over first because they came to an agreement."

On January 16, Lita again woke early. Her mind was racing ahead to that afternoon's hearing when the pivotal question of the post-nuptial agreement would be decided. Her lawyers did not anticipate any problems; the judge's rulings had all been going their way—he had already tossed out Sullivan's demand to have the case heard in Florida. They were confident the document would be torn up and the preliminary date of January 26 confirmed for the start of the trial before a Fulton County jury. And that jury, Schiffman believed, would be very sympathetic to Lita's testimony about the stress of her interracial marriage, her husband's cheapness and his constant cheating.

Lita was glad Schiffman was so confident; all the same, she would be glad when the day was over, and hoped that Jim would stay in Florida and let his lawyers do the talking. "Actually neither party had to attend and we assumed that Sullivan would not show up," says Schiffman. "It wouldn't have made a lot of sense for him to appear, although he certainly could have chosen to. We had debated with Lita the day before whether she was going to come to it and finally decided, yes, she was. It was just a hearing, just an oral argument, no evidence was going to be presented."

She would be glad when the whole wretched business was done. She was tired of the wrangling over money. She'd taken Jan Marlow's advice about overspending to heart and asked her friend to open a secret bank account where Lita could stash part of her allowance. "Be very careful, Lita," Jan had said. Recently she had become more than a little spooked. Several times she had noticed a van in her rearview mirror. The first time, she had blamed imagination, but after it tailed her a third time, she was convinced that Jim was having her followed.

God, how that $7,000 a month must be eating him up, she thought. She knew it killed him to write out the check, because he had immediately fallen behind with the payments and had been absolutely livid when, on November 25, the court in Atlanta ordered him to pony up the extra $2,500 and pick up her outstanding lawyers' bill of $7,500.

She dozed on and off until around 7:30 A.M. when she heard the shower in the bathroom along the hall. Poppy must be up, she thought as she swung her feet over the side of her bed and fished around for her slippers. Yawning, she pulled back the drapes to look out the window. It was a gray morning, and a steady drizzle was falling. Perfect, she thought grimly, what could more suitable for the miserable day ahead than storm clouds? She cheered up a bit when she heard little Ingrid babbling to her mom. Poppy had offered to go to the courthouse with her, but Lita had assured her, "No, I'll be fine." Still, with the 6:00 A.M. battering on the front door the previous Sunday and the mysterious van hanging around, she was glad to have Poppy's company. Thank God this hell would soon be over; another ten days and she would be a free woman.

A few minutes before 8:00 A.M., less than a mile away, Randall Benson arrived to open up the Botany Bay flower shop where he'd started working a month before. He switched on the lights, unlocked the front door and went into the back of the store to retrieve the register cash from its hiding place in the cooler. He looked up when he heard the sliding door and went out front to greet his first customer of the day. Outside, a white Toyota with North Carolina plates had pulled into the parking bay.

Benson looked at the man at the counter. He was wearing a flannel shirt and work pants. His customers were the dapper businessmen stopping off on their way to the office to treat a treasured secretary to an impressive bouquet. This guy was around mid-thirties, he reckoned, nearly six feet tall and had curly hair framing a pasty face which was fringed by a sparse beard.

"Can I help you, sir?" he asked.

"Gimme a dozen roses. In a box," the customer growled.

"What color, sir?"

"Don't care."

"Well what sort of occasion is it?" asked Benson, trying to be helpful. "If they are for your wife or girlfriend, you would want red, if it is for an anniversary, you'd want yellow."

"Don't matter. Just gimme a dozen roses," the surly-looking man snapped.

Benson showed the guy the selection, but his customer was running out of patience.

"I don't care what they're like, and I haven't got much time," he said.

Benson picked twelve of the nicest pale pink blooms. Would the gentleman like them in water, or in a box? he asked.

"A box."

He began sticking a piece of wire into the heads, to prevent the flowers drooping after a few days, but the man was making him nervous, drumming his fingers on the counter and staring.

"You don't have to do that," he said.

"Well, if I don't, they're not going to hold, you know, hold up," began Benson.

"It's not a problem. Just give me them."

With only five of the flowers secured with the wire, Benson placed them in a long white box and tied it with a pink satin ribbon. He was about to slap on a decorative sticker with the store's name and address, when the man stopped him.

Benson asked, "Do you want a card?"

The man said he didn't and began digging in his pockets for change while the clerk rang up the purchase.

"That will be twenty-five dollars," he said.

"Hold on a minute," said the man, turning on his heel and going out to the car.

Benson became uneasy. Was this a stick-up? He followed the man to the door and eyed him warily as he walked around to the passenger seat and asked the occupant for some money. The guy in the car reached into the back and began rummaging through what looked like rolled-up sleeping bags, he testified at Sullivan's trial. All the while the engine purred, as if the driver planned to make a quick getaway.

Benson stood watching, occasionally checking behind him to make sure he could beat a hasty retreat out the back of the store. The open car door gave Benson a good side view of the bearded passenger. The man came back to the shop, threw $25 on the counter and left without exchanging another word or pocketing his receipt.

At 8:15 A.M. the doorbell on the Buckhead townhouse rang. Lita opened an upstairs window. She peered down on a scruffy-looking individual with thinning hair and a flower box under his left arm. "What is it?" she asked.

"Flower delivery, ma'am," he called back.

"Okay, I'll be right down," she told him. When she unlocked the door, he thrust the box at her. "You need to sign for them," he said. Lita told him, "Come in, I'll find a pen." He followed her into the foyer, the door partly closing behind him. Seconds later, three shots rang out.

SEVEN
The Finger of Suspicion

First on the scene was Bob Christenson. A few minutes
earlier, as he was taking out the garbage before leaving
for work, he had noticed a tall, balding, middle-aged
man striding purposefully across the courtyard towards
Lita's porch with a box of flowers. After dumping the
trash at the far side of the house, Christenson walked
back to his own porch to pick up the morning paper. As
he glanced up, he saw that the man was just a few feet
from Lita's front door.

Instinctively, Bob started towards him. Later he remembered thinking that something was not quite right;
it was far too early to be delivering flowers. Ever since
Lita had moved in next door, he and his wife had felt
protective towards their pretty young neighbor, knowing
she was going through a nasty divorce. The guy was
staring up at the house until he heard Bob's footsteps behind him and turned around. Something made the former
soldier stop and take an involuntary step backwards. The

stranger was a rough-looking character, with dirty blond hair scraped back off his forehead. He was wearing a green jacket and gray pants, and he gave off an air of pure malevolence. His eyes narrowed menacingly as he fixed them on Bob and began to head in his direction.

Ducking his gaze, Bob walked quickly back to his garage and leaned against his car, waiting for his wife to join him for the ride they shared to work each morning, hiding behind his paper. A few moments later, he heard a voice and looked up. Lita had stuck her head out of an upstairs window and was calling, "Wait a second, I'll be right down." Then he heard the three shots, fired in rapid succession. He ran out of the garage and around to the gable side of his house, where he dived for cover behind the wall; the Vietnam vet knew that what he had heard was gunfire. Crouched out of sight, he felt his gut twist in fear. He had looked the shooter square in the eye; would the guy come after him next? A few seconds later, he saw the gunman go tearing out of The Coaches, slipping on the wet road as he turned onto Slaton Drive.

Picking himself up off the ground, Bob feverishly turned over his options. He could chase the man he believed must have shot at Lita, but if he did that, he couldn't help her. It really was not much of a choice; the fleeing man was armed and dangerous, and Lita might be in desperate condition. Sick to his stomach, fearing what he might find, he ran back around to her driveway. The front door was ajar and when he gingerly pushed it open, he saw her, lying on her back on the floor of the foyer, still in her nightdress. Blood was oozing from a gaping wound in her head, the box of pink roses lying beside her.

He described the gory scene at Sullivan's trial: "I

have had some military training and though I am no medic or anything like that, you do know some things you are supposed to do for trauma victims, so I looked to see if she was still breathing. She was, not well, but she was still breathing and she seemed to be unconscious. It looked to me as if she had been shot in the face. I knelt down beside her and opened her mouth to see if she had swallowed her tongue, and put my arms— my hands—underneath her head to see if I could find any wounds. Then I could see there wasn't a whole lot I could do for Lita. I called 911." He looked at his watch. It was 8:20 A.M.

When he put the phone down, he went into the kitchen to get a towel, which he folded and put under her head. He was sitting dazed beside her when the emergency services arrived a few minutes later. What Bob did not know was that, while he was frantically trying to make Lita comfortable and get help for her, there was someone else in the house. Upstairs, a terrified Poppy Marable was hiding. When she'd heard the first shot, she had scooped up little Ingrid and dived into a linen closet in the bathroom, where she shielded her child with her body, until she heard the police sirens.

An ambulance pulled into the driveway. The paramedics felt for a pulse and worked to staunch the bleeding and keep her airway open as they tried to stabilize Lita for the trip to the hospital. "She's still breathing," one of them told a cop, but he was shaking his head as he said it.

Poppy called the McClintons' home, where JoAnn was getting dressed.

"I was getting ready to talk to the therapist about my mother, who was in the hospital having broken her hip, when the phone rang. Poppy was screaming, 'Lita's been shot! Lita's been shot!' I couldn't take it in. I asked her to say it again. I called Emory, he asked me to repeat it. 'Lita's been shot.' Emory's office was a five-minute ride from Buckhead. He told me to meet him there. All the way I was thinking, Was it a robbery? Did she have a gun in the house? Lita hated guns. Was she shot in the arm, her leg? I didn't think for a moment she was dead. When I got to the driveway, the ambulance passed me with Emory behind it. I turned the car and followed him to Piedmont Hospital. We went in to the doctor's office and after a few minutes, he came in and said Lita had died. Right away Emory said, 'It was that son-of-a-bitch Jim Sullivan.' "

They stood in stunned silence, unable to comfort each other, and struggling to make sense of the situation. It had to be Jim who had done this, but how could it be? He was a thousand miles away. After a time, they went back to Buckhead. "It was the loneliest ride," says JoAnn. "Emory had driven his car, I drove mine. When we got there, there was yellow ribbon around the house. The place was full of detectives, police, media. The blood was still in the hall, we had to step over it. I went straight upstairs to Lita's room. Although I had stopped smoking, I asked someone, 'Please get me a cigarette.' Then I called Valencia and my son."

"I knew instantly Jim had done it. The second I heard she'd been shot, I knew he had done it. Who else would want to kill her?" says Valencia. "Lita was just a trophy. The McClinton name had power in Atlanta and even in Macon, and he felt he could be part of that power when he lived here. In Palm Beach, the power base was totally changed. He didn't need her anymore to have any status or power at all. And why pay her a penny to get rid of her, when for $25,000 he could have her killed?"

The townhouse was now a crime scene. Forensic technicians swabbed for evidence and dusted for fingerprints. All that remained of the horror that had taken place earlier was the blood on the marble floor of the foyer and pieces of gauze left behind by the paramedics in their fight to save Lita.

Two uniformed cops, Officers Thrall and Bowden, had answered the signal 50, the Atlanta Police Department's code for a homicide. Detective Welcome Harris and his partner, Detective George Jackson, arrived shortly after. When they reached the house, Lita was already in the ambulance, five emergency medical personnel, two cops, a fireman, another detective named G. C. Lovett, a traumatized Poppy, a frightened toddler and a very shaken Bob Christenson were at the scene. The EMT personnel told Harris and Jackson that the victim was a young woman who had sustained a gunshot to the head. From the eyewitness reports and from what they discovered in the preliminary search, the killer had shot three times.

The box of roses, which lay six feet from where Lita had fallen, was covered in residue from the gun, and splattered with her blood. From the measurements they took and from where they found the casings and nose of one bullet, Harris and Jackson figured that the shooter had first aimed at her and missed. Lita had then tried to scramble to the stairs holding the box up to protect her face from the horror of what she must have known would surely come. She managed to get a few feet away, then he fired again. The second shot had gone clean through the box, struck her squarely on the left side of her head, and exited through her right ear. The third whizzed by her as she fell. The bullet they found behind the door had come from a 9mm Smith and Wesson. The gunman had taken the weapon with him as he fled, and they had no way of knowing how many rounds were in it.

Richard Schiffman got the news as he was getting ready to leave for work. "I got a call early in the morning, around 7:30 A.M., 7:45 A.M., from Poppy Marable. She was hysterical," he says. "She kept saying, 'They shot her.' I kept trying to ask her questions, like 'Did you call paramedics? Did you call Lita's parents?' She told me those things had been done and she wanted to get out of there, she was terrified for her child. Then Lita's mother called me and told me that Lita had died."

He knew he had to take care of some immediate business. "When Poppy called, it was absolute disbelief. I'd never had a client murdered before, or since, and I thought, What do I need to do?" he recalls. "I called Jack Turner and Wilbur Warner [Sullivan's divorce attorneys] to let them know what happened, and then notified the court. I wasn't going to tell the judge until we got down there that afternoon, but I warned people from the security standpoint to keep their eyes open a little more than normal, because we had no idea what the story was."

The quiet neighborhood was thrown into a frenzy. Across the street, corporate lawyer Homer Deakins, Jr., told the cops that he had also noticed the flower deliveryman as he was standing in his kitchen drinking coffee. "I was on the sofa in my breakfast room facing away away from Lita's house when I heard two noises; they sounded like steel hitting steel, and I saw this guy running out of the neighborhood. I saw that Lita's door was open, and I didn't go out immediately. I waited a couple of minutes, then I walked over to Lita's porch, looked inside and saw her lying there. I didn't go in, I walked back out and met Bob Christenson. He had already called the police.

"The guy I saw at her door was tall, at least six feet," Deakins told the police. "I would say he was in his fifties, he had a receding hairline. His hair was brown, but light, and he wore glasses, I thought they were steel glasses that looked more like aviator glasses. He had on a light jacket and was kind of shabby, he certainly didn't look like a business person."

As the killer fled, he ran in front of Margaret McIntyre's car. She was on her way to the Feed Mill in Buckhead to keep a regular breakfast date with friends, and narrowly missed knocking him over. She had driven on, but an hour or so later, on her way back from the restaurant, she saw the emergency vehicles and stopped. She gave a description of him to the cops.

Just after 9:00 A.M. the phone rang in the Sullivans' Palm Beach mansion. It was a collect call and whoever answered told the operator he would accept the charges. The call lasted about a minute.

Sullivan maintained that he'd found out about Lita's murder when his lawyer called him around 9:30 A.M. Suki told investigators that he phoned her a half-hour later: "Hey, guess what? She got killed." When Suki did not answer, he said impatiently, "Lita got killed. After all, it's better for us." He spent the rest of that morning fending off calls from the press. As soon as the story had hit the news wires, he was besieged by reporters clamoring for a comment; it had not escaped them that his estranged wife had been murdered on the eve of a bitter divorce trial that he was likely to lose.

Just after noon, Jim spruced himself up to keep a long-standing lunch date in town. That afternoon, Richard Schiffman was contacted by Sullivan's lawyers.

"Jack Taylor called saying he wanted me to call the McClintons and tell them not to steal anything from the house," he says. "I remember telling him to go to hell. I told him that if he thought I was going to call her parents the day their daughter was murdered and say, 'Don't steal,' they were crazy. I wouldn't do it. I know Wilbur Warner well enough, he's a good guy, he must have been getting a great deal of pressure from Jim Sullivan to do it, because Wilbur is not usually that crass, it's not his style."

During that afternoon and evening, Lita's family and friends gathered in an upstairs bedroom. They had drawn the drapes in the downstairs living room to shut out the bank of TV cameras trained on the house and filming through the window. It was then that Detective Harris discovered that the bullet that had gone through the French windows had also pierced the curtain.

Bob Christenson remembers hearing for the first time that night, that somebody had been hanging around Lita's house three days before. With a jolt, he recalled that January 13 was the day that Jim Sullivan had rung asking if he'd noticed anything suspicious and looking for Lita's unlisted phone number.

The Wheelers had heard about Lita that afternoon. "I had just gotten in and my wife received a call from a friend who told her, 'Look at the news, there's something about Jim Sullivan and Lita.' We turned on the TV and there it was, on the 5:00 P.M. news. I was just, uh . . ." says Ed. "The first thing I did was to call my priest, Bob Gibson, who had been our vicar in Macon, and tell him. It was instinctive. He had known Jim, and Lita, too. He had met them at our house. I told him Lita had been murdered. We talked for a bit before I hung up. Next, I thought, I have to call Jim.

"I rang him and said, 'I have just heard about Lita.' Then I asked him, 'How do you feel about this?' I remember him saying, 'I feel stunned,' but he didn't sound stunned, he sounded mechanical. I remember asking, 'What do you know about this?' I must confess I was instantly on guard, I don't think that contract murder was the first thing I thought of, but I wanted to know how he felt. I can also recall asking him, 'What do you know about the details?' He told me that his lawyer had called."

That night, the suddenly single Sullivan celebrated this incredibly fortunate stroke of luck with Suki. They nibbled on caviar swilled down with champagne at Jo's, his favorite French eatery in Palm Beach, oblivious to shocked expressions of their fellow diners, whose chattering tongues wagged for days about his conspicuous lack of sorrow. Even if he was glad to get rid of her, you do not go out on the town with your sweetie on the very same day your wife of ten years has her brains blown out, clucked the local mavens. It was horribly insensitive.

But nothing could dampen Sullivan's celebratory mood. Lita's untimely death freed him from all sorts of constraints: he no longer had to go through an expensive divorce to marry Suki and he certainly would no longer have to hand over a large chunk of his assets to Lita, and therefore, his oceanside pile and his millionaire lifestyle were safe. No wonder he was breaking out the bubbly.

"Lita was a mistake, she was an impediment, she was black and she had to go," Lita's friend Aida Flamm later told the TV show *48 Hours*. "I'm sure he thought it was the perfect crime. I'm sure he thought he had it covered."

Next day found him busy with his arrangements for a party he was throwing on Sunday to help boost Mayor

Marix's re-election kitty. In Palm Beach most politicians relied on wealthy backers who opened their homes for informal fund-raising events. Some supporters held breakfast or lunch affairs; those with more money, like Jim Sullivan, were expected to host cocktail parties. When no word arrived from Sullivan about canceling the Sunday bash, the mayor made a call.

"Deedy was in a panic," remembers the recipient (who asked not to be named). "She wailed, 'We've got a cocktail party scheduled there for tomorrow night for my campaign.'

"I said, 'Oh my God, I'd completely forgotten about that,'" says Marix's phone pal.

"'I think I'd better not have it,' she said.

"'Probably not,' I agreed.

"Then she said, 'The newspapers are calling asking for statements from me and I don't know what to say.'

"I told her, 'You know what, why don't you just say, "Who knows who did it?" What, are they thinking Jim did it? Lita was living up in Atlanta, she'd been living up there for quite a while, maybe she had some high-profile guy that was not yet divorced and it was very possible that she was going to court, and that would have come out and he'd be found out. Maybe they should look in Atlanta. Why just look down here, at Jim Sullivan?'

"'Oh,' said Deedy, 'that's a good idea.'

"It was true. At that moment, they didn't know anything. They had no idea about that telephone call then."

Sullivan's first wife got the news about Lita's death from her kids, who had been told by a relative who'd heard the news while she was at work and called her house. Catherine picked up the phone and called her ex-husband. "It's true," he told her matter-of-factly. "Lita was murdered in Atlanta this morning."

Her call set off alarm bells for Jim; he had to talk to his mother and father up north before the news of Lita's murder hit the headlines. Cutting short the usual niceties, he told them that the daughter-in-law they had known nothing about had been blown away in the most horrible circumstances, and that the police were looking for her killer. "Of course," he reportedly told his speechless parents, "I had absolutely nothing to do with it."

In Atlanta, the McClintons were getting ready to say goodbye to their daughter. In accordance with JoAnn's wishes, there was a simple and moving service at Turner's Funeral Home in Decatur, not far from the home they had bought after the children had grown, which Emory had jokingly dubbed "JoAnn's Tara" after the mansion in *Gone With the Wind*. The chapel was packed with family and friends; mourners spilled out into the parking lot.

Messages of condolence came flooding in, but there was a deafening silence from Lita's husband. "As a matter of fact, Jeff had to call him," says Valencia. "Since they were still married, Jim was her next of kin, and by law, her family could not have her cremated without his permission. So my husband called down to Palm Beach and spoke with him, and I will never forget the look on his face when he came back into the room. He said, 'I cannot believe that man. It was like, "Why are you calling me? Leave me alone. Yeah, yeah, do what you like with her.'" Jeff was upset for the rest of the day.

"Jim never called, he never came to the funeral; it was the talk of the funeral," she remembers. The McClintons, who regarded Lita's stepchildren as part of the family, have kept in touch with Sullivan's children ever since, and a couple of years ago when Dierdre got married, she sent them a wedding invitation. "His children were very upset. They called, Catherine called. They sent cards and flowers. I don't know what they were thinking or what they said, but they were upset," says Valencia.

"I was four months pregnant at the time and couldn't take any tranquilizers or alcohol to calm me," says Valencia. "I couldn't stop crying, I would wake up in the night crying and get up and walk around the neighborhood. I don't remember anything about February. My parents would not talk about it at all, not at all. My mother just shut down. She and my father, as far as I know, never grieved it. Maybe they were afraid if they started, the tears would never stop. You are never supposed to bury a child."

Ed Wheeler was contacted by the police. When he arrived at the station house, he was questioned by a detective who had pictures of the gruesome crime scene spread out on his desk. "One of them was of Lita lying on the floor, a terrible picture, and next to her, was a postcard I had written her splattered with blood, almost like a calling card," he recalls. "I remembered immediately it was the one I wrote telling her I couldn't testify for her. Evidently she had gotten it the day before. As you walked into the foyer, there was a little table where she kept her mail. She must have put it there and when she fell, she knocked it off onto the floor.

"I was a suspect, everyone was a suspect, and he doesn't know anything about me and he doesn't know my name is inches from her body."

"This picture bothers you," said the detective.

" 'Yes, it bothers me, I don't mind telling you it bothers me.' I told him. 'It's my postcard with her blood on it, and she was a very dear friend of mine. It bothers me to see my postcard near her dead body.' "

"At that point he said, 'Do you want a lawyer?' And I said, 'I am a lawyer.' "

In the days that followed, the McClintons tried to help the police track down Lita's killer. Their gut feeling was that their former son-in-law was behind her death. But James Sullivan was a white millionaire with a slick tongue, and they felt he had the Fulton County authorities eating out of his hand. Firstly, he had a cast-iron alibi—nobody disputed that he was at home in Florida at the time of the murder. His lawyers had wired him to a polygraph machine and he had passed with flying colors. Warren Holmes, the Miami polygraph expert who'd conducted the test, maintained that his results showed that Sullivan was telling the truth when he said he had nothing to do with Lita's death.

Then the police began asking them about Lita. Was there anything about her life, or anything she could have done to invite such violence? What about her friends, were any of them involved in criminal activities? Her parents quickly cottoned on to, and deeply resented, the implication that a black girl could not have been living in such a luxurious, tasteful home unless she was up to no good.

It was their son-in-law's poisonous insinuations that had prompted this line of questioning. He had told the police that Lita was heavily into drugs, suggesting that maybe she had been murdered by a dealer. Despite the lack of evidence to back up his allegations, the cops followed up every misleading clue he threw their way. Plainly, they liked him, and that was unpalatable to Lita's anguished parents.

"I was told, 'Mr. Sullivan is a very nice man,' " says JoAnn. " 'A real gentleman.' We found out that he was not taken to the police station like everyone else. Jim was interviewed by detectives at his attorney's office."

The police were looking at the statement that Sullivan had given just weeks before, as part of the couple's on-going divorce proceedings. In it, he had painted a devastating picture of a greedy and adulterous wife. He told the police that he had followed her as she snuck out to keep alleged trysts with various men. He said he had noted it all down in his diary.

"I have records that I made of numerous incidents of adulterous rendezvous which Mrs. Sullivan made, particularly in Palm Beach," he had said. He named two men he claimed had been her lovers. He admitted he had never caught her in the act, and offered no proof that what he was claiming was anything but a stack of lies or the product of his self-absorbed imagination. He said he knew she was having affairs because, "Mrs. Sullivan had a complete lack of interest in me."

In another statement he produced for the investigators in the week following Lita's murder, he also claimed to have seen her buy one hundred dollars' worth of white powder. "I took it to be cocaine. I went absolutely berserk," he said. "I told her that if she ever did that again, it would be curtains. I was bitterly opposed to it." They heard how he had accused her of stealing diamonds he had stashed away for his retirement, having the real stones replaced with fakes and hawking them to a Palm Beach jeweler for $7,000; of maxing out her credit cards; and cashing checks made out to him.

"If that isn't the definition of somebody in need of money for a bad habit, then I'd like to know one," he had declared. "Understand, I'm a simple layman who has done nothing but work hard for my money, nickel and dime at a time. And to see someone steal from the mail in the amount of $21,000 at a clip, or to take jewelry that doesn't belong to her and hock it and leave phony zircons behind, is certainly fit for contempt."

The Wheelers were appalled by this turn of events. Ed got the first inkling of how Sullivan was going to smear his wife's reputation during a phone conversation just after she died. "It was either that first call, or maybe a call soon afterwards, but he insisted she had been killed by a 9mm pistol which he made a point of saying was the choice of drug dealers. I thought it was a cruel characterization of the murder," he says. "At the time I got that information, I didn't know what type of weapon had been used, but I thought, frankly, that was a hell of a characterization. You didn't have to to be a genius to put together where he was going."

When his drug theory went nowhere, Sullivan came up with another culprit in his wife's death, and the McClintons found themselves under suspicion. A couple of years before her death, Lita had taken out an insurance policy and named her parents as her beneficiaries. Now they found themselves in the incredible position of being investigated for killing their own daughter for money. "She had taken out insurance prior to going to the Orient," says JoAnn, "and here he was saying we could have done it for the insurance. We were told they [the investigators] had to look into everything."

A month after Lita's murder, on St. Valentine's Day, Sullivan pulled another despicable stunt. "Jim had his attorney arrange for Emory and I to be deposed at his attorney's office," says JoAnn. "While we were there, he emptied the house. He cleaned out the entire house, took everything, all of Lita's personal belongings, things that

Emory and I had given her over the years, the special dishes that I had lent her for the party she was throwing that Saturday night for the Cystic Fibrosis Foundation ball committee. He even took her make-up."

A few weeks after Lita died, an anonymous source offered a $15,000 reward for information leading to the capture of her killer. In September, with no arrest on the horizon, that amount was raised to $20,000, $3,000 of which was also donated anonymously. The remaining $2,000 came from Georgia Governor Joe Frank Harris.

Emory and JoAnn set up the Lita McClinton Scholarship Fund to award college scholarships to eight students every year. Their neighbors built a memorial garden for Lita in the yard of her parents' house.

Sullivan's callous behavior and complete lack of sympathy for his dead wife's grieving family bolstered their suspicions that he had somehow arranged her murder. He was going on with his life as if nothing had happened. In fact, financially, things looked better for him than they had for months. In March, he went back to the Barnett Bank and applied for another loan. This time he took Lita's death certificate with him as proof that he no longer needed her signature. Without further ado, the bank advanced him $956,000 with which he paid off the two existing mortgages on the mansion. The Buckhead townhouse was put on the market. He accepted an offer of $575,500 and pocketed a tidy profit of $135,000.

With his Florida home secure, money in the bank and the glamorous Suki on his arm, Sullivan resumed his social climbing. Five weeks after Lita's funeral, he hosted a large reception at his Palm Beach home to raise money for his alma mater, the College of the Holy Cross.

Over 100 alumni who lived in the area gathered in his living room to listen to a speech by the school's then-president, the Reverend John Brookes, before being asked to dig deep into their wallets. Father Brookes found Sullivan curiously untroubled about the murder of his wife. "He said to me, 'I presume you know Lita is not here?' and then he started talking about the stock market," he reportedly said.

Ann Mulligan got to hear of an exchange that took place between Sullivan and one of the alumni. "One guest asked, 'I hear your son wants to go to Holy Cross. When you have all this money, why on earth is he applying for a scholarship?' I don't know what answer Jim had for him, but I know the kid did not go to the school," she says. What makes his son's plea for financial help even more bizarre is that for years, Sullivan gave an annual donation of $50,000, making him the college's biggest single contributor. "Jim was very generous to them, he held parties at his home, fund-raisers, he really walked the extra mile for these people. He could have done it for self-serving social reasons, but for whatever reason, he helped them out a lot," says Ed Wheeler.

He also threw a rescheduled party for Mayor Marix which again raised meticulously groomed eyebrows in the snobby little town. The timing stunk was the consensus. Even though you were in the middle of divorcing your wife, you don't polish the silver and break out the champagne a few weeks after her murder. Appearances are everything among the privileged classes, and this was tacky by any standards. Yet the same affronted locals turned up to enjoy his hospitality, and gossiped about him all the way home.

He was still a regular fixture at the Palm Beach Tennis Club, but most of its wealthy members wanted no more to do with him. "He was never at any parties I was at. The only place I ever saw him was at the tennis court," says Jonathan Commander. "I never heard anything nice about the guy. He stalked the women over there. He had a particular taste for Eurasian women, and if there was anyone of that description around, he'd be hovering over her. He was not very socially acceptable and although you are surprised when anyone kills somebody, I think anyone that knew him, the first thought they had was, 'He did it.'" Their suspicions that Sullivan was as guilty as sin may have been bolstered by one member who played him on the day the decision about the divorce trial venue had gone against him, and reported that Jim erupted in a psychotic rage when he got the news.

While Sullivan was living the life of Riley in Florida, the Atlanta police, who had been sidetracked for a while by his insistence they check out his former wife, refocused their investigation. They had been struck from the start by how convenient Lita's death was for him. And basic detection held that in any wife's murder, no matter the socioeconomic circumstances, the husband is always the first suspect. Bob Christenson had told them how Sullivan had tried to weasel Lita's phone number from him three days before she died. Why?

On May 7, five months after Lita's death, the Palm Beach State Attorney's Office, at the request of the Atlanta authorities, subpoenaed Sullivan's home phone records for the previous year. They also wanted the records from Suki Rogers' condo. The Palm Beach Circuit Court ordered the phone company to hand over all billing and long distance charges information.

Six days later, Detective Harris and Lieutenant Horace Walker, head of Atlanta's Homicide Task Force flew to Florida to question Sullivan. Although artist's sketches of the two men in the flower shop and of the gunman had not resulted in their being identified, the cops were convinced that three hoods were part of a hit squad hired by Sullivan, who, they now admitted, was the main suspect.

The interview lasted for an hour. It was the first time they had talked to him since the week of Lita's death and his answers did nothing to alter their belief that he was behind the murder, although publicly they claimed to be open to other theories. "I have ruled out nothing and no one," said Detective Harris. "The only person I know for sure didn't kill her, was me."

Before returning to Georgia, Harris and Walker assured the McClintons that they would not rest until their daughter's killer was brought to justice. "It may take twenty-five years," said Lieutenant Walker, "but we'll still be following leads. We want the killer to know that. This case will remain open." Then, via *The Palm Beach Post*, he issued a warning that must have kept James Sullivan awake nights:

"If I were the person who hired the killer, I'd be very nervous right now. He's open to blackmail for the rest of his life. If I were the person who hired the killer, I'd want to get rid of him. I'd want him dead. And if I was the man who did the killing, I'd be nervous knowing someone now has a good reason to want me dead. If that gets someone nervous—good. I want this to be nerve-racking for someone."

With Lita out of the way, Sullivan stepped up his pursuit of Suki. She was not going to stick around forever as his girlfriend, and anyway, it was fun to see the reaction of the Palm Beach Old Guard when he'd walk by dangling her on his arm. She was so drop-dead gorgeous that marrying her would make him the envy of every man with a set of working eyes. Suki was quite amenable to the suggestion of a wedding, but she had one condition—she was not going to be mistress of the Casa Eleda if none of it belonged to her.

Why would a man who had fought tooth and nail with his ex-wife over every dime be prepared to sign away half of his mansion to a woman he had been dating for only a few months? Suki told Sullivan that she had asked Rogers to add her name to the deed of their home on Tangier Avenue and when he refused, she had taken up with him.

EIGHT
Storm Clouds

At the beginning of September, Sullivan heard that the reward money for information about Lita's death had been raised to $25,000. On the 15th, he and Suki picked up a marriage license from the Palm Beach County courthouse. Later, in another part of the municipal building, Suki watched as he signed the papers that made her a co-owner of the Casa Eleda. Eleven days later they were married; Sullivan's entrepreneur pal George Bissell stood up as best man; a friend of Suki's, Xiomara Ordonez, was the maid of honor.

Since it was the third time around for both, they opted for a no-fuss ceremony at the Royal Poinciana Chapel on Cocoanut Row, the little church built in 1894 by Standard Oil magnate, Henry M. Flagler, on the grounds of his Royal Poinciana Hotel.

In those first heady months, Sullivan showered his new bride with lavish gifts of diamond and sapphire jewelry; her closets were bursting with designer gowns and cocktail dresses, couture suits and sinfully expensive shoes. To the newlyweds the extravagant shopping sprees were a form of foreplay, as he snuck into changing rooms to take off her clothes. "Jim liked to go shopping with me," Suki said. "He liked to come in and help me undress, if the clerks said there were other women undressing, he would tell them, 'Then we are not buying. C'mon, let's go.'"

When he was caught up in an occasional business lunch or a meeting of the Landmarks Preservation Commission, Suki would take herself off to the beauty parlor to keep her size 2 frame buffed and polished. At night they would surface, Suki drawing leers from the men and envious stares from the women, while her new husband smirked by her side. Decked out in their party duds, they became fixtures in *The Shiny Sheet*, showing up at the gala events favored by the rich, and the even filthier rich; they vacationed in Europe and Asia, and she drove Lita's silver Mercedes—their daily routine smacked of an episode from *Lifestyles of the Rich and Famous*. When Suki was not drowning in "caviar dreams and champagne wishes," she would knit, clacking away with needles and a ball of yarn, or play with Coco, the little brown dog Jim had bought her for Christmas.

She also introduced her new husband to the joys of Asian food. One of their favorite restaurants was Daika in Lake Worth where Hyun and Hiro Sun Moon were working. "She would talk to me in Korean and we got friendly," says Hyun. "One time we went with her and Mr. Sullivan for dinner at Shangri-La, a big Chinese restaurant. We stayed there until it was late and then she asked us back to the house. It was like a castle."

They were invited again, this time to a formal dinner

party. "It was so nice," says Hyun. "They didn't seem to have staff. I saw just one lady working there. I think Suki did the cooking, because she served the food. We ate in the dining room and afterwards went into another room for drinks and dessert. Suki showed us around the house—and out into the courtyard where the swimming pool is. Then Mr. Sullivan took us into the tunnel which runs under the road from the house to the beach."

When the Moons opened their own restaurant, KYO Sushi, on South Military Trail in West Palm Beach, Suki and Sullivan were frequent customers. "She was a very nice, pretty lady and just desperate to talk. I think she was very lonesome—no friends, there were no other Koreans in Palm Beach then," says Hyun. "When we saw them together, he was nice to her. One time I remember she had some problem with her leg and she couldn't walk, she was in a wheelchair, and Mr. Sullivan pushed her everywhere, he even took her to the bathroom."

A year after their marriage, Sullivan was appointed chairman of the Landmarks Preservation Commission. According to lawyer Brad Moores, who later represented the McClintons in their civil suit against him, Jim managed to alienate half the town with his imperiousness. "He has this thick but superficial layer of charm and if you get to know him, you see through him. Here's a guy who is a sociopath, but he can get along in Palm Beach society. I know people who battled him when he was on the commission. In fact, when my [then] boss was building his house, Sullivan was hassling him. I don't think he was very well liked."

But his enhanced role got him invited to all the A-list parties, and gave him an excuse to drop by his neighbors' homes offering to grant them landmark status. Not everyone welcomed the suggestion, since even basic home improvements then turned into a nightmare of red tape, but at least in theory, it did send the value of the property soaring.

By the end of the year, the *Palm Beach Daily News* was describing him as "a potent political force." He received a letter of commendation from Town Manager Robert Doney, which read, "On behalf of the mayor and town council, please accept my sincere thanks for your willingness to continue serving Palm Beach in this most important capacity." Despite the rumors swirling around Lita's death, he had managed to hang on to some powerful supporters. "Sullivan is a very intelligent guy. He had all he wanted. Why would he ever have that done [his wife's murder] just hours before the divorce?" asks Deedy Marix. "I've always wondered about that. Why wouldn't he have had it done long before?"

Another neighbor who asked not to be named, fearing a backlash in a community that has long since turned its collective back on Jim Sullivan, says she was never convinced of her former friend's guilt. "I did like Jim. He was always very nice to me—I don't have any gripe with him at all. He loved dogs and anyone who loved dogs was fine with me.

"I always wondered. I give anyone the benefit of the doubt, and I did that with Jim. I know that collect call came into his house forty minutes after the murder and that it came from Atlanta, or right outside, and it came right into the house, but you know what? Suki was living there at that time. Why did the police all of a sudden assume it had to be Jim? They almost had to, because of the telephone calls, but Suki was living there, and she knew damn well she would marry him."

For a while it seemed as if the blue-collar boy from

Boston had it all. He had an incredible home, a beautiful wife, he was trim and fit and he had finessed his way into a position of authority in the town where he so desperately craved acceptance—his appointment to a second three-year term on the Landmarks Preservation Commission was carried unanimously at a May hearing. He was never out of the papers.

He was also never out of the court. While he threw money around to impress his friends, he still hated parting with it for the more mundane necessities of life. He made a habit of quibbling over every invoice and being late with his taxes. By the end of the decade he was being sued for unpaid bills by a local locksmith, the Good Samaritan Hospital in West Palm Beach, architectural window specialists Blumer and Stanton, who had installed the new windows in the house, and the State of Florida Revenue Department. The lawsuits were like a hobby to him, an exercise to sharpen his intellect and hone his skills as an amateur lawyer. His social life was a dizzying whirl of tennis, evenings at the ballet, art gallery openings, charity galas and meetings of the Landmarks Preservation Commission.

The only blip on his radar was the loss of his wheels; in April 1989, an exasperated traffic court judge banned him from driving for five years after Jim appeared in front of him on his eighteenth violation; in six years he had amassed eleven speeding tickets and seven other traffic citations.

But storm clouds were beginning to gather. His finances, which for a brief period after Lita's death had seemed so rosy, were beginning to come under scrutiny. The woman who bought his house in Macon, and for whom he held the mortgage, had made her payments into trust fund accounts Sullivan had set up, ostensibly

for his four children, in 1980. Eighteen months after
Lita's death, in July 1988, he got in touch with his 22-
year-old daughter Dierdre and asked her to sign away
her claim to the trust fund she had no idea existed, for a
lump sum of $15,537.

According to *The Palm Beach Post*, Dierdre showed
the document to her mother, who called a lawyer. He
discovered that Lita had been named trustee of the fund
and that Dierdre had been legally entitled to all the
money accrued in her name when she turned 21. The
attorney filed to recover the full amount: "In the light of
the lack of contact between the Sullivan family and
James Sullivan, Catherine and Dierdre were, at best,
shocked and, at worst, suspicious about the letter and
legal papers they had received from Mr. Sullivan," he
said in court papers. It wasn't the first time he had
raided his children's nest eggs. JoAnn McClinton says
that Lita had been horrified to discover that he had financed their vacations from his kids' trust funds.

The Atlanta authorities were beginning to connect
the dots in their ongoing search for Lita's killer. In
April 1990, a federal grand jury was convened to begin
hearing testimony. The panel was told that the police
had taken the box of roses to the florist's where the
sales clerk had given a detailed description of the man
who had bought them, and his creepy sidekick in the
car. They had, he remembered, headed off towards
Buckhead.

It also heard that the occupants of the small white Toyota had checked into a Howard Johnson's three days before the murder and that telephone records seized by the
police showed calls from their room to Sullivan's home
in Florida. Sullivan's subpoenaed phone records had

To the outside world, Lita Sullivan had it all: beauty, brains, and a wealthy husband. But behind her happy smile she hid the heartbreak of her crumbling marriage. (both family photos)

LEFT: Living the high life: Jim and Lita Sullivan at the racetrack. (family photo)

BELOW: McClinton family picture at Poppy Marrable's wedding. *Left to right:* Emory, JoAnn, Lita, Valencia. (family photo)

LEFT: Lita's sister, Valencia McClinton, at Aisle Five, her vintage clothing store in Atlanta. (Marion Collins)

BELOW: JoAnn and Emory McClinton's Decatur home.

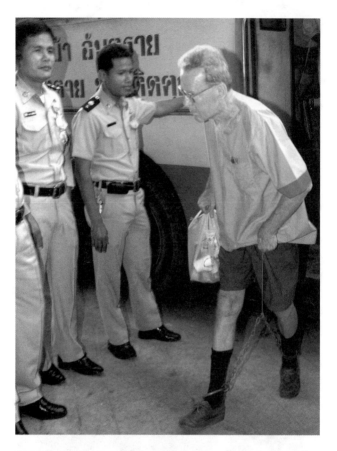

ABOVE: James Vincent Sullivan arrives at court for an extradition hearing in Bangkok, Thailand, Sept. 16, 2002.
(AP Photo/Sakchai Lalit)

TOP RIGHT: James Sullivan declares he's the innocent party in his bitter divorce from Suki.
(Jeff Greene/*Palm Beach Post*)

RIGHT: Suki Sullivan is cross-examined by her husband's attorney, Joel Weissman. (Allen Eyestone/*Palm Beach Post*)

Social climbers: Jim and Suki Sullivan partying in Palm
Beach. *(Palm Beach Post)*

LEFT: Lita's Buckhead house. She called down to her killer from the upstairs window. (Marion Collins)

CENTER: Turner and Sons Funeral Home in Decatur, where Lita's memorial service overflowed into the parking lot. (Marion Collins)

BOTTOM: Sullivan's pride and joy: the Casa Eleda mansion in Palm Beach. (Marion Collins)

Life on the lam: Jim at a restaurant in Thailand, unable to
make eye contact with the camera. (Jane Podd)

coughed up one vital clue—the collect call to his home from the Suwanee truck stop 40 minutes after Lita had been shot. This escalated the investigation to a federal case, since the cops now believed it proved the connection between Sullivan and the hit squad; because the call had crossed state lines, it fell under the jurisdiction of the FBI.

Greed was the motive, the grand jury was told. It was also persuaded that there was other circumstantial evidence linking Sullivan to the men who killed his wife. But without the murder weapon, or the capture of one of the hired gunmen, the Fulton County district attorney believed his chances of nailing Sullivan were iffy at best. After taking everything into consideration, he decided not to press for an an indictment until he had more tangible evidence. The McClintons were disgusted. "We do not think the D.A. pursued this in a very diligent manner," Emory complained.

By the end of 1989, Sullivan was faced with chronic money troubles, having been sent into a financial tailspin by a huge investment which went down the toilet. George Bissell had roped him into a get-rich-quick scheme that suckered in dozens of investors who woke up to discover they had lost their shirts. In 1983, using his Palm Beach house as collateral, Bissell got a $100,000 loan to buy a nursery near Orlando, where he grew orchids and dwarf palm trees. With some of the money intended for DewKist, Inc., he made mortgage payments on his home.

Bissell targeted on his Palm Beach friends and acquaintances at the exclusive Everglades Club and the Bath and Tennis Club: put down some money now and when the plants mature, they will reap a healthy profit and your investment will pay huge dividends, went the line. He was so convincing that around thirty Palm Beachers, including Sullivan, anted up around $30 million. But when some of the investors became suspicious when no profits were forthcoming, and Bissell fobbed them off with excuses about bad weather, the police were called.

They discovered that the surefire deal was nothing more than a clever pyramid scheme cooked up by Bissell and his partner, Charles Donohue, to resell the same plants over and over, using money wheedled out of new investors to pay off the original backers. The pair was promptly arrested and 63-year-old Bissell was charged with fifty-seven felony counts of racketeering, securities fraud and the sale of unregulated securities. The cops also found that, despite the millions of dollars they had raked in, the company coffers were empty. Sullivan, who claimed to have sunk over a million dollars into DewKist, was cleaned out. It was scant comfort to him that his former buddy was facing a prison term of up to 40 years. In an ironic twist, the bilked investors turned to Sullivan to be their spokesperson when the orchid business went belly-up. They did not recover a single cent.

In July 1990, Bissell went on trial in Orlando, charged under Florida's Racketeer Influenced and Corrupt Organizations act (RICO) with defrauding 200 gullible investors out of more than $14 million over a ten-year period. Sullivan had been called upon to testify against his former buddy, and on the stand, he gave an Oscar-worthy performance; the prime suspect in a murder blinked back tears as he told his story to the court. He had met Bissell at the Bath and Tennis Club in Palm Beach, where the master scammer had made his pitch.

He had fallen for the spiel: give me $50,000 and I can promise you a 30 to 40 percent return on your investment, Bissell had urged him. Sullivan, blinded by greed, had forked over $1.6 million.

The debacle left him with little room for maneuvering; his beloved Casa Eleda was put up for sale. It was advertised in *Town and Country* and *The Wall Street Journal* with an asking price of $3.9 million. When it had not sold by March 1990, he upped the price tag to $4.9 million and re-advertised it in *The Palm Beach Post*.

Although the Atlanta prosecutor's office made no charges, the strain of being an ongoing suspect, coupled with his dire financial situation, was taking its toll on Sullivan's new marriage. Suki turned a deaf ear when he yelled at her that he could no longer afford the luxuries she craved; neither was she interested in putting herself on a budget. To her, the man who had wooed and married her had changed out of all recognition. It had been months since they had gone on one of their fun-filled shopping trips. Instead, she found herself living with a bad-tempered tightwad. As he ran around the mansion switching off the lights and the air conditioning, complaining, "They are eating up too much power," she began to think that maybe his previous two wives had done the right thing when they'd dumped him.

This was not what she had bargained for when she walked down the aisle. She called her former husband, crying that she had made a terrible mistake and wanted to come back. "He won't even let me flush the toilets, because it uses up too much water," she moaned. Leonard Rogers listened sympathetically, but is said to have told her he could never trust her again.

His fiscal difficulties did not go unnoticed by dinner party guests who snickered that social gatherings at the

Casa Eleda were becoming pretty frugal affairs without the sumptuous choice of food and drink they were accustomed to. *Spy* magazine writer John Connolly claimed it was common knowledge that Suki was already looking around for a more solvent domestic partner. At dinner parties, he wrote, "Suki's hand would drift onto the leg of her male dining companion, particularly if he had more money than Jim." And in Palm Beach, that left a lot of fat chickens ripe for plucking.

By early summer of 1990, the marriage was over—at least as far as Suki was concerned. Not only had Sullivan run out of money, he had turned downright nasty. In early June, she turned up at attorney Ronald Sales' office and told him she wanted to sue her husband for divorce. "The night before, she had had a fight with him and she had run out of the mansion terrified," says Sales. "It was a Gothic scenario. The fight took place in the middle of a storm, and with thunder and lightning flashing around her, she fled from the house and hid outside in the bushes. Enraged, Sullivan came after her, beating the greenery trying to find her. When he couldn't locate her, he gave up and went back indoors. Suki first went to a friend's house, then took a hotel room for the night."

She called Leonard Rogers, and he recommended she talk to Sales, who had represented him in his divorce from his first wife. Too afraid to go out alone, she arrived at his office with a friend in tow. Sales was entranced by his young client. After listening to the whole sorry tale, he felt she had been through a traumatic experience and was genuinely scared. "Suki was beautiful, stunningly exotic and petite," he recalls. "She had married a much older man and she seemed to have no woman friends outside the one she ran to on the night she fled to escape Sullivan's fury."

Sales also did not like her husband. "Sullivan was hellbent on gaining entry into Palm Beach society. He joined lots of boards," he says. "I never understood why she was with him. He wasn't worth a look, he was mean-spirited and conniving. He was so tight with money. If she wanted to buy a bra, it was a struggle. She had to go to him for the cash. He was crazy in a warped sort of way, very jealous, very controlling. Suki just wanted some of his money to get out of town. She was deathly afraid."

Although she returned home the next day, after first checking that he had calmed down, twelve days later she walked out for good. She waited until he left for a meeting of the town council, where he caught his colleagues off-guard when he announced that he was taking the summer off from the Landmarks Commission, citing "personal reasons."

Later that day, June 12, Suki filed for divorce. She claimed that she had been forced to go into hiding: "My husband follows me about, watches my every move and makes me account to him for every moment of my time. He calls me foul names. A year ago, he told me that I was dealing with a dangerous person [him] and that I had better watch out. He throws things at me. His previous wife was murdered in Atlanta. His behavior is so aberrant and threatening to me, albeit he has not hurt me physically, he has left me in a highly nervous state and very scared."

She asked for $9,459 a month in temporary alimony to sustain the lavish lifestyle the couple enjoyed. "Mrs. Sullivan is in need of sufficient money to leave the area, and it ought to be arranged so that her husband cannot discover her whereabouts," Sales wrote in court documents.

The suit sent Sullivan scurrying to his own divorce lawyer, who issued a statement the following day. "Mr. Sullivan is surprised at the allegations from his present wife and hopes it is a mistake and wants to reconcile," it read. The statement also disputed Suki's assertion that she needed nearly $10,000 a month for expenses. "The husband is disbelieving that the wife would require the amount of money she claims. The husband has a right to inquire as to where, how and to whom, the wife is paying the money and why."

A week later, motions containing accusations and rebuttals were flying thick and fast. Attorney Joel Weissman assured the court that his client was very much in love with his wife and asked the judge to order them into marriage counseling. In answer, Ronald Sales claimed that "Mrs. Sullivan is deathly afraid of her estranged husband. She is in hiding and is unwilling to make her deposition in person, she would prefer to phone it in. Furthermore, contrary to his assertion that he is in love with her, [her husband] denigrates her, he has called her the F word, the C word, 'stupid bitch,' and 'bloodsucker.'" That was why, he continued, "I don't want anyone to know where she is."

Sullivan countered via his lawyer: "If he could only talk to Mrs. Sullivan in an atmosphere of reconciliation as opposed to dissension, then she would realize she had nothing to fear," said Weissman. Suki's attorney was having none of it. "Mrs. Sullivan is extremely subservient . . . even to the extent that she might be compelled by him to act against her own interests," he demurred.

Circuit Court Judge Hubert R. Lindsey made his preliminary ruling. Sullivan won one round but lost on three more. Suki had to give her deposition at Weissman's office, deathly afraid or no. Sullivan had to allow a video-tape inventory of the contents of the Casa Eleda to be shot the following Friday. Counseling was put on on hold and Suki was granted a temporary restraining order.

In July, Sullivan fought back. He asked the judge to throw Suki out of town. "She travels in the same circles that the husband travels in. She travels to the same stock brokerage account firm that the husband has. Because of the court-ordered ban on his client contacting his estranged wife he is fearful that the wife is going to claim some type of misconduct on his behalf that will jeopardize his position in this lawsuit." And so, Weissman argued, "In order to ensure that the husband does not have any contact with the wife, the court ought to enjoin the wife from residing in the town of Palm Beach."

The request had Sales up in arms. "It's the craziest thing I've ever heard. Our Constitution abolished writs of banishment," he objected. The judge agreed; Suki could stay in town. Next they squabbled over who was responsible for Suki's legal expenses stemming from what started as a minor fender-bender, but this one suddenly spun out of control.

A few days before she fled, Suki had taken the rap after Jim was involved in a three-car pileup at the corner of South Ocean Boulevard and Peruvian Avenue, a few blocks north of their home. He had been stopped for oncoming traffic when a Jeep Cherokee driven by an heir to the Woolworth fortune rear-ended a 1978 Cadillac, which hit Sullivan's 1973 Rolls-Royce.

When the police arrived, Sullivan was cited for driving with an invalid Georgia license and an expired registration tag. He told the arresting officer, Michael Nauth, that his license and registration were at home. At a May

7 arraignment, he assured County Court Judge Robert Schwartz that Suki was the one at the wheel. After she was cautioned about the penalties for lying under oath, Suki was sworn in, backed her husband's version of events and the summons was dismissed.

When Officer Nauth learned that Sullivan had gotten off, he refiled the ticket. Eyewitnesses and the other drivers involved confirmed that Jim was alone in the car. Suki was arrested at the Casa Eleda on May 23 on charges of perjury and found herself facing 5 years in jail and a $5,000 fine. After spending an unpleasant day at the Palm Beach County Stockade, she was released on $10,000 bail.

On June 7, Jim was recharged with driving with a re-voked license and an expired tag. Eleven days later he was back in traffic court with a high-priced lawyer who managed to get a trial postponed until November 9.

NINE
The Best Show in Town

They could have sold tickets for the divorce of James and Suki Sullivan. Their messy split had Palm Beachers salivating for months, just as they had drooled over the airing of dirty linen that had made the Trumps' and the Pulitzers' divorces so compelling. Since her marriage to Leonard Rogers, Suki had been a topic of local gossip. The scandalous affair with Sullivan and the subsequent death of his wife had Palm Beachers muttering, "I told you so," over their canapés and cocktails. Now they gleefully anticipated what could be a delicious diversion until the social season got into full whirl.

The lurid details had already been splashed across the local papers when, on September 5, Sullivan's lawyer demanded that Suki return personal items he claims she packed along with her own belongings, including: two pairs of Ray-Ban sunglasses, the gizmo for opening the garage door, and jumper cables.

Among the items he said she had looted from the house were:

> a Cuisinart food processor,
> Van Cleef opera-length pearls,
> 24.8-carat topaz ring with diamonds,
> a 35mm Canon camera,
> a membership card for the Olympiad Health Club, and
> Coco, the Maltese terrier

Five days later, Suki submitted her response:

- The wife does not have a radar detector
- The wife does not have possession of the husband's slacks
- The wife does not have possession of 100 25-cent stamps
- The wife does not have possession of an electric glue gun
- The wife does not have possession of a bronze Thai ashtray in the shape of a cross-legged priestess . . .

She had already filed her wish list. She had adjusted her original demand to $8,000 a month, citing, among other things, $2,000 for rent, $850 for a maid, $2,000 for clothes, $350 for beauty treatments, and $200 for Coco's groomer. She also wanted subscriptions to *Vogue* and *Cosmopolitan* magazines.

It was obvious that they were about to bicker over every last teacup. What had gone on behind the walls of the Casa Eleda was about to become common knowledge; the natives had not enjoyed this much juicy entertainment since the Kennedys were behaving badly and screaming headlines accused Roxanne Pulitzer of performing an unnatural act with a trumpet, an allegation that surfaced in her divorce from Herbert Pulitzer. What made it even more titillating was that the opposing lawyers, Ronald Sales and Joel Weissman, were former partners who now heartily detested each other.

Preliminary proceedings got under way on Thursday, September 13, at Palm Beach Circuit Court as the two sides met to fight over how much money Suki was to receive in temporary alimony. Immediately, Sales lit into Sullivan over the murder of Lita. "Where were you on January 16, 1987? Do you know who killed your second wife? Did you benefit financially from your second wife's death?" Furious, Weissman leaped to his feet. Circuit Judge Hubert R. Lindsey upheld his objection and told Sales: "Your questions may be very interesting, but they aren't relevant." Next day he awarded Suki $2,500 a month in temporary alimony. Along with her investment income of $2,400, he figured she could get by.

With the money settled, the two lawyers lashed out at each other. Sales was the senior of the two, a rumpled, low-key figure, who reportedly wore an elastic band around one wrist and a Mickey Mouse watch on the other. Brooklyn-born Weissman was a flashy dresser with a weakness for jewelry and clipped an 18-karat Montblanc gold pen into the pocket of his expensive suit. Outside the courtroom, he jokingly told reporters that his wife checked him out every morning for excess baubles. If she thought he was over-decorated, she would remove at least one piece.

Former partners, they had fallen out New Year's Eve 1983, when Sales accused his junior associate of forging his name on seventeen checks amounting to $30,000. Sales demanded he agree to repay every penny and leave town. The seething Weissman refused and was charged with thirty-eight counts of forgery.

During a bitter three-week trial, Sales claimed: "When he came to me, he was making thirty thousand dollars a year and he didn't have a car. When he left, he was making close to two hundred thousand dollars a year and he had a new Cadillac." Weissman insisted that Sales had given him the checks to sign and was seeking revenge because he wanted to bust up the partnership.

Unable to decide unanimously who was telling the truth, the jury stalled. Rather than face another trial, Weissman agreed to accept a majority verdict—the vote went his way, five to one. He never forgave Sales for trying to ruin him and relished every opportunity to humiliate him across a courtroom.

The trial proper started the following Monday, September 17, 1990, and the gloves were off from the start. Amongst the spectators in the courtroom were investigators from the Palm Beach County State Attorney's Office, who were especially interested in hearing what Suki had to say. Any relevant developments would be passed on to the district attorney in Atlanta.

At stake were the Casa Eleda, which was appraised at $3.6 million, its contents and a $99,000 bank account. Sullivan's net worth was estimated at $3.1 million, Suki was said to have assets amounting to $600,000. Weissman told the court that the trial was entirely about money. "Only in America could a woman with $360,000 who was married for about a year [in fact they were wed thirty-one months] have the chutzpah to say she can't live without taking money from her husband.

Suki Sullivan is a true success story. When all she has to do is look nice, dress nice and go to social parties, enough is enough," he railed.

Stabbing an accusing finger at Suki, who was dressed from head to toe in a demure black two-piece suit, black stockings and black high-heels, the sapphire earrings Sullivan contended she had pilfered from him twinkling in her ears, he called her, "The Black Widow of Divorce." "This is her fourth divorce," he said. "Every time she divorces, she doubles her bank account. She got married not for love, but for dollars, and when the dollars ran out, so did she." He blamed the $1.6 million that his client had lost in the DewKist scam for his marital woes. He insisted that Suki's departure had broken James Sullivan's heart. "She was not only his wife, but his whole life. Her entire life has been about the pursuit of money."

Ronald Sales' opening statement was even more shocking. In a bombshell announcement, he said that Suki would testify that Sullivan admitted that he had arranged to have Lita murdered. "He told her he had made some terrible mistakes. He cried, he said God would punish him for that." The confession was made on the night that Suki was charged with perjury after she had lied, at his insistence, to keep him out of jail, he said. Weissman accused Sales of making the allegations to force Sullivan to settle. Well, he wouldn't, declared the pit-bull attorney. "Our answer to this veiled threat has been the same all along: take your best shot."

Next day, in a conservative dark suit and red tie, Jim Sullivan took the stand and painted a picture of himself as a duped husband, bereft at having found that the woman he loved had been planning to leave him for months. She had sneakily hoarded clothes, perfume and pantyhose, hiding them under beds. When she left, she had taken almost anything from the house that could be pried loose, he maintained. She had gotten into a basement vault and made off with Van Cleef gold-and-diamond necklaces, a string of pearls, a diamond ring and cash; she had stolen the very earrings she had the gall to wear in court, he said with a look of weary betrayal. He said he would bring some of the items she had squirreled away into court to show the extent of her greed.

"You mean we are going to get to see the pantyhose?" asked Sales.

"I promise you," said Sullivan.

"Oh," said Sales, shaking his head in disgust. "For shame."

Next morning Sullivan trundled Suki's purported stash into the court, piling 187 pairs of pantyhose, 17 pairs of shoes, boxes of Clinique cosmetics, a two-foot-high mountain of knitting yarn, bottles of Chanel and Cartier perfumes, and a flacon of Dior Poison under the judge's bench.

He told the court he'd found the hidden trove when an ankle support fell out of his tennis sneaker and he bent down to pick it up. The jewelry was not hers to keep; it had been bought as an investment, he said. He'd had most of the gems before their marriage. He kept them in the basement safe in purple velvet-lined boxes. When Suki had wanted to wear an item, he had gone downstairs to get it for her. He complained that she spent $800 a month on clothes, but the impact of his outrage was somewhat diluted by the titters that erupted when a local matron sniffed loudly, "Well, that's not very much at all!"

On cross-examination, Sales asked why he was painting his wife as an out-of-control shopper when Sullivan had told him that his wife spent very little on clothes and make-up. "When I said those things to you, it was a week after Suki left me. I was in a very bad mental state," he explained. "I have since learned much more and I am wiser now. She had an American Express card which gave her independence, and she used that independence. The records show an awesome amount of spending. Suki had nine walk-in closets in the house, and every one of them is crammed full of dresses and gowns."

He said he was worth $4 million, two million less than he had when he had married her. His losses in DewKist forced him to dip into his $1.1 million investments to pay the bills, his insurance company had cancelled his homeowner's policy for nonpayment and now the bank had given him thirty days to satisfy the mortgage. He had already lost his wife, now he was going to lose his home, he bleated to the court. He had tried for a reconciliation, but had since finding out that his wife was nothing more than a greedy gold-digger. What he couldn't live without was the pet they had shared. He begged to be allowed to keep the little Maltese terrier. "The dog is the only thing I have left. I found Coco, I bought him, he needs me, I need him," he pleaded.

Shaking with emotion, he insisted he still loved his wife. When Sales questioned him about Suki's limited grasp of English, he denied that it helped him deceive her; everyone in the room gasped as he mistakenly called her by his dead wife's name. "I think everything Lita does, she does beautifully. She was my whole life."

Sales asked Sullivan why he had made Suki co-owner of his house in November 1986, two months before Lita was murdered. "Why did you convey the house by a deed to your intended wife when you were still a married man?"

"I don't know," Sullivan replied.

"Was it because you planned to have Lita's life on earth terminated?" he asked.

Weissman jumped up and told Sullivan not to answer. Sullivan trotted out his Fifth Amendment right not to incriminate himself, then blurted out, "I intended to give her the house if I died before she did, to protect her, but not to give it to her if we divorced."

Sales next disputed his claim that they'd lived on on a budget of $2,000 a month. He asked incredulously, "You are telling the judge that you and Mrs. Sullivan are rattling around in a 4.9 million mansion on two thousand dollars a month?"

"Between two thousand dollars and three thousand dollars," replied Sullivan, apparently forgetting he had just described Suki as a proliferate spender who had brought him to near-ruin.

Suki's alleged lack of understanding of legal documents was at the heart of Ronald Sales' case. Psychologist Linda Werner told the court that Suki read at a third-grade level and that her comprehension of English was even more inept. Therefore it was doubtful that she really knew what she was signing when she inked the quitclaim by which she gave up any right to her half of the mansion on divorce.

Suki testified across the pile of her belongings. In her polished black pumps, she tiptoed nervously to the witness box. Barely audible, and in fractured English, she said: "I just signed what he told me to sign, what he put in front of me. I trusted him." She then maintained that she had grown afraid of Sullivan after he confessed that he'd had Lita killed. Avoiding his penetrating gaze, she told the court:

"It was the night I had been released on bail after being charged with perjury. I was in the sitting room when Jim came in and said he wanted to talk to me. I had been crying. I said, 'We have to tell the truth about the driving or I have to go to jail.' Jim turned the TV high so nobody could hear our conversation," she recalled. "He said I had to protect him because if they put him in jail for his driving habits, then he was afraid he would never come out because of what he did to his ex-wife."

The judge started in his seat, then asked, "What do you mean by 'did'?"

"He hired someone to get rid of her," she said.

"Sorry?" asked the judge.

"He hired someone to get rid of her," she repeated. "He said, 'So let's sell this house as quick as possibly, move to a different country, or anywhere you want to live. We'll just get out.' I knew I had to do something. I left the house without letting him know."

Suki denied that they'd fought over her spending; her husband had often joined her on her splurges, happily whipping out his American Express Gold Card to pay for them. She stored clothes under the beds because they frequently rented out rooms in the house, and because she was tidying for a film crew who were due to shoot a Victoria's Secret catalog at the house after making a deal with Sullivan for $5,000. She also told the court about Coco: "Jim gave me him for Christmas," said Suki. "I had wanted a fur coat."

She said she would like to visit the dog. That is why she had taken a pillow with the dog's picture on it. She

swore she had not taken any of Jim's things. What she
wanted was only fair. She wanted half the house; Jim
had promised her it belonged to both of them. She had
seen him put her name on the deed. She did not remember anything about signing a quitclaim.

Having swallowed up three days of court time, the
case was put on hold until November and the warring
Sullivans had no alternative but to sit and stew. Sullivan
was still bound by the restraining order not to contact
Suki, who remained holed up a few miles south in Delray Beach. But she did emerge from hiding to fly to Atlanta to testify before the Fulton County grand jury
impaneled to investigate Lita's murder. For three hours,
she repeated her allegations about her husband's com-
plicity in Lita's death.

When she returned, she drove over to the Casa Eleda
to pick up the rest of her possessions. With her was
gumshoe James Hegarty, hired by her attorney to make
sure Sullivan didn't do anything to her.

Despite the grandeur of the mansion, Hegarty was
unimpressed. "That was one of the dreariest houses I've
ever been in," he says. "The courtyard in the center had
just gone to hell. It was really a drab, moss-covered,
dingy-looking place and it had a lot of mold. Suki and I
were going up and down those stairs and in and out of
the various rooms with Sullivan following behind us
ranting, 'Look, I've let her take her prescription drugs.'
I said to him, 'Are they her prescription drugs?' He said,
'Oh yeah,' and so I asked him, 'Well, what's your com-
plaint?'

"As she removed her clothes and personal items and
he kept saying over and over, 'Look, more pantyhose,'
or he'd just stand there with a faraway look in his eyes.

Then he'd say again, 'Look I'm letting her take those drugs.' 'What's so generous about that? They're hers,' I asked him and he started again with, 'Oh, here she comes with more pantyhose.' I have to tell you, she did have a hell of a lot of pantyhose."

The six-week hiatus did not diminish interest in the trial that had overshadowed every other event in town that fall. When it resumed on November 5, the local papers reported that senior citizens from the Century City retirement village crowded onto a bus to attend; some spectators brought picnic bags to sustain them throughout the proceedings. Fearing the trial was turning into a circus, Judge Lindsey turned down a request from a teacher at a local school who asked if she could bring her class.

The trial reopened with another round of monstrous accusations. For over an hour, Weissman chipped away at Suki's motive for leaving Sullivan, her lapses of memory and her poor English. Then he hit her with his tactical battering ram: She had had Lita killed for fear the divorce court in Atlanta would award the mansion to her. "You had as much to gain from the death of Lita Sullivan as he did, true?"

Suki was bewildered. "How?" she asked.

"Where were you when Lita Sullivan was killed?" Weissman said.

In her confusion, Suki stumbled over her words, her language skills deserting her. "She got killed that morning. I . . . with Mr. Sullivan that night. I don't know until I see in paper."

"You received a call from someone in Atlanta in Mr. Sullivan's house?" asked Weissman.

"Me?"

"You."

"Isn't it true that you are the individual that hired Lita Sullivan's killer?" Weissman asked.

"Me? Why? Why? I did not hire. No!"

"Is it true that you paid someone in Chicago with money from your first divorce to kill Lita Sullivan?"

Nervously, Suki began to giggle. "No."

Sales immediately called Sullivan back to the stand. "Did you hire someone to kill Lita? Do you know who hired someone to kill her? Are you suggesting it was little Suki who hired this killer?" he hammered. Once again pleading the Fifth, Sullivan said nothing. During a break, an outraged Suki suddenly recovered her facility with English and told reporters, "I think I will sue Weissman."

Next morning Sullivan was back on the stand. Sales asked if he thought Suki was a killer. Did he believe that his wife caused Lita's death? Why did he continue to live with her if he believed that? Again Weissman was on his feet protesting.

Sales then honed in on the quitclaim deed Sullivan had made her sign. Suki is virtually illiterate, and had no idea what she was agreeing to, he contended. This tack upset Sullivan, who lashed back, his voice quivering: "Of all the things Mr. Sales has accused me of, I don't think he's ever called me a mental vegetable. I would be incapable of falling in love with someone who is a mental vegetable and I did fall in love. Suki is extraordinarily intelligent. She is literate, intelligent and unusually perceptive.

"She reads *Vogue* and *Cosmopolitan* magazines and clips articles from them. She's financially astute, she went from zero—having not a penny nine years ago—to six hundred thousand dollars today, of which three hundred and sixty thousand dollars is in cash. She did this in large measure through her stocks, including reading her monthly financial statements and trading stocks. You don't achieve that kind of success in today's market through luck. She read the market quotations and she understood them."

As for the house, there was nothing confusing about what he had done. "It was pretty clear, there was nothing complex about it," he maintained. She had signed one quitclaim as Suki Rogers and it wasn't witnessed; he had asked her to sign another after they married.

As for the contested $99,000 certificate of deposit, he had used his own money to buy two CDs totaling just under $200,000, and had put half the money in his wife's name, since FDIC insurance would cover up to $100,000. Suki had agreed to sign it back to him when it matured.

Before the trial drew to a close, the couple's feuding lawyers could not resist one last opportunity to publicly snipe at each other. Weissman was forced to defend the claim that he was charging Sullivan exorbitant fees.

The ugly scene was sweet revenge for Weissman, who later bragged, "I've been waiting a long time to do that." While the squabble between their attorneys was at full pitch, the animosity that had been building all week between Sullivan and Suki spilled over. Several times they sniped at each other, and one time Suki got up and shouted, "Shut up, you are just bad all the way," and fled the courtroom in tears with sales chasing after her.

In his summing up, Sales told the judge knew about the exchange. "I believe Mrs. Sullivan is in some little danger from him, and I want a permanent injunction to keep him from coming around. Money had nothing to do with her leaving Sullivan. It was fear that had driven her away. She left him because he began to act spookier and spookier," he said. "My client is not the Black Widow and she's not a gold-digger."

Weissman defended his harsh treatment of Suki. "I referred to her as 'the Black Widow' because it meant she was a seducer of men. She gains from men what she can and the next day discards them in the trash." As for his theory that she, and not Sullivan, was behind the murder, Weissman asked: "If none of this is true, why did she wait until September 19 to tell the world that James Sullivan was the person responsible for Lita Sullivan's death?"

The case was now in the hands of the judge. The day after the divorce trial concluded, Sullivan pleaded no contest in traffic court to driving with a suspended license and an expired tag, and was sentenced to six months' probation and 90 days house arrest. Because he had not been sworn in on the day he lied about Suki, he escaped being charged with perjury.

A couple of days later, Suki was back in court facing the serious charge of lying under oath about the fender-bender on South Ocean Boulevard. She pleaded no contest. In mitigation, her lawyer, David Roth, tried to convince the judge that his client had been caught between a rock and a hard place. The reason she gave the testimony she did was out of fear, he said. She was sentenced to one year on probation, fined her $265 in costs and ordered her to give a truthful statement about the March 8 incident within seventy-two hours.

A month later, on December 10, Judge Hubert Lindsey came down firmly on the side of James Sullivan, who got everything, even Coco. Lindsey had not bought for a minute the argument that Suki was virtually illiterate, since she had been in the country for seventeen years, read the local newspaper every day, entertained English-speaking friends and played the stock market.

Under Florida law, he ruled, there were no marital assets except for the jewelry Sullivan had given her. If they were feeling the financial pinch, that was because they had spent freely. "They traveled extensively, attended parties, dined out frequently and in general, had a grand time during most of their marriage," said the judge. That, along with bad investments, had eaten into Sullivan's fortune. Suki got to keep her $42,000 engagement ring and her $1,200 platinum wedding band, and a few other pieces given to her during the marriage, but she was ordered to return all other jewelry, including the sapphires she had worn to court. She also had to give back Lita's silver Mercedes. Lindsey made Sullivan pay $30,000 of her costs and upheld the permanent injunction warning them to keep away from each other. An ecstatic Sullivan could barely contain his glee.

TEN

Out of the Frying Pan . . .

Less than twenty-four hours after his stunning victory in divorce court, Sullivan was in jail. The next morning two burly investigators from the state attorney general's office showed up at his door to arrest him on charges of perjury. They allowed him just enough time to scrape together $2,000 in cash for bail, before hauling him off in handcuffs. Suki may have been the loser the day before, but it was she who put him behind bars.

She had now testified twice that he had forced her to lie under oath. In her compulsory statement, she went into details of how they had fooled the traffic court judge. Sullivan had taken her to the spot where the accident had happened, he had drawn a map so she would know exactly where each car was positioned and had her practice what she would say; that she was the driver and had moved the car because she had panicked. When the arresting officer had insisted Sullivan was the driver, Palm Beach County State Attorney's Office investigators Lieutenant William "Buzz" Patterson and

Robert Plouffe re-interviewed witnesses and the other two drivers. Helena Woolworth Guest repeated what they had said at the scene: Sullivan was driving and there was no one else in the car. She [Suki] was nowhere around. The driver of the Cadillac, Paul Gottschalk, agreed that it was a male behind the wheel. There was no way he could have mistaken James Sullivan for his petite Korean-born wife.

What Sullivan did not know is that when Suki was arrested back on May 23, she had burst into tears on the way to jail after Plouffe recited her Miranda rights. She was not behind the wheel, she was not even in the car, she had wailed. While she was locked up in the stockade, he'd tried to help her contact the lawyer Sullivan had hired to defend both of them, but he had already left for the day and Sullivan was out of town on a business trip. When he and his partner were about to take off, Suki dissolved into tears again. "Don't leave me here alone," she had pleaded, "I'll tell you what really happened." According to Plouffe, "Mrs. Sullivan then advised that she would like to tell the truth about this whole thing, but was very frightened of what her husband might do to her if he found out she was talking."

She was also upset because she was supposed to be at Palm Beach International Airport that afternoon to pick up her husband on his return from his trip. "Don't worry," Plouffe had comforted her, "we will meet him instead."

As Sullivan's eyes scoured the waiting group of limo drivers for his wife at the airport exit, Plouffe stepped forward. "James Sullivan? Your wife won't be meeting you tonight. She's in jail on perjury charges." Sullivan began rooting around in his pockets for a quarter to call his lawyer and came up empty. Plouffe's partner, Patterson, tossed him the 25 cents. When he arrested him seven months later, Sullivan handed him a quarter.

Over the winter, Sullivan's lawyer battled to keep his atrocious driving record out of the upcoming perjury trial, along with the evidence that had convicted him in the suspended license case. He also persuaded the court to allow his client a daily break from his domestic incarceration to smack a tennis ball around.

Although Sullivan was still under house arrest for driving without a license, it did not seem to curb his social life. Indeed, his detention had become the talk of the town. For one thing, he never seemed to be off the tennis courts. "It is good for him," his probation supervisor, Will Agnew, told *The Palm Beach Post*. "He has a doctor's letter that says tennis is therapy for him." Despite having described himself as retired on his 1989 tax returns, he was allowed to leave home every weekday to go to work, and he was somehow able to ignore his curfew and turn up at parties. At one point, the prosecutor went back to court to ask that he at least be restricted to a few of the mansion's twenty-four rooms.

The situation came under further scrutiny when an incident at the house ended up with the police being called. According to Sullivan, local teenagers had taken to taunting him and trespassing on his stretch of private beach. He said he'd chased them because they were vandalizing the cabana; the parents of the kids claimed he'd assaulted one of them.

In March, at a pre-trial hearing for his perjury case, Sullivan tried to stop Suki giving evidence against him, citing Florida's marital privilege law. Pillow talk should be protected, he argued; the fact that they were now divorced was irrelevant. Judge Marvin Mounts reluctantly agreed. "In my own view, the privilege should not exist if the husband and wife are talking about planning a criminal act," he said. But although he ruled that Suki need not divulge her private conversations with her husband, she could still be a state witness.

In the end it didn't matter. Suki did not have to face her ex-husband in a courtroom, because on May 30 Sullivan pleaded no contest to two counts of perjury, despite the judge's advice to take his case to a jury. His excuse was that he could not face any more publicity. "I appreciate your consideration," Sullivan told him, "but unless you were the victim of the press as I certainly have been, one cannot know the extent of the pain." Judge Mounts sentenced him to a year in jail and a year of probation.

What was to happen concurrently with his house arrest was left up to the discretion of the Florida Department of Corrections, which again opted to let him also serve out this new jail time at home. But this time around Judge Mounts told the sheriff's office to impose tougher restrictions.

Before Sullivan's sentence began, he took a trip to Orlando, where he was due to testify once more against George Bissell, who, along with his wife Pilar, was fighting the seizure of his $1.6 million home on Brazilian Avenue under the tough RICO laws, which allowed the state to grab property used in racketeering. At a June 27 hearing, prosecutors claimed that Pilar Bissell had helped her husband snare investors for his scams by throwing parties for likely victims at the house. She bristled at the suggestion that she'd reeled in suckers at her soirees: "Business is never mingled with social friends," she sniffed. "It's always rude to discuss business when ladies are present."

She swore that she had signed papers put in front of her by Bissell without bothering to read them, because her husband had said that the documents were for setting up a trust fund for their daughter, Dominique, and both parents' signatures were needed.

Bissell was out on bond pending an appeal of his 10-year sentence. The couple glowered at Sullivan as he refuted her testimony, claiming that Pilar was involved up to her neck. He said he had met them on many occasions between 1985 and 1988, 109 to be precise. He was able to be exact about this because he kept diaries in which he noted down every appointment. He added that he had been to their home many times and that business was often discussed there. At one dinner, in July 1988, he had queried late payments on his investment, and Mrs. Bissell came up with an explanation which showed she clearly understood what was going on. She angrily dismissed his claim: "Mr. Sullivan is lying again."

Whether Pilar Bissell was guilty or not, few people in Palm Beach believed that Jim was an innocent dupe. According to Brad Moores, "Sullivan was involved with this orchid scheme. George Bissell ended up going to prison, but Bissell told me that Sullivan was involved in all kinds of stuff and he and somebody else—I don't want to implicate anyone who has not been officially implicated—went to Bissell and threatened to do something to his family."

While Sullivan was trying to bury his former friends in Orlando, Palm Beach Assistant District Attorney Dan Galo was arguing against house arrest. Sullivan had abused the program, he said. He was out playing tennis, attending social gatherings, and in two trespassing incidents, there were even allegations of batteries.

This time would be no picnic, promised Lieutenant James Holland, the officer appointed to oversee Sullivan's in-house lock-down. He would be allowed to swim in his pool, but nighttime parties were out. Alcohol was forbidden for the duration of his detention. He would have to wear an electronic ankle bracelet with a transmitter device that would immediately signal the sheriff's office if it was tampered with. He was restricted to the ground floor of the mansion and would be allowed out, for business meetings only, Monday through Friday between 9:00 A.M. and 7:00 P.M. and he had to call when he left the house and again when he arrived at his destination. "We have made his house a jail cell," said Holland.

What is incredible is that Sullivan was able to meet the criteria for house arrest in the first place. To qualify, the detainee has to have a job. A letter is then sent out from the sheriff's office to the employer informing him that the employee is under arrest and advising him to notify the office immediately if he turns up late for work, or takes an early pass. Sullivan produced a amateur-looking piece of headed note paper identifying him as the president of an outfit named Progressive Funding, which claimed to provide a variety of financial services to the direct mail companies, hotels, convention centers and entertainment concerns he claimed were clients. In fact, Progressive Funding, which listed Lita as a co-director, was wound up in 1982.

Despite complaints that he was just another rich man who believed himself to be above the law, and had been cut too much slack, the then–50-year-old Sullivan found himself confined to his home, his every movement documented, increasingly strapped for cash, and still the prime suspect in the 1987 killing of Lita.

In the four years since Lita had died, the Atlanta police had continued to look at other suspects. Convinced her death was a contract killing, they had checked out a bunch of bumbling thugs based in Knoxville, Tennessee, whose specialty was murder-for-hire. The ringleader, Richard Savage, and a sidekick, Sean Doutre, had recently been convicted in the slaying of Anita Spearman, another Atlanta woman. Her husband Robert, who'd paid them to kill her, committed suicide in prison after he had been caught trying to hire a helicopter to break out of jail. But the Knoxville crew was soon dismissed as being too stupid—they had practically left calling cards behind them. Lita's killers were a tad more professional.

In July, the Bissells' lawyers subpoenaed all of Sullivan's personal diaries, records and calendars from January 1, 1985, to December 31, 1989. Sullivan immediately fired off a letter saying that to comply would be an invasion of his privacy. "My diaries and calendars contain extensive and highly personal data having no relevance whatsoever to the testimony I gave at the trial," he wrote. His objection was endorsed by Florida's Assistant Attorney General Ann Corcoran, whose help he tried to enlist to skewer his former friends. In August, he wrote to her claiming that Pilar Bissell was stalking him:

> Dear Ann,
> At approximately 2:00 P.M., I was driving away from the Post Office, I noticed a metallic blue automobile swing in closely behind me. At the stop sign at Ocean Blvd., I saw the driver to be [Pilar] Dora Bissell. She tailgated me the entire two miles to my home at

*the corner of Via Bellaria, a small dead-end
street with only seven homes on it. When I
made my turn, so did she. I thereupon stopped my car at my front door. She stopped behind me and after a minute's delay, swung
into the circular drive of my neighbor across
the street and engaged his gardener in conversation. I made a three-point turn and continued my errand but a half-hour later when I
returned, I asked the gardener what she
wanted. He said she told him that I was following her and acted upset, although he admitted being puzzled because she was behind
me. I then called you but you were not in.*

*I do not know what she may have been or
is planning. But knowing the Bissells' devi-
ousness, I believe it prudent to ask you for an
Order of Protection filed on my behalf to pre-
clude my being victimized by them in any
way.*

While he was trying to further incriminate Pilar, the
Atlanta police were stepping up the pressure on him.
They also talked frequently to the McClintons and repeatedly assured them that the case would not be closed
until the person responsible was behind bars.

On September 5, Marvin Marable, who police suspected of being one of Sullivan's accomplices, agreed
to talk in return for immunity. Detective Welcome
Harris said: "We still believe that the forty-two-year-
old Marable was the go-between for Sullivan to get
his wife killed. I'll bet my life on it."

But despite being granted freedom from prosecution,

Marable stopped short of implicating himself. He told the Atlanta cops that he had bugged his home phone in December 1985 after his marriage began to break up. Over the next eight months, he had recorded some forty tapes that provided ample evidence that his wife's best friend, Lita Sullivan, was leading her astray. He said he had confronted Poppy "about her errant ways during her association with Lita," but his ruse had backfired when Lita called the cops. He pled guilty to illegal wiretapping and was put on probation.

He said he had called Sullivan telling him he had information that would help him in his case against Lita. Sullivan offered him $30,000 for the tapes, which he sent by courier. After Sullivan listened to them, he returned 35 of them through an attorney. When Marable asked where the missing tapes were, Sullivan and his lawyer claimed to be baffled as to their disappearance. He had no more contact with Sullivan until he called him three days before the murder. He asked if Lita was still driving the same car, if anyone was living with her at the Buckhead townhouse. Marable said he thought Sullivan was about to unleash a private investigator on his wife. He found out about the murder when an attorney called him. But while Marable was happy to rat out Sullivan, he steadfastly denied being the middleman in a murder conspiracy.

On the morning of September 6, agents from the Georgia FBI arrived in Palm Beach armed with a sealed search warrant for 920 South Ocean Boulevard. They were accompanied by Florida FBI officers and two motorbike cops from the Palm Beach Police Department. When they arrived, Sullivan was out running errands. They went over every inch of the mansion, unearthing four guns, including a 12-gauge L.C. Smith shotgun, a

.22-caliber Winchester short rifle, a 12-gauge bolt-action Mossberg and a .38-caliber Smith & Wesson revolver. By 11:30 A.M., just as the convoy of FBI vehicles was preparing to leave with boxes full of papers, files and the four guns, Sullivan pulled into the driveway in his Mercedes.

The search was part of the ongoing grand jury probe into Lita's death, which had been overshadowed by Sullivan's very public divorce and perjury trial. It was Sullivan's own testimony at George Bissell's fraud trial that he kept copious diaries and files which had tipped off the Georgia investigators, who then obtained a warrant. They also contacted Allstate Insurance Company, which provided them with a list of items amounting to $217,000 that Sullivan had claimed were looted from the Buckhead house in the aftermath of Lita's murder. Allstate disputed the claim, the case was later settled out of court and a gag order was imposed on the outcome.

The tip that there might be firearms and other incriminating evidence in the Florida house had come from John Connolly, who had spent a bizarre week as Sullivan's house guest, and then written about the experience for the now-defunct *Spy* magazine. It is not quite clear why Sullivan would invite the retired New York cop-turned-scribe into his home and his life. One theory put forth by Connolly is that Sullivan thought, with the perjury trial looming, that he could tweak the article in his favor. It turned out to be one of the worst decisions he ever made.

The two were thrown together inadvertently by Sullivan's ex-friend and business associate, now his sworn enemy, George Bissell. Connolly had been commissioned to write a piece on the multimillion-dollar orchid scam for *Forbes* magazine, and had been told that James Sullivan was still smarting from losing his investment. When he was contacted, it was clear that not only was Sullivan anxious to badmouth his former friend, but he also seemed to know where all the other bodies in Palm Beach were buried, and became a source on other stories.

They met in April of 1991 at Testa's, while Connolly was covering the latest scandal in town, the William Kennedy Smith rape case. That summer, when Sullivan was visiting the Long Island, New York, home of his friends Allan and Millie Resnick, he'd called Connolly at his New York apartment and invited him for the weekend.

They'd spent Saturday afternoon playing tennis, and in the evening drove to a local restaurant. For the writer, by far the most memorable event of the weekend was the trip back to the Resnicks' after dinner, when, he claims, Sullivan suddenly went ballistic at an oncoming driver who blinded him with his high beams. The unreasonable intensity of Sullivan's anger made Connolly see his reliable source in a new light.

Sullivan then asked Connolly to spend a week in August at the Casa Eleda, which was still on the block and listed with Sotheby's International Realty of Palm Beach. As he drove up to the mansion, like everyone else, he was impressed; once inside, it was another matter. Connolly was appalled to find that the man who, until his current disgrace, had headed up the Landmarks Preservation Commission was living in squalor. "It was dirty, dusty and in terrible disrepair," he wrote, "and one upstairs bathroom had a foot-and-a-half hole."

"The whole place was very dark and forbidding," maintains Connolly. "There was one high four-poster thing, very ornate, made of some type of wood in the living room, with a silk or satin type sheet on it, which I guess you used for, whatever. I think he bought the furnishings with the house." He also saw evidence of the irrational stinginess that had driven Lita and Suki to despair as Sullivan saved the plastic wrapper from his *Wall Street Journal* to use in the microwave. And despite the debilitating heat and humidity that shrouds Florida in August, the air-conditioning was always off.

As Connolly prowled around the house, he noticed that Sullivan was obsessively neat about his papers, which he kept piled on a bed in one of the eighteen bedrooms. He clipped newspaper articles, and kept a daily journal of his every activity. No detail was too small to be overlooked. He bragged to Connolly that he had documented the minutiae of his life for decades and never discarded a single notebook.

When he wasn't scribbling in his diary, Sullivan's day was filled with domestic chores. Nights were spent in the bougainvillea-scented courtyard sitting by the pool that he cleaned out himself. Over a glass of wine— he had no qualms about flouting the no-alcohol rule of his detention—he opened up to the author.

The news that their former son-in-law was in trouble with the law again, and this time with potentially very serious consequences, brought some satisfaction to the McClintons. As a convicted felon, if he were found guilty of these new gun charges, he could kiss his sweet deal of a house arrest goodbye and spend the next few months in jail, where they firmly believed he belonged.

On September 11, Sullivan pleaded not guilty to possession of an illegal short-barrelled shotgun and of another firearm. His latest legal team of Michael Salnick and Barry Krischer took the line that the guns were not his, and claimed he had no idea how they had gotten into his house. Salnick told the court that other people had lived at and visited the mansion, naming, in particular, Matt and Jean Houston.

The couple, who had been friendly with him for five years, were incensed at the implication they had stashed guns at his home. Matt Houston said he had never seen any weapons during his frequent visits to the mansion and contended that he and Jean had used one of the rooms for storing nothing more dangerous than a baby crib, two gaming tables and some other personal items.

Salkin told the court that his client needed to get out of jail to pay off an $830,000 debt on his house, or risk losing it. The bank had called in the entire mortgage after discovering that Sullivan had no insurance on the mansion. When prosecutor Dan Galo requested that bail be denied, Judge Marvin Mounts asked, "Where is he going to run? Madagascar?"

At any rate, the point was moot. Anyone arrested on the house arrest program is no longer eligible for bail, Sheriff's Deputy Brian Hern told the court. Salnick tried again. Sullivan could lose his home, he pleaded. But no mitigating circumstances could affect the outcome of this hearing; he had run out of breaks. Dressed in dark blue prison duds, his hands cuffed behind his back, he was led off to a cell to finish the remaining nine months of his one-year sentence for perjury.

A week after his incarceration, Sullivan was mulling over an offer for his house which was fast becoming an eyesore. Earlier that year, in May, before Connolly's visit, he had received a warning letter from the town complaining about the state of his lawn. There were strict rules about garden neatness in Palm Beach: grass had to be no more than eight inches high, bushes and other foliage had to be kept neatly trimmed. Tidy it up, he was told, or the Code Enforcement Board would hold a public hearing about it.

To compound his misery, the FBI released its theory of what had happened the day Lita was shot. A sworn affidavit from agent Todd Letcher, who had taken part in the search of the Casa Eleda, spelled out what he believed was Sullivan's motive for killing his wife, how he'd hired accomplices carry out the murder, and the incriminating evidence that led back to him.

Greed was the motivator, said Letcher. Sullivan could not risk a divorce trial in which he was going to have to hand over a chunk of his fortune to Lita. She had refused to sign the loan application, therefore, he would lose his mansion. Telephone records of calls between Atlanta and Sullivan's home three days before the murder, and on the day Lita died, and a tape-recorded call describing the murder weapon—details the Atlanta police had never made public—placed him squarely in the middle of a murder-for-hire plot.

The same day as the damning document was made public, Joel Weissman was back in court asking Judge Mounts to let Sullivan sign legal papers to sell the house. A week later, he accepted an offer of $3 million. Even though it was way below his asking price of $4.9 million, it had been on the market for well over a year and he was running out of time. After years of legal woes, he needed the money to pay his attorneys' bills.

As soon as the McClintons got wind of the transaction, they filed a motion to stop Sullivan from pocketing the cash. They planned to sue their former son-in-law in civil court for the wrongful death of their daughter and wanted to stop him from getting access to money that could well be awarded to Lita's estate. "They have well-founded fear that Sullivan would attempt to conceal, dissipate or remove from the jurisdiction of this court, the net proceeds from the sale to avoid the payment of any verdict rendered against him as a result of the civil action," their lawyer claimed at a meeting. The judge granted them a restraining order and ordered that the proceeds from the sale of the house should be placed in an escrow account.

When he heard about the ruling, Weissman was furious and denounced it as laughable. He had not been notified about the hearing, nor had there been any civil suit raised against his client.

But at last, events were beginning to turn in the McClintons' favor. On the same day Weissman had approached Judge Mounts about the sale of the mansion, and Todd Letcher's affidavit had been released, the FBI nabbed Thomas Bruce Henley at his home in Acworth, Georgia. He was charged with using interstate phone lines to call Sullivan from a rest stop on Interstate 85 in Suwanee, at 9:00 A.M. on the morning of the murder, after having been identified by Randall Benson as one of the men who bought roses at his store, fifteen minutes before Lita was shot. He also drove a white Toyota.

Henley had a lengthy rap sheet which included forgery, assault, car theft, impersonating a police officer and possession of a firearm by a convicted felon—he also worked less than an hour by car from the rest stop. He had been released from prison in February after serving a stretch on gun possession charges, and had been ratted out by a snitch, Johnny Turner, who told cops that Henley had bragged about the murder during a trip they had made to Florida. Turner claimed that Henley

and an accomplice named Clinton Botts had killed Lita.
Marvin Marable was the go-between who'd set the
whole thing up, he said. Botts had pulled the trigger.

It all seemed to tie up, but not everyone was buying
the bureau's scenario. His boss came to Henley's defense. She said that on the mornings of January 13 and
16, he was working as a handyman in Kennesaw, a suburb of Atlanta, thirty minutes after the FBI said he'd
made the call from Suwanee. Henley's lawyer argued
that it would have been almost impossible to drive from
the rest stop to Kennesaw in thirty minutes in rush
hour traffic. He also lashed out at the government's
songbird, calling him a con man with a history of fabri-
cation. Botts was picked up in Smyrna in the early hours
of late September 15 on an unrelated charge, possession
of illegal drugs. He told the cops he had heard his name
being linked to Lita Sullivan's murder on the TV news
and also branded Turner as a liar.

More problems for Sullivan surfaced at the end of
September when the FBI said a videotaped inventory of
the contents of the Casa Eleda filmed at the time of his
divorce from Suki clearly showed a rifle propped up
against a wall in his second-floor office, where it had
been found by the agents who searched the house. Joel
Weissman denied it was the same weapon. He had been
in the house when the video was shot, and to his recollection, no firearms were mentioned or inventoried."

The next loss for Sullivan as he languished in jail
was the decision of the Property Appraiser's Office to
deny him a tax break. He had petitioned to have the
$2.9 million assessment levied on the Casa Eleda re-
duced to $1.8 million because it needed $1.5 million in
repairs. Along with his letter he included a contractor's
report. The house had leaking window frames; cracks

in the columns that held up the balcony; the roof and plumbing were in such a bad state that both needed to be totally replaced.

On October 16, a judge upheld Sullivan's right not to be deposed by the attorneys representing the McClintons in their wrongful death suit. By the end of the month, the McClintons were denied their request to tie up the money from the sale of the mansion until the outcome of their wrongful death suit was decided. They had cited Suki's testimony but without a suit having actually been filed, the judge had no option but to lift the temporary ban. Sullivan could unload his home, but he and his attorneys were warned not to engage in "transferring, secreting or removing assets from the sale of the house outside Palm Beach County."

ELEVEN
With his Foot in his Mouth

Whatever Jim Sullivan was thinking when he asked a former ten-year veteran New York detective to scrutinize his life, the ploy backfired horribly. When the November issue of *Spy* magazine hit the stands in late October, the effect on Palm Beach was electric.

And if the blistering article, which was fittingly entitled "The Prime Suspect," had his neighbors reeling, Sullivan must have been sick to the point of panic when it appeared. It had to be painfully clear to him that he had gravely miscalculated. According to John Connolly, Sullivan had believed that, if he could successfully snow him, the respected ex-cop would exonerate Jim in the death of Lita.

Instead, the very people he had tried so hard to impress, the moneyed snobs who'd had to come begging for his permission to landscape their lot or install another bathroom, were now clucking over the scathing magazine piece, which posited that he had not only orchestrated the murder of his wife, but that there was good reason to believe he had also killed his uncle.

He had damned himself. There, in his own words, was his cruel rant that he had never loved Lita, and the lunatic insinuation that her gentle and law-abiding parents had had their beloved daughter bumped off to cash in on a $250,000 life insurance policy. Then there was the laughable suggestion that Weissman's deplorable trial antic asserting that the pint-sized Suki did it had some actual merit; and Sullivan's claim that she had worked as a hooker in Chicago.

"Jim, did you arrange to have Lita killed?" Connolly had asked him point-blank one night. When Sullivan did not answer, Connolly had tried again. "Well, who do you think murdered your wife?" That was the moment when Sullivan shifted the blame onto his former in-laws. "Did I tell you about the life insurance her family received?" he asked. "You are not suggesting her parents were responsible?" queried Connolly. "They did get all that money," he replied.

Worse still, it was Connolly who had presented the Atlanta police and the Georgia FBI with the ammunition they needed to carry out the search which had led to his arrest on illegal firearms possession and landed him in jail where, according to the cops and the McClintons, he was in the right place for the wrong reason. Connolly told them about the stacks of meticulously kept weekly planners and leather-bound diaries in which Sullivan chronicled his every waking minute, prompting the author to comment, "I think he's so pathological, I don't think he can help himself."

What emerged was a picture of an obsessive personality consumed with every minute detail of his own life, which is why he was able to say without a shadow of doubt that he had visited the Bissells' home exactly 109 times. Yet it was not the fascination for facts and figures that began to worry Connolly. During the week he spent with Sullivan, he began to sense that his host was barely suppressing a sociopathic streak that could place him in real danger. "I felt he'd shoot me in the back. He would never confront me face-to-face but I was concerned he would shoot me in the back," Connolly says.

"I must say that I underestimated him, in that he had hubris, which is always dangerous. But he was under house arrest and I couldn't imagine that he would be that brazenly stupid, to squirrel away a couple of guns in that 17,000-foot mausoleum. I thought that would be incredibly stupid. And I was very wrong because when he was arrested he had four guns, including a sawn-off shotgun." Sullivan's nightly alcohol consumption was against the rules of house arrest, but Connolly kept that to himself. "It would have been too cheap and petty to turn him in over a bottle of wine," he says.

As copies of *Spy* flew off the shelves, the locals learned for the first time of Sullivan's preposterous allegation that the sweet-natured Lita had somehow degenerated into becoming a drug mule for a man whom she had dated after leaving Jim. In a town where everybody knew when anyone sneezed, they wondered how they could have missed the wild affairs he accused her of having; no one could remember ever seeing or hearing about her with another guy.

Sullivan had another theory he ran by Connolly which found its way into print: Marvin Marable could have murdered Lita out of revenge for having him arrested for illegal wiretapping when she discovered he had been listening in on her phone calls for weeks on end.

The writer's conclusions about the fate of Frank Bienert, whose untimely death had catapulted Sullivan into millionaire status, were just as alarming. After he left Sullivan's mansion, he had gone to Macon and interviewed employees of Crown Beverages. There he was reportedly shown a lengthy report Frank had written on December 30, 1984, which listed all of Sullivan's shortcomings and confirmed that the old man had intended to fire his nephew and cut him out of his will. According to the people Connolly spoke with, Sullivan had known about the letter and of his uncle's resolve to oust him from the company; with the emergence of such a strong motive, Connolly concluded in the article that Bienert's curious death was no accident.

Connolly even offered clues as to how Uncle Frank's demise might have been engineered. When Sullivan's first wife was pregnant with their first child, she had undergone surgery to remove blood clots. She had also been prescribed the anticoagulant drug coumadin. He described how Catherine, who, all these years later, was so wary of her former husband that she agreed to meet the writer only after much cajoling and in another city, told him that at the time, she had been struck by Jim's morbid interest in the drug; he had questioned her doctor at length about it and seemed especially fixated on its propensity for causing hemorrhaging.

Connolly is convinced that this was a secret she had held close for years and that it had deterred her from hauling her millionaire ex into court to force him to provide for their children. "Catherine was a nurse; he's a manipulative son of a bitch, and I'm willing to bet he said to her, 'I need coumadin for a customer' and she got it for him. [When she realized what he had done,] he warned her: 'If you ever say anything about me, I'll say you were in on this.' I've met the woman, I'd be shocked if she was, but I believe he would say that," says Connolly. He then contacted Dr. Michael Baden, who from 1960 until 1985 was New York City's medical examiner and is currently co-director for the Medicolegal Investigative Unit of the New York State Police, and asked him if Uncle Frank's symptoms were similar to those suffered by victims of coumadin poisoning. Baden said they could have been.

With no autopsy, there was no evidence, and, according to Connolly, Sullivan had Bienert cremated before anyone had time to ask any questions. To Connolly, it was no coincidence that Catherine left the next week. She told him that at least one family member maintained, "I always thought Jim killed Uncle Frank." Although the Macon police looked into the allegations, no charges were ever forthcoming.

Whatever passed between them when Frank Bienert died, it haunted Catherine. Ann Mulligan now says that "Cappy" consciously avoided doing anything to antagonize her former husband. "It's always been a long, ongoing struggle for her. Cappy was always afraid of what Jim had gotten involved in. She was afraid that if she said something about him, they [his hit squad] would come and everybody would be slaughtered."

The story was devastating. Most of the people Sullivan had counted on as friends never again took his phone calls. Nowadays they barely admit to having known him at all and stress that he was never really "one of us." Stewing behind bars, Sullivan complained bitterly that he had been stitched up. "He called me from jail," says Connolly. "I told him, 'Jim, you got what you deserved,' and he made some sort of ominous sounds. I don't remember what they were, but I had no regrets about what I did."

On October 13, Sullivan's attorney was back in court. This time, he wanted to be transferred to solitary confinement, arguing that the Georgia authorities might plant an informant in his cell in their desperation to nail him for Lita's murder. Sullivan's request for private accommodation was denied.

With his client in county jail, Weissman handled the closing of the Casa Eleda, which finally went under the hammer on December 11, when a Boca Raton couple snapped it up for the bargain basement price of $3 million—in cash. Apart from $100,000 he owed in unpaid county property taxes, Sullivan pocketed the lot, having paid off the outstanding mortgage debt a few weeks before. Shortly after, he bought a place in The Sanctuary, one of Boca Raton's luxurious waterfront communities. It was an undeniable step down from the mansion on South Ocean Boulevard, but it was still an enviable address. The 107 single-family, 4,000- to 12,000-square-foot homes scattered over half-acre lots between the Intercoastal Waterway and private canals nowadays fetch between $700,000 and $5 million.

In December, to fight the firearms charges and hopeful of getting sprung from jail, Sullivan hired yet another high-profile lawyer, Richard Lubin, who immediately appealed for sympathy. His client was not faring well in his new role of millionaire convict.

One of the problems Lubin had to overcome was that the videotape had clearly shown the gun in Sullivan's office. Since the camera does not lie, his only hope was to argue that the raid was illegal and the charges should therefore be thrown out. He also claimed that the FBI had pulled something slick on the judge who had issued the search warrant. Agent Todd Letcher's affidavit was, "replete with misstatement, half-truths and omissions that would have affected whether the warrant was issued." The FBI sources were questionable, he argued. John Connolly was hardly a disinterested party, since he was working for *Spy*. Johnny Turner was a convicted forger who had concocted his story to get out of jail.

Lubin claimed that Turner had first told Fulton County prosecutors in March 1988 that he had valuable information about the death of Lita Sullivan, and he would be willing to give it up for a free pass. His offer lay dormant until 1991 when the FBI wired him up with four thousand dollars' worth of surveillance equipment and set him loose. But instead of leading them to the weapon and the killers, he skipped town. He was tracked down and charged with stealing FBI equipment. The FBI knew that Turner was a liar and yet, on the basis of bogus information, they were able to search Sullivan's house a month later. Furthermore, Lubin charged, Turner had a history of lying. In 1988, he had claimed he knew all about a plot to kill the Savannah D.A., and that had turned out to be false. He also accused the FBI of using excessive force; they waited until Sullivan went out, then broke down the door, he said.

Letcher told the judge that he had relied on Lita's case file in seeking the search warrant. He believed that what was in the file was true. James Sullivan was the number one suspect in his wife's murder, and it was on that basis that he had applied for the order.

The McClintons derived some small comfort from their former son-in-law's unhappiness at having to spend Christmas in jail. On December 23, 1991, they made the holiday season a little worse for him when they filed a wrongful death suit, charging that he had "solicited and conspired with others to commit the murder of Lita McClinton Sullivan." They put him on notice that they would be seeking damages in excess of $10,000.

The couple contacted veteran investigator Pat McKenna, and asked him for help in finding a lawyer to take on their wealthy son-in-law. McKenna had worked on many high-profile investigations, including the successful defense of William Kennedy Smith, who was accused and acquitted of raping a young Jupiter mom in 1991. "They contacted me looking for someone to help them in the wrongful death suit. I thought of Brad Moores. We were both trying to build up a business and neither of us could really afford to do it—the McClintons were ordinary people. They didn't have the kind of money you need to hire high-powered legal staff. We knew the case would cost a lot to put on, but it was the right thing to do. As soon as I spoke to Emory McClinton, I was hooked. He and JoAnn are wonderful people. What was incredible to me was that they believed in the system even after all these years."

Moores flew to Atlanta to meet them and was equally impressed. He contacted Atlanta lawyer David Boone, who also warmed to the couple. "I liked them very much," he says. "They are very, very upstanding, wonderful people and they believe in themselves, in the system, they believe in justice, in right and wrong, and they want to do the right thing for the right reason. And they are tireless in their pursuit of justice. God bless them."

By the time January 1992 was over, Sullivan was facing a murder trial, a wrongful death civil suit and the ongoing firearms case. He began to fight back, starting with a counterclaim for slander against his former in-laws. They had made him lose $100,000 on his house by displaying a "wanton disregard" for his rights by seeking a temporary restriction on the sale of the property. They had interfered with the contract negotiations, and their suit had been frivolous and abusive, he whined.

Then he wanted the wrongful death suit tossed out of court, since, he said, it left out the names of the real perpetrators who had killed his wife. He denied again that he had had anything to do with Lita's murder. His lawyer dismissed the suit as being "total hogwash," and in an incredibly nasty jibe, he added: "I think it is sad that the McClintons are trying to get rich from their daughter's death."

On January 3, Sullivan testified that he did not need Lita's signature on a bank loan, since he had around $1.5 million in cash and a further $1.5 million in retirement funds. Although he owed nearly $1 million on the mansion, he could easily have stumped up the dough. (In fact, he was two months late on a penultimate payment of $750,000 and the interest was compounding daily.) The FBI had tricked the judge into signing a search warrant. Bob Christenson had told him what kind of gun had killed Lita. He was looking for ammunition to use against her in the divorce and had merely called to find out if his wife had a string of boyfriends.

A week later the guillotine fell. On January 10, Jim Sullivan was indicted by a grand jury in Atlanta. The charges were:

- COUNT 1: Using interstate phone lines between his Palm Beach mansion and the residence of Marvin Marable in Atlanta at 7:02 A.M. and on January 13, 1987, to arrange and pay for the murder of Lita McClinton Sullivan.
- COUNT 2: Using interstate phone lines between room 518 at the Howard Johnson Motel at 5793 Rosewell Road, Atlanta, and his home in Palm Beach at 7:44 A.M. on January 13, 1987, to arrange and pay for the murder of Lita McClinton Sullivan, a call which lasted between two and three minutes.
- COUNT 3: Using interstate phone lines between his home in Palm Beach and the Howard Johnson Motel in Atlanta at 10:33 A.M.
- COUNT 4: Using interstate phone lines between the Suwanee Rest Stop in Sandy Springs, Georgia, and Palm Beach at 9:00 A.M. on January 16, 1987, to arrange and pay for the murder of Lita McClinton Sullivan.
- COUNT 5: Causing others to use a firearm.

Also cited were the calls he made to Christenson's office in Atlanta at 8:58 A.M. and again at 9:31 A.M. on January 13, 1987.

"You wait for this so long—I was in a shambles," JoAnn told the *Palm Beach Daily News*. "I was so elated, yet so depressed, because it is so close to the anniversary of Lita's death, and this brings it all back." When the news broke, the press descended on their home in hordes. Ten minutes after pushing past the crush of cameras, they fled to an out-of-town cabin with no phones or television. Later they watched a videotaped recording of the press conference in which the indictment was read by United States Attorney Joe D. Whitley.

Predictably, Sullivan's lawyers began howling. "It is ridiculous," puffed Lubin. "Shocking," said Joel Weissman. "It just doesn't add up," he told the paper. "But that's in Atlanta, and there must be something we were unaware of here in Florida. But you can present anything you want at a grand jury; they only get one side of it. I am sorry for him. I wish there was something I could do for him."

On January 24, the state attorney's office released statements made by Sullivan on the day his home was searched. "The polygraph I took showed I was telling the truth, but I don't remember the questions," he told FBI agent Robert Ingram, adding that he was upset over being accused of Lita's death. But he never offered an explanation in answer to Ingram's query why he'd called the Howard Johnson motel in Atlanta. He said it was "to make reservations for an upcoming trip." Yet his call had been put through to room 518 instead of the reservation desk. As for the call to the mansion forty minutes after the shooting, he denied having gotten it.

In spite of the serious charges he faced, Sullivan had not shrunk away from the petty legal wrangles that seemed to appeal to his combative nature. At the beginning of February, he sued the driver of a truck he said had knocked him unconscious while he was riding his bicycle to the tennis courts the summer before, claiming $2,000 in medical costs—incidentally, the same amount that West Palm Beach's Good Samaritan Hospital was suing him for unpaid bills. He wanted $228 to repair the bike, $121 for ruined clothing, $45 for shoes, $90 for his tennis racket and $110 for his racket bag.

On February 26, he got into a scuffle with his cellmate Paul O'Brien. The scrap erupted in a hallway outside the cell after Sullivan supposedly called O'Brien a snitch on learning that he had been subpoenaed by the prosecutor in the firearms case. "He came out of a meeting with his attorneys, red in the face and furious, and said he would get me," said O'Brien, who had been charged with his wife for a series of armed robberies. Sullivan got the worst of the scuffle that was broken up by two other inmates, Randy Turner and Richard Babayan. Immediately afterwards, O'Brien asked for a lawyer. Sullivan was in too much pain to give a statement. "Mr. Sullivan has a broken nose and had to have stitches behind one ear," said Robert Ferrell, a spokesman for the Palm Beach Sheriff's Office. "There will be aggravated battery charges filed against Mr. O'Brien."

On March 1, O'Brien's home at 22,275 S.W. 57th Ave. in the Sandalfoot Cove area of Boca Raton, went up in flames. With damage estimated at $20,000, the Fire Department investigators labeled the 7:45 P.M. outbreak "suspicious." Five days later, O'Brien was sentenced to 15 years for armed robbery by Judge Marvin Mounts, the same justice who was, coincidentally, presiding over Sullivan's firearms case. O'Brien's wife, Janyce, got five years probation for driving the getaway car. The arsonist was never caught.

Palm Beachers opened their papers on March 9 to find Sullivan embroiled in yet another court dispute. Despite his incarceration, he had found himself a new girl-friend. On December 18, the same day that the mansion was sold, the woman, Karen Griner, rented a three-bedroom house at 377 Seabreeze. She paid $2,500, and Sullivan ponied up the remaining $3,050 for three months' rent in advance. According to the house's owner, Frances Oyler, Griner then stopped payment on her check. Oyler then sued for $3,700, or two months' rent. Sullivan and Griner countersued, claiming, among other things, that the place was overrun with roaches and mice.

On April 3, Sullivan was taken from Palm Beach County Jail and flown to Georgia by U.S. Marshals to answer the federal charges. Facing the judge, he said what he had always said: "I plead not guilty, Your Honor." He hired veteran lawyer Ed Garland and his partner Don Samuels to defend him. Garland met with reporters after the arraignment and told them, "I doubt if there is enough evidence that would allow this case to go to a jury. Jim denies his guilt as vehemently as he can, and he will testify on his own behalf. The prosecution has nothing to go on but innuendo, suspicion and a desire to end an unsolved crime. Many others had motives to kill Lita Sullivan."

For JoAnn and Emory McClinton it was a huge relief that their former son-in-law had been arraigned just three days before the five-year statute of limitations expired on his alleged accomplices. They were present to see him hauled into court in handcuffs; it was the first time they had laid eyes on him since before Lita was murdered, and it was clear that his time behind bars had knocked off some of his glamor. The Palm Beach tan had been replaced by ashy gray prison pallor and despite his smartly pressed business suit, he looked just like any ordinary felon.

With just two weeks to go until his release after serving his sentence for perjury, prosecutors, at a bond hearing held on April 16, said that Sullivan constituted a serious risk of flight. The magistrate agreed and froze $2.9 million of Sullivan's assets. His new girlfriend, who chimed in on his behalf in court, said they'd met when she was working as a property manager in Macon. (Sullivan had unloaded his Macon business two years before Lita packed up her car and left him.) Griner said Sullivan had paid her $1,500 a month as his "personal assistant," and they were talking about getting married.

Back in Palm Beach Circuit Court, prosecutor Dan Galo produced a sworn affidavit from Suki identifying the guns as her former husband's. Richard Lubin wanted to question Detective Welcome Harris and Georgia FBI Agent Robert Ingram.

Galo said he couldn't force Harris and Ingram to cooperate and risk compromising the case in Atlanta. Judge Mounts disagreed. Produce the agents within forty-five days or he would throw out the charges against Sullivan, he warned. Meanwhile, Suki, having successfully completed her probation on her perjury conviction, had her record wiped clean.

Since both the firearms case and the conspiracy to murder charges in Atlanta hinged so much on what had been retrieved at the mansion, his lawyers kept hammering away at the legality of the search. Sullivan had every right to expect privacy in his home, Lubin argued. Sullivan gave up that right by committing his earlier offenses, objected Galo. "He was a jail inmate who was incarcerated and then transferred to his residence, subject to constant surveillance and on-site inspection. Mr. Sullivan was told his residence was a penal institution. He signed a contract agreeing to the conditions, which included wearing a monitoring device and having his home inspected by sheriff's deputies."

While the wrangling over the search of his house went on, the rent case was resolved with a loss for Sullivan and Karen Griner.

In late April, Sullivan enjoyed a brief spell of freedom. He was released from county jail, where he had been held since March 31, and instantly put on a budget of $8,000 a month to cover the cost of his own home, $1,500 for the rent of his lover's new digs, a garage apartment in Palm Beach, and her compensation as the manager of his beleaguered finances. He would also be reimbursed for travel costs for him and his attorney to go to Atlanta for the upcoming trial.

The bond was set at the proceeds of the sale of the house. The money (the $2.9 million frozen by the court) was put in an escrow account and Sullivan's lawyers were warned not to disburse any funds to him. "He will lose the full amount if he flees," said Assistant U.S. Attorney William McKinnon, Jr.

Sullivan was returned to Palm Beach County Sheriff's Office to complete the last few days of his house arrest sentence, then moved in with Karen Griner. In July, she became the next woman to dump him when she went back to live in Georgia. He gave up the garage apartment, sold the property he had bought in Boca Raton, and rented an apartment in Mariner Village, Boynton Beach.

Sullivan spent the summer huddled with his defense team. One of his neighbors in the complex was Barbara Brackett, who had no idea he was the James Sullivan whose soap opera divorce had been splashed all over the front pages and TV news. To her, he was just the quiet guy down the block. "He was a very nice gentleman, he kept very much to himself. I really only spoke to him when he was walking the dog; he had a cute little dog. I didn't know who he was," she says, "I'm not from Palm Beach."

Back in county jail, Randy Turner, the inmate who had helped break up the fight between Paul O'Brien and Jim Sullivan, was giving a deposition. Richard Babayan, O'Brien, Sullivan and he had sat at the same table at mealtimes and hung out together, he said. Allegedly Sullivan had talked freely about Lita's murder to them. Turner described how, when he'd pulled O'Brien off Sullivan, Sullivan had crawled away on his hands and knees.

Sullivan was excused from testifying by Judge Mounts, who fretted that compelling him to talk would give him immunity in the murder trial. "O'Brien talked to Georgia officials and that's what started the fight. Immunity for Sullivan is not my client's headache," said his lawyer, after being warned by Mounts to confine his questions to what had happened one hour before the fight. "There's a history—these men were cellmates for months. I have no ax to grind with Mr. Sullivan."

With Sullivan failing to show up, charges against O'Brien were dropped. On October 9, all charges were dismissed against Thomas Henley. His lawyer claimed that Henley had been able to prove he was at work when the call had been made from the Suwanee rest stop. Atlanta prosecutors refused to give any explanation but confirmed that he was still a suspect in Lita's murder.

Nor did they bring charges against Henley's alleged accomplices, Marvin Marable or Clinton Botts, who, while still under investigation, served 6 months in Cobb County Jail, Georgia, for threatening a man with a knife. Two years later, he was arrested and convicted of making terrorist-type threats against his wife and sentenced to a 3-year term. After he was released from prison in 1997, his son Christopher beat him so badly that he ended up in intensive care with a ruptured spleen. The teenager had punched him unconscious, bitten him in the chest, then lashed out at the cops who came to arrest him. At his son's sentencing, Botts admitted that he had provoked the young man.

A week later Sullivan's right not to be deposed by the attorneys representing the McClintons in their wrongful death suit on Fifth Amendment grounds was upheld. Now he could give his complete attention to defending himself against the federal charges in the murder of Lita. "Jim is looking forward to his day in court," said Lubin.

TWELVE

High Noon in Atlanta

At noon on November 2, Sullivan made his first appearance before Judge Marvin Shoob having been granted special permission to leave his new home in Boynton Beach, where he was still under house arrest, to attend his trial.

He was impeccably decked out in a smart gray business suit, a pale blue shirt and dark red tie. His shoes were shining, his fading reddish curls neatly trimmed and slicked back. His summer of liberty, which had lasted from his release from prison in April until his reincarceration in September on the firearms charges, had put some color back in his face and filled out his skeletal frame. Striding into the courtroom he looked every inch the Palm Beach millionaire—six months before, as he pled not guilty at his arraignment, he was just another seedy jailbird in prison garb. If convicted, he was facing life behind bars and a $1.25 million fine. Watching him impassively—at least on the outside—was JoAnn McClinton.

"James Vincent Sullivan is a cheap and miserable man, who is so preoccupied with his wealth, it was the be-all and end-all of his existence. He arranged to have his wife murdered," began U.S. Attorney Robert F. Schroeder. "He arranged to have other people commit the brutal execution of his wife. He is cheap and miserly, he didn't want to lose anything. Lita was gunned down just hours before a divorce hearing that could have resulted in her being awarded a substantial chunk of Sullivan's fortune. He wasn't about to take that risk." In vivid detail, he described how the trusting Lita had opened her front door and found herself looking into the eyes of "someone that would have sent shivers down the spine" of a battle-hardened Vietnam vet. Clearly it was a contract murder.

The government would prove that Sullivan had masterminded the hit on his wife, said Schroeder. The FBI had connected Sullivan to her murder after being tipped off by an informant who named three men involved in a plot to kill the black wife of a white millionaire in Florida. Phone calls placed from the Atlanta area to James Sullivan's Palm Beach mansion tied him to the murder. The jury would learn how Lita was killed on the second try. Someone rang her doorbell early in the morning of January 13, but she did not answer. Shortly afterwards, a call was made to her husband's home from a motel, not far from Lita's townhouse. Less than three hours later, somebody in Sullivan's home placed a call to room 518 at the motel where the hit men were staying.

"Sullivan would have you believe that he was trying to book a room for an upcoming trip," Schroeder told the jury. "This is not a Howard Johnson man, this is a Ritz-Carlton man," he mocked. "Surely, if he was trying to book a room, he would have talked to the desk clerk about a reservation? . . .

"There was another call that morning," he continued. "Sullivan called Lita's neighbor, probing for information about her. That night, another two calls went from the motel to the Florida mansion. On the last of these, he was overheard asking tersely, 'Why not?' and then saying, 'Get flowers.' On the morning Lita was gunned down, another call was placed to the mansion from a rest stop forty minutes' drive from Lita's home, forty minutes after the slaying, that informed James Sullivan that his inconvenient wife would trouble him no more.

"These four phone calls that went between the motel room in Sandy Springs, Georgia, and Sullivan's Palm Beach mansion, would prove his connection to the murder. When the hit failed at the first attempt, he sent the killer back with the order to get the job done. The defendant's problem was how to get her to answer the door. You will hear testimony that Lita Sullivan loved roses. A witness will testify that at a dinner party the following evening, she heard Sullivan tell the caller, 'Get flowers.' " Sullivan made a note of the remark in his diary, said Schroeder.

Jurors would hear testimony about a taped phone call in which Sullivan described the gun that killed his wife as a 9-millimeter weapon. "But the police did not tell the defendant that it was a nine-millimeter and the gun was never recovered, so nobody knew the gun had nine rounds but the defendant and Lita's killer," Schroeder maintained. And they would hear from James Sullivan's third wife, Hyo-Sook [Suki] Sullivan, who would tell them about the night he confessed his role in Lita's death.

The trial had begun with jury selection the previous

morning. Out of sixty potential jurors, sixteen survived the screening process. Of the twelve who were selected, eight were men, four were women and the group included two schoolteachers, an engineer, an office manager, a software analyst, a geologist, a state of Georgia employee and a comptroller for the city of Douglasville. Two of them were black.

The jurors and four alternates listened intently as Ed Garland got to his feet. "This is a case of how an innocent man can be charged with a crime he did not commit," he began. "The prosecution's case lacks solid evidence or believable witnesses. The investigators have blinkers on—they look at the facts and see only speculation and guesswork and what they want to see. You will not be told any details about the telephone calls made between the mansion and the motel. You will not know what was said or who said it, because all they have is speculation. There's no proof about who made the calls and what was said. You will not be told what was said. What you have here is a theory."

Garland downplayed the couple's bickering over their divorce. "It was no more bitter than most. They had grown apart," he said. Despite their differences, during their marriage Sullivan had showered his wife with expensive gifts. This was no miser; his client had given Lita a $75,000 diamond-and-ruby necklace, she had $300 a week for personal spending, and he'd bought a $440,000 townhouse in Atlanta to make her happy. "He had no motive to murder her, having spent lavishly on her," he maintained.

Then he launched an attack on Lita. She had brought her death upon herself. The defense would show that Sullivan was not the only partner in the marriage who was unfaithful. Lita started cheating in 1980, four years after their wedding, and had since surrounded herself with drug users and dealers. "She was leading a double life in the fast lane, she put herself in a dangerous situation," he claimed, then softened the diatribe by adding: "The death of Lita Sullivan was a great tragedy. She didn't deserve to die under any circumstances. That is not the issue here; I am not trying to slander her."

With the jury mulling over the two portraits, one of the greedy millionaire who'd had his wife murdered to avoid parting with his money, and the other of a pampered woman who was dead because of her unsavory associates, the prosecution called its first witness. Attorney Robert Christenson, Lita's next-door neighbor, said he'd met Sullivan at the courthouse in Macon and had begun talking to him. "I told him I had just bought a home in Buckhead and Sullivan said, 'You know, I'm in the process of buying a home in Buckhead, too.' After comparing notes, it turned out we were buying right next to each other."

At first, the Sullivans were mostly in Palm Beach, but after Lita started spending more time in Atlanta, the two couples had gotten friendly. The last time he had seen Sullivan was when he came up to try to reconcile with Lita in 1985.

Christenson was near tears as he described seeing the gunman at Lita's door. "The hair stood on the back of my neck. I got a very bad feeling from this guy," he testified. He compared his gut reaction of impending danger to his service with the army in Vietnam. "It was like the instinct you had on patrol when you're feeling you are going to get hit," he said. "I just had this instinct—just stay away from him." Then he had heard Lita call out. "I couldn't make out the exact words," he said, "but it sounded like she was greeting somebody."

Ten to fifteen seconds later, he heard the shots. Fighting back tears, he described how he had run to Lita's home and found her unconscious, blood oozing from the wound in her head. He'd wanted to help her, but when he realized there was nothing he could do, he ran to the phone and dialed 911. He had glanced at his watch and noted it was 8:15 A.M. When they arrived, he'd led the police to where Lita lay mortally wounded.

He told about receiving the messages that Sullivan had left for him at the law firm where he worked, and about the conversation in which her estranged husband had asked for her phone number three days before the murder. After she died, he had seen a U-Haul moving van draw up in front of Lita's townhouse. He saw a group of men climb out of it and recognized one of them as Wilbur Warner, Sullivan's divorce lawyer.

Next on the stand was Homer Deakins, Jr. He told the court he had been in his kitchen at number 8, across the street from Lita's house, when he saw the man ring her doorbell. "I heard two noises that appeared to be steel hitting steel," he said, "then I saw this guy running out of the neighborhood."

Margaret McIntyre described how the gunman had streaked across the road in front of her. She remembered thinking how out of place he looked in the tony neighborhood. "He was not a Buckhead jogger. He was running as fast as he could go, like a bat out of hell," she said. "The streets were damp and as he swerved to turn towards West Paces Ferry Road, he almost slid into my car. I veered to get out of the way." Her description of the gunman jelled with those given by Homer Deakins and Bob Christenson. "He had on a plaid shirt and some sort of windbreaker jacket and street shoes."

The prosecution produced phone and hotel records

obtained by the police. A Southern Bell employee testified about the four calls at the crux of the government's case. Schroeder then called on lead investigator Detective Welcome Harris to explain why he believed Lita's murder was a hit. Witnesses had given police accounts of three men, the two who'd bought the roses, and the shooter. Three men fitting those descriptions, traveling in a white Toyota with North Carolina plates, had checked into room 518 of the Howard Johnson Motel at 7:24 A.M. on the morning of January 13, 1987. The man who paid the bill had signed the motel register as Johnny Furr and gave a fictitious address in Raleigh. "It appears all three acted in concert to carry out this deed," he said.

"But although Lita ended up dead, the goons who killed her were a bunch of amateurs," he added. "The shooter had taken the gun with him. A professional hit man would have used a stolen gun that could not be traced back to him, and dropped it at the scene. In Harris' twenty years as a homicide cop, a 9mm gun was rarely the weapon of choice he said. "It is a semiautomatic weapon and once it's fired, it ejects shell casings, and therefore you leave these things lying at the scene" he said. "In most instances that I'm familiar with, a small caliber weapon is used, a revolver, something like a .22. The casings remain inside it when it is fired."

Harris maintained that a real pro would never have gone inside the house. "This was a very critical factor simply because it appears that the assailant penetrated the home over approximately fifty feet. Normally I would think that, using the flowers to gain entry, the shots would have been made right at the doorway. But Mrs. Sullivan's body was discovered approximately seventeen feet or better, back into the foyer. There could have been somebody else at home and he would have put himself in jeopardy," Harris said.

The first thing Harris had found when he arrived at the crime scene was the nose of a bullet lying on the walkway, a couple of feet before the first step up to Lita's front door. In the foyer, he'd seen a copper shell casing lying in the middle of the floor. He'd spotted another shell casing to the rear of the door. After warning the jury that they would be difficult to look at, Schroeder produced a sheaf of police photographs. Harris identified each one: the gauze pads swimming in the pool of Lita's blood, the pink-ribboned flower box six feet away from her body. He pointed out the bullet hole in the box, the one in the French doors and then, as they held pictures in their hands of Lita lying on a slab in the police morgue, he showed the jury where the bullet had torn through her head.

He described how he had traced the flowers to the Botany Bay store where the clerk had helped a police artist draw a composite sketch of the two men who had bought the roses. Neither he, nor anyone else in the APD, had released any information about Lita's death until he had spoken to the McClintons, around 10:00 A.M.

Schroeder then questioned Detective Harris about the conversation he'd had with Sullivan at his divorce attorney's office on January 25.

"Did you ask the defendant where he was on January sixteenth of 1987, the day Lita Sullivan was murdered?"

"Yes, sir."

"What did he tell you?"

"He said he was at home in Florida alone in bed."

Harris was asked about the trip he took to Palm Beach on May 13, 1987, to obtain Sullivan's telephone toll records.

"Specifically, did you learn of a telephone call, a collect telephone call to the defendant on January sixteenth of 1987?"

"Yes, sir."

"Where did it come from?"

"It came from Buford, Georgia. And it was a rest stop on the I-85 near Suwanee." He told the court how, on the following day, he had driven from Lita's home to the phone booth at the rest stop.

"How long did it take you?" asked Schroeder.

"Exactly thirty-eight minutes."

Then Schroeder asked Harris if, at any time, he had revealed to anyone outside law enforcement that a 9mm gun had been used to kill Lita. "No, sir," said Harris. "It is the Atlanta Police Department's policy never to give out the type and caliber of a weapon used to commit a crime."

Harris was cross-examined by Richard Lubin, who nit-picked over the police measurements of the shooting and raised again the defense's main theory that Lita had been slain by one of her alleged junkie pals. He tried to shake Harris's belief that Lita had died as the result of a contract being taken out on her life. A professional would have fired from close range to avoid missing, wouldn't he? Wouldn't he have used a smaller gun? And Lubin insinuated that the media had found out about the caliber of the gun from either him or someone else in the police. He quibbled over whether the florist's clerk had told him that the car that had parked outside his store was a Toyota or a Honda and whether it was clean or mud-splattered. But he did not manage to fluster the veteran cop.

Trying another tack, Lubin said that Sullivan had flown to Atlanta to talk to Harris voluntarily and Harris, at the time, had been satisfied that he had answered all his questions, right? Detective Harris nodded, "Yes, sir."

"And on the subsequent interviews?"

"Yes, sir."

Lubin asked if the majority of drug killings were carried out using a 9mm semiautomatic weapon.

"They have been used, right," said Harris.

"And as a matter of fact, because of that, you had the strong belief that this was a drug killing, didn't you?"

"I wouldn't say I had a strong belief that it was a drug killing, but by the same token, I didn't dismiss anything," he replied.

"You knew that Ms. Sullivan was seeing a man named Bob Daniels, correct?"

"I later found that out," agreed Harris.

"And you knew that Bob Daniels threatened to kill her, didn't you?"

"That was the information contained in the police report, yes, sir."

"And you knew that less than two months before she was killed, he had driven his car through her garage. And when he was arrested, he said, 'I'm going to kill the bitch.' Correct?"

"Right. According to the officer, he was drunk when he made the statement," said Harris.

"Okay. You're also aware that during the week of her killing she received flowers on other occasions from a man named Michael Hollis, correct?"

"Yeah, from Ansley Mall. I believe they were roses. I don't know that it was exactly on the week of her death. It was her birthday."

"And you knew that Michael Hollis was also seeing Lita Sullivan?"

"Yes, sir."

Lubin then linked Lita to Stephen Brumley, whom Harris confirmed had been arrested on drug charges, and asked, "Did you take in to account that the night before she was killed she was with Bob Daniels?"

"Did I take it into account? Yes, sir."

"And that he brought her two roses that night?"

"That's new to me," said Harris.

"Did you take into account that the autopsy confirmed that Ms. Sullivan had cocaine in her system when she died?"

"Yes. I found out when the lab reports came back, and yes, I took that into account."

When Lubin finished, Schroeder leaped to his feet and urged Harris to tell the court about Bob Daniels. Harris then said he had investigated all the men Lita was said to have dated. Daniels had been a suspect, but he had been eliminated.

"He had just undergone quadruple bypass surgery, heart surgery, at the University of Alabama, Birmingham. We contacted the physicians at U.A.B. and they said it was physically impossible for him to have been running anywhere."

"On January sixteenth, 1987, in the course of your investigation, did you determine where Bob Daniels was?" asked Schroeder.

"Yes, sir, at home. . . . in his pajamas."

Harris said he had also pulled Daniels' telephone records, but could find nothing to link him to Lita's death.

Then Schroeder asked, "Did you also investigate Stephen Brumley?"

"Yes, sir."

"Where was Stephen Brumley at the time the murder occurred?"

"In jail."

On Thursday morning, November 5, the prosecutor played a tape of a conversation from February 19, 1987, a month after the murder, between Clyde Marlow and Jim Sullivan. Marlow testified that Sullivan had called him at home and asked him to call back when his wife was not around. "What should I do?" he had asked Jan. He had not talked to Sullivan since Lita moved back to Atlanta, because they had pretty much taken her side in the divorce. "Go to your office and call him, but make sure you get him on tape," Jan had said. When Marlow returned the call, his old friend wanted to talk about the murder—and what he said about the murder weapon had prompted Marlow to contact the police.

As the tape rolled, the jury heard Sullivan say, "This is what is called a nine-millimeter automatic pistol. The police tell me that the weapon that was used, Clyde, is a weapon never seen in Atlanta."

"Really?" said Marlow.

"It apparently has nine shells or cartridges, whatever you call the bullets, instead of the normal five or six. It's automatic, and it is the weapon of choice of Colombian and Cuban drug-hit people."

Detective Harris had sworn under oath that the police had never told Sullivan what type of weapon had killed Lita, and ballistics expert Kelly Fite of the Georgia State Crime Lab had told the court that the bullet that had killed Lita came from a Smith & Wesson semiautomatic. Unless he had actually seen the gun, there was no way Sullivan could have known how many cartridges were in its clip.

Throughout the playing of the tape, Sullivan took copious notes. Although the tape implicated him, it put Lita in such a bad light that even the judge questioned the decision of the prosecutor to include it. Out of earshot of the jury, Judge Shoob cautioned Schroeder, "The jury is not to hear about the character of the defendant."

When the tape resumed, the court heard Marlow ask Sullivan how he was doing. "Oh, you know, so-so, I guess," he had replied. "I had been looking forward to just having the divorce finalized and getting it over with and behind me as of January, and then this thing happened."

He offered Marlow damaging evidence about Jan. "The shit is unlimited," he said. Then he maintained that both Jan and Lita were using cocaine, and said he would provide evidence of Jan taking coke if Marlow ever wanted to use it against her.

His own marital infidelity would pale compared to what he had on Lita, Sullivan boasted. "And all of her cocaine stuff was—my ace in the hole." Professing to having been shocked by the murder, he went on, "But this is an extension of what she and Jan were messing around with, Clyde. They were messing around with drugs." He started to complain about Lita's parents, accusing them of swiping over $300,000 of property from the townhouse on the day of the murder.

When the tape finished, defense attorney Ed Garland asked Marlow if he and Jan were having their own domestic difficulties at the time.

"Yes, sir, we certainly had some marital problems."

With transcripts of the tape handed out to the jury, Garland drew his attention to the part of the conversation where Sullivan had taunted him: "Your wife is cheating on you, just as Lita is running about on me. What do you think the girls get up to in Palm Beach?" Sullivan talked about trips the women had taken with boyfriends. It will come out on the credit card bill, he had said ominously.

When asked to explain what he thought Sullivan meant by this, Marlow said this part of their conversation had stemmed from an occasion when an airplane ticket had been charged to his credit card. It was from Palm Beach to Savannah—he owned a house on Hilton Head Island—and as he could not remember buying the ticket, he had contacted Delta Airlines.

"I found out the name of this person was Christopher Brandner. I didn't know him," Marlow told the court. "The Delta Airlines lady then made some inquiries— when you get a ticket you have to leave a phone number, and that was answered by Brandner's sister Bridget. She said, 'Oh yes, that's a legitimate ticket because Jan is his girlfriend,' and the airline reported this all back to me."

Garland continued reading from the transcript. "Mr. Sullivan asks, 'You remember once when you and I were driving down from Macon to Palm Beach in the Rolls?' and you reply, 'Hah, what was the individual's name, do you recall?' And Sullivan says, 'His name was Christopher [Brandner].'"

Garland went on: "Mr. Sullivan said to you, 'Sure, he was her twenty-year-old lover down there,'" and, looking at Marlow, he went on, "You say, 'Both of them?' and Mr. Sullivan says, 'No, uh, Lita was going with a guy by the name of Stephen Brumley, who was a soccer player for the Fort Lauderdale Strikers.' Then he said, 'Now you've got one in Macon.'

" 'Really?'

" 'Yes.'

" 'You know who it is?'

"Yes, sir."

He read on: "Mr. Sullivan asked you, 'Haven't you noticed, uh, new pieces of jewelry popping up. Like, let's see . . .'

"And you say, 'New pieces of jewelry?'

" 'Yes, he gave her a necklace in the summer for her birthday.'

"Then you ask, 'Why did you wait so long [to tell me this]?' and Mr. Sullivan tells you, 'Because I needed—I couldn't jeopardize the surprise element of my information because of my own divorce. That's why I needed to get her deposition, needed to get Jan in deposition, so I could put it all out on the public record.' "

Again the judge shook his head in disbelief. During another huddle at the bench he scolded Schroeder: "I don't see why the government put that tape and this transcript into evidence. The only thing I can see that would support the government's case is the reference to the gun, and I think the government has injected all of this alleged adultery and drugs into the case with this transcript. Why couldn't the government have gotten the information about the gun directly from the witness?"

Schroeder told the judge he had thought long and hard about it before deciding to go ahead. "I don't know whether the defendant is going to take the stand or not. Shortly after his wife's murder, he's having these conversations, both about his wife, also about the supposed affairs of another individual's wife, and I think it gave the jury an eye towards how this individual operates."

THIRTEEN
Sex, Lies and Audio Tapes

Secret tapes were also at the center of testimony given by Marvin Marable, who had refused to testify at all until the district attorney granted him immunity. The former New York State trooper, sometime Avon salesman and linen supplier, told the court that Lita had introduced him to his wife at her parents' house and after their marriage in 1982, the two couples had often socialized. When his relationship with Poppy began to founder, he had bugged his home telephone, hoping she would reveal something he could use against her in a divorce. He had confided in his lawyer, John Taylor, who was also representing Jim Sullivan in his divorce, and had offered to share with the attorney any damaging information he uncovered about Lita. He said Taylor knew that Poppy and Lita were unaware they were being taped illegally. At Taylor's suggestion, Marable called Sullivan.

Sullivan was very interested in what Marable had to say. When he wanted to remove the device, Sullivan

implored him to keep it in place. "He was very pes-
simistic about the outcome of his divorce. He didn't feel
the [post-nuptial] agreement would hold up in court,"
said Marable. "He felt the courts in Atlanta would, I
guess, be more liberal than the courts in Florida, and he
felt she would receive what she was asking for."

Marable testified that Sullivan had offered him
$30,000 for tapes that allegedly proved Lita was seeing
other men. He had handed them over, but had taken no
payment. "I sent them in the spring of 1986. Three or
four weeks later I received them back at my attorney's
office. Several were missing." Marable called his lawyer,
he called Sullivan's lawyer, then he called Sullivan. All
of them denied knowing anything about the missing
tapes.

When the bug was discovered, Lita called the police,
Poppy filed for divorce and her husband pled guilty to
criminal charges of invasion of privacy in Fulton County
Court, where he got two years' probation. The tapes
were destroyed. "I threw them away back in '86 when I
learned that the Fulton County D.A.'s Office was at-
tempting to prosecute me," Marable said.

He testified that he'd had no further contact with Sullivan until they spoke again just three days before the
murder. "He called me around 7:30 A.M. He was very
nervous; he sounded desperate. He said, 'Marvin, I need
some information. Do you know if Lita is still living at
the same place, or in the townhouse? Do you know if
she has the same car? Do you know if anyone is staying
with her, or just any information you might have.' "

Marable's memory failed him when the defense tried
to nail down specifics. He admitted telling Sullivan about
trips Lita had taken and parties she had been to. But
when Ed Garland asked about her alleged numerous

affairs, he recalled her dating only one man. She knew Steve Brumley, Maurice Spencer and Michael Hollis, he agreed, but he had no proof that she had slept with any of them; they were just men she talked to. All he had done was given Sullivan the identities of people whom he could subpoena in his divorce case. He could not recall telling Sullivan that his wife was doing drugs, he had just been told that she did. Neither could he remember a private investigator in a little green car. To his recollection, the gumshoe who was tailing Lita drove a two-tone Dodge van.

After the weekend break, Jan Marlow took the stand. She had known the Sullivans during the eight years they'd lived in Macon, and the friendship had endured after they moved to Palm Beach, where she visited them regularly. She told of being in the kitchen at the mansion and noticing a crumpled piece of paper towel hanging from the empty roll. She went to throw it away and was stopped by Lita. "I said, 'Lita, this looks like it has been used, we need to clean it up.' 'Lita said, 'Leave it alone, Jim will get mad. He uses it to wipe his hands.' She told of seeing the ledger in which Sullivan entered every cent he spent on food and drink for which Lita had to reimburse him out of her household budget. "It was a long list. One item was for a fifty-nine-cent bottle of ginger ale. He was very, very stingy."

Jan also told the court about Sullivan's bizarre attitude toward his appearance. "The way Lita described it, he didn't have a maintenance concept. He had wonderful business suits, but with his casual things, he liked to wear things completely and totally ruined or lost or worn totally out, and then he would replace them, but he didn't maintain them. He wore shirts that were ragged, things that were faded, things that were torn. One time, when we were at the Nottingham Drive house, Lita told me he had inherited his uncle's underwear. I asked her if he was wearing it, and she said yes."

Despite his stable of luxury automobiles, he grudged paying for gas. "There was usually a problem," she said. "There were three cars, a Rolls, a Mercedes sedan and a roadster. The roadster was considered Lita's car, and she would keep gas in it. If Jim left first to go out of the house, he would take her car. There would never be any gas in the other cars and she would have to fill whatever one she was driving. He kept them close to empty. I even ran out of gas in one of them. I had borrowed it to go to a beauty salon half a mile from the house. I got two blocks and ran out."

Later, under questioning from Ed Garland, Jan admitted that Sullivan also spent what she described as "tremendous amounts of money" entertaining his flashy new friends. She was staying with Lita in 1985, when he threw one of his fund-raisers for Deedy Marix. The food and wine had flowed as the guests milled around the cabana bar overlooking the ocean.

She said she had accompanied Lita on shopping trips while a maid cooked and cleaned for them, and that she had seen Jim splurge on expensive gifts for his wife. She had been on one spree where Sullivan had swept them into a jewelry store and told Lita to pick out a bracelet. She'd left the store wearing twenty-six thousand dollars' worth of diamonds on her wrist. He had bought her a sixty-inch pearl necklace, a stunning ruby-and-diamond necklace, a 7.5-carat ring and flawless diamond earrings. Lita also had a mink coat. But it was all to impress other people, Jan claimed. "He spent money with other people in a show of friendship, to be a gracious host, but he wasn't generous with Lita except on those rare occasions. She used to call it a life of periodic deprivation."

Jan said that Lita had started salting away money in a secret account she had opened for her friend using her own name. She said she had worried about Lita's safety when she decided to challenge Sullivan over the divorce. "I told her she should be very careful and very serious about it, because Mr. Sullivan was going to be a tough adversary. I told her, 'It's not a merger, it's a takeover and somebody could get hurt."

Battling the judge and Schroeder's objections every step of the way, Garland went on the attack. Hadn't Lita squandered her husband's money on drugs? he asked. "We tried cocaine together one time when I was staying in Palm Beach, just to see what it was like, but I never saw her take it again," Jan replied. She swept aside his claim that boyfriends stayed over at the Casa Eleda when Sullivan was out of town. She denied that Lita and she had a pact to cover for each other and lie to their respective husbands. After she had split from Sullivan and returned to Atlanta, yes, Lita had dated several men. Jan had never spoken to him again.

Jan was followed on to the stand by FBI Agent John Kingston. He had conducted the investigation into the incriminating telephone calls and interviewed Sullivan on April 7, 1988. Sullivan told him he had not listed himself as being single on his loan application, but whether he had or not, he didn't think it was important. He also said he could not remember getting a collect call on the day his wife was murdered. He also claimed his lawyer said he would win at the divorce hearing regarding the post-nuptial agreement.

Garland asked Kingston if Sullivan had told him that Lita was dating Michael Hollis during the divorce proceedings.

"I believe so," said Kingston.

"And he told you that he had listened to tape-recorded conversations between his wife and Poppy Marable which revealed the activities that Lita was having with Michael Hollis, didn't he?"

"Yes, sir."

"And he told you he had gotten those tapes from Marvin Marable?"

"Yes, sir."

"And he intended to use that information in his divorce case. In your report, you write that Sullivan advised that Lita had an affinity for cocaine and she used it during their marriage, didn't you, sir?"

"I believe so, yes, sir."

But when he'd tried to locate the tapes, Marable had destroyed them. Kingston said he could find no evidence that any of what Sullivan alleged was true. He did not have to. Judge Shoob ruled that Sullivan's statements were hearsay and inadmissible, and so were Lita's conversations with Jan Marlow.

Ed Wheeler was called next. He remembered his friend's fear of being taken to the cleaners in the divorce. "I recall commiserating with Jim and saying, 'I know this has been rough on you, I know you've worked hard for where you are in life, and I know that losing some of it is bothersome to you, deeply bothersome.' I knew Jim Sullivan. He had been a successful businessman in Macon and he worked hard at it."

Wheeler also remembered when Sullivan's griping over Lita became obsessive. "Jim said, 'You just wouldn't believe what she is trying to do to me.' "

"You understood him to mean what?" asked prosecutor William McKinnon.

"What Lita was doing to him financially, is my understanding."

"In the divorce action?"

"That's correct."

Ed testified that after the couple split, he and his wife stayed friendly with Lita. McKinnon then asked, "During the time of the divorce, was Lita having problems financially maintaining the home on Slaton Drive and maintaining herself, financially? Was there a time when Ms. Sullivan came to you and your wife and asked, in essence, for a loan?"

"Yes," said Wheeler. "It was mid-1986 and Lita had called Fran and asked if we were interested in either purchasing or holding a diamond ring she had. As I recall, it was a two-carat ring. I told her that I really did not want the ring. It was her ring. If she needed—I am not a man of great wealth—but if she needed a modest loan, that we could arrange that, but I didn't really want to get into the business of buying or holding her ring."

"How much was she asking you to loan her at the time?" asked McKinnon.

"I seem to remember the sum of $2,000. The ring was worth more than that. I think that is why I felt uncomfortable about it."

Wheeler went on to describe other jewelry that Lita owned, including a striking ruby necklace. "The color of it," he marveled. "I had never heard the term 'pigeon-blood red.' I guess it is a way of describing fine rubies. She had lots of nice jewelry and a good wardrobe, always made a fine impression." It had never occurred to him that the gems were not Lita's to keep, he added.

The next day Judge Shoob cleared the court while the opposing sides fought over Tonya Tanksley, who was refusing to testify against her former lover. At issue was what Tanksley was alleged to have told former prison guard and police dispatcher Joan Amos Gleaton from Macon, Vickie Durden from Gray, Georgia, and another friend, Judy Thompson. According to police and FBI accounts, Tanksley told the trio that, when she told Sullivan about his wife's threat to haul her into court, he had said, "Don't worry about testifying, I am going to take care of things." And after Lita was murdered, he had said to her, "See? I told you I would take care of it."

Durden and Gleaton had told the police they had been scared into coming forward after finding roses taped to the windshields of their cars. Now Tanksley had clammed up. Prosecutors argued that she was taking the Fifth because she was more scared of Sullivan than of the consequences of committing perjury. There had been two suspicious fires at her apartment in Macon since Lita's murder, and Vickie Durden claimed that Tanksley had said, "Oh God, I might be next." If Tanksley will not talk, let us call the friends, the prosecutors pleaded.

With the jury still out of the courtroom, Don Samuels argued, "The witness is on the stand, she's right here. The fact that she is not testifying in a way they like does not make her unavailable." And Tanksley's own lawyer told the judge that it was the government who was threatening his client, not Sullivan. She had been warned she might be prosecuted for lying if she denied her friends' story, he claimed. That was why he had her exercise her Fifth Amendment rights. Judge Shoob ordered Tanksley to answer some questions.

With Sullivan's eyes boring into her, she told the court she had known him for twelve to fourteen years after bumping into him at a store, and that they had been intimately involved for seven of those. It was not like they went out on dates, she said. Apparently the relationship was purely sexual. They had had sex at the Macon home dozens of times when Lita was away; he would call or go to her place and pick her up. She would go to his office at Crown Beverages to get money from him. Sometimes they would spend a few hours at the Guest Quarters hotel in Atlanta. Once they had stayed the whole night. After he moved to Palm Beach, he had arranged a prepaid ticket to fly her to Florida to have sex in the mansion.

She had known about the divorce, but was not worried about being called as a witness. She denied that Lita had ever confronted her, but admitted she had met her once. When her trysts with Sullivan ended, they talked frequently on the phone. She had called him as soon as she heard that Lita had been killed. "He said he couldn't talk right now and hung up," she said.

The prosecution asked if she had told the police on October 22, 1987, that Sullivan had also had a sexual relationship with Vicki Durden, and with Judy Thompson at the Nottingham Drive house. She said that, although she knew that Durden and Thompson had gone there once, she didn't know if they had had sex with him there.

It was not the only statement about which her memory was fuzzy. Schroeder read a report from the Bibb County Fire Department Investigation Office on the mysterious fires at her home, blazes inspectors clearly attributed to arson. "On both occasions, Ms. Tanksley expressed the opinion that she thought someone may have set the fire, but stopped short of naming any enemies or persons to have a motive for harming her." Tanksley could not recall telling the firemen that.

She also denied having a conversation with Joan
Amos Gleaton's policeman boyfriend, Lieutenant
Charles Grant, in November 1987. He claimed she had
called him asking for protection. "She begged me to
check on her apartment, she was scared to death, she
knew what happened to his wife. From the way she was
talking, I got the impression she was afraid that would
happen to her."

On the advice of her lawyer, she repeatedly took the
Fifth Amendment and could not remember prior testimony she had given to the grand jury. Lubin immediately pounced on Gleaton and Durden. Both, he claimed
were substance abusers. He asked Tanksley to list Vickie
Durden's drugs of choice, "Coke, meth, purple microdot
[LSD]," she said. She had seen Durden inject herself
with crank (an amphetamine cocktail), draw blood out
of her veins and shoot it back in. For her part, Durden
had previously testified that she had tried to commit suicide twice and had been treated for severe depression.
Schroeder contended that Durden had been rehabilitated
and had cleaned herself up four years before the conversation with Tanksley had taken place. She had repeated it
to Joan Gleaton, who felt compelled to go to the police.

The following morning Judge Shoob ruled that
Gleaton and Durden would not be called. All the jury
got to hear about was Tanksley's admission about her
sexual exploits with the defendant. The decision made
Sullivan break into a big grin that lasted pretty much
the whole day. As he left the courthouse, on a day which
had been disastrous for the prosecutors, he laughed and
joked with his legal team.

The next day Schroeder called Pamela Orhart, who,
with her husband, had stayed at the mansion for a month
while Lita was out of town. She said that during that

time Sullivan had brought several women back to spend the night.

She was followed by Lita's divorce attorney, Richard Schiffman. He told the court that he was convinced that Lita would have won her bid to have the post-nuptial agreement thrown out. "The judge had already cleared his calendar for a trial January 26 and indicated there were questions of fact about the agreement that should go to the jury."

He described how Sullivan had bought the Palm Beach home without Lita's knowledge and had not allowed her to see it before they moved in because he was afraid his bid would be turned down if it were known his wife was black. "Lita was not accepted in Palm Beach," Schiffman said. "She was not comfortable there and did not want to live there. She was never welcomed from a social standpoint."

She had fled after a year of unhappiness in a community that despised her because of the color of her skin, and to escape a loveless marriage. She had told him that she and Sullivan had not had sex since 1980. He was a multi-millionaire and all she had wanted from their divorce was the Buckhead townhouse, the silver Mercedes and $200,000 in cash.

Schiffman said he would have introduced evidence of Sullivan's chronic infidelity. The jury would have been told that the gifts he had infrequently bestowed on Lita were bought because of his repeated philandering. "She testified that every time she would catch Mr. Sullivan in an affair, he would buy her a very expensive piece of jewelry. He cheated on her often and blatantly—he would bring women into their bed when she was in Georgia visiting with her folks—and would try to woo back her affection with a gift," he said. She had amassed more than $100,000 of jewelry in this emotional trade-off.

Schiffman said the divorce court would have heard that Sullivan, by his own admission, had offered Marvin Marable $30,000 for any damaging tidbits that would hurt Lita in court. "It would have been a dynamite piece of evidence. It would have shown the length Sullivan would go to in order to win the case." The court would also have heard how Lita suspected he'd fathered another woman's child.

Sullivan had fought tooth and nail to get the case heard in Florida and to block his wife's temporary alimony of $7,000 a month, but had lost. "Georgia is the only state in the country that allows a jury trial to decide economic issues in divorce. The jury could award her anything. And that is what had Sullivan worried stiff. He knew the jury would hear how he started having affairs right after their 1976 wedding, and how he expected his wife to live on fifty dollars a week and made her drive from Macon to Palm Beach while he flew his mistress there," Schiffman said.

Next, the jury learned that, six months before Lita died, Sullivan had applied for a loan to pay off the $1 million mortgage on the mansion. Rhonda Paxton, the lending officer at the Margaretten Mortgage Company testified he had given his income as $22,000 a month, with another $18,000 in dividends and interest. When she checked, the $22,000 was actually $21,000 and came from the non-compete agreement he had signed when he sold Crown Beverages. He claimed he had $520,000 in his bank account when, in actuality, there was just $22,057. "I didn't question him about the discrepancy, since he had enough cash to cover our costs," she admitted.

On January 14, two days before Lita's death, Sullivan got a loan from the Barnett Bank with the proviso that he must produce Lita's signature or proof that they were divorced. "A few days after the murder, he called me and informed me as to the death of his wife. He wanted to know if we could possibly proceed with the consummation of the loan," Howard Stekoff, a former officer at the bank, told the court.

It was Donna Wooten of Bank One in Lexington, Kentucky, who had written to Sullivan to remind him that his mortgage payment was overdue. What would the bank have done if this second loan had fallen through and he was unable to pay? she was asked. "We would have foreclosed on the property," she replied.

The trial was entering its third week when Suki took the stand. At 40, she was still beautiful and she looked like she would rather be anywhere else than having to face her ex-husband across a courtroom again. She testified that Sullivan had complained about Lita's demands, and his fear of the trial taking place in Atlanta, where Lita's parents were influential. "He said the laws are a lot better for woman's side in Georgia; he said he would lose his property, his lifestyle." And as she had done two years before in her divorce trial, she claimed he'd confessed to killing Lita.

Nervously wringing her hands and dabbing at her eyes with Kleenex, Suki repeated, in a voice that barely rose above a whisper, what she had told the divorce court and the grand jury. Her ex-husband had turned up the volume on the television because he was sure the house was bugged by the police. "People can hear through telephone, your conversation," she remembered him telling her. " 'I know it, I know they are listening,' he said. He said he hired someone to kill Lita," she said.

"He was afraid. He doesn't want to go to jail because he'd never get out." And just as she had done in the Palm Beach Courthouse, she said he'd pleaded with her to run away with him.

The prosecutor asked if she'd prodded him any more about Lita's murder. "This is terrible," she replied, shaking her head, "but I didn't ask. I'm too scared of this person." She had not left right away because her brother and sister were staying with her. When they went home, she walked out the door and never went back.

She suddenly halted and asked for a break and asked if she could speak to the prosecutor. Calling for a ten-minute recess, Judge Shoob cleared the room. Suki told McKinnon she was bothered by Sullivan, whose eyes had been trained on her the whole time she testified.

"It is scaring her," he told Shoob.

"If he's staring at her and frightening her, I would suggest he not do it. You can look, but don't stare, Mr. Sullivan," said Judge Shoob. Sullivan shrugged his bony shoulders and smirked.

On cross-examination Ed Garland branded Suki a liar. To make sure the jury got the point, he wrote in block capital letters, "ARRESTED FOR PERJURY MAY 1990 on a large board propped up by an easel." Over McKinnon's objection, he said he was merely trying to keep track of confusing dates. But even as Suki recounted how Sullivan had blurted out the confession as he tried to persuade her to lie for him in traffic court, and when she admitted the lie and had been slung in jail, the damning label was facing the jury.

Garland chipped away again. "She was bitter, still smarting from the divorce trial in which she had come away empty-handed," he suggested. Did she concoct this confession story to exact a measure of revenge? Why this sudden fear; hadn't she known when she married him that Sullivan was a suspect in Lita's murder?

Garland pointed out that in 1987 Suki had said under oath that she couldn't remember whether he had told her about Lita's death by phone or personally.

"I'm not trying to lie," she told him. "How could I say this? I was at home."

"Are you saying that this was a lie?" asked Garland.

"I don't intend to lie, but this is not true," she replied.

The chief investigator for the Palm Beach County State Attorney's Office, Lieutenant William "Buzz" Patterson, followed Suki on the stand. He told of taking her to jail the day she was arrested for lying for Sullivan over the fender-bender. "In the car she was extremely disturbed, crying, her body shaking and in fear," he recalled. He said she'd told him that what she knew [about Lita's death] made her afraid for her safety. Before Patterson left her, he had given her his card and told her to call him if she needed help. "She rolled it up tightly and hid it in the lining of her coat so that her husband wouldn't find it," he said.

The next witness was Pilar Bissell. She told the court that she had been a guest at a small dinner party at the Casa Eleda on the evening of January 14, 1987. "He [Sullivan] was very agitated, extremely nervous, very jumpy, though I would say he tried to put on a good face for the other people in the room," she said. The phone had rung three times during the evening. "In the second call, when we were having drinks in the study, I saw him turn toward the wall and say, 'Why not? You let me know . . . keep me informed.' " Later that evening, about 10:30 P.M., the phone rang again and she overheard Sullivan say, "Get flowers."

Richard Lubin attacked Bissell for not coming forward with this information until her husband was in trouble. He also explained away the "Get flowers" instruction she had overheard Sullivan give to the unidentified caller. He did buy flowers, Lubin said, but they were for the party he had thrown for Mayor Deedy Marix after Lita died.

The last witness for the prosecution was FBI Special Agent Todd Letcher, whose affidavit had triggered the chain of events that resulted in this trial. He told the court that when he had searched the mansion in September 1991, he had been struck by Sullivan's lack of sorrow over his wife's brutal death. With prompting from the prosecutor, Letcher laid out the scenario that had led to the murder: the phone calls, the information gleaned from the diaries and records that had been removed from the home. "Sullivan planned the whole thing," he said.

As soon as the prosecution rested, the defense moved to have the case thrown out. Judge Shoob took an hour-long recess to mull over the motion before announcing that he was withholding his decision for the time being. "I have no problem with the motive," he told Schroeder and McKinnon. "I think the government has established enough to take to a jury. But I haven't seen any evidence that the telephone calls facilitated the murder."

The defense lost no time trashing Suki. Three Palm Beachers testified that she'd lied her head off. "I find she had great difficulty in telling the truth," said James Gordon Beekman, who had appeared for Sullivan at his divorce. Joel Weissman, who had won the crushing victory for Sullivan in that trial, was still in a take-no-prisoners mode. "The confession was invented," he claimed. "Suki Sullivan is the most manipulative woman I have ever met, a sheer fabricator of the first resort. For example, I asked her during the divorce proceedings if she was aware that Sullivan had offered to give her $500,000 to settle out of court, and she replied, 'I would no say about Lita if I were.'"

Schroeder asked Weissman about his allegation that it was Suki, not her husband, who had arranged to have Lita murdered. "Why didn't you tell the authorities?" he asked.

"I felt that she either committed the crime or was involved in it, but it was merely a theory," Weissman replied. "I felt I shouldn't impugn her character without proof."

He claimed that Suki would have settled her divorce if Sullivan had coughed up the $500,000. Suki swore that she had never been told of any settlement offer—which landed his old foe Ronald Sales nicely in the soup, according to Weissman's way of thinking, since keeping a settlement from a client violates the Florida Bar Ethics Code.

Weissman confirmed that he did not like Sales. He also admitted that he was a good friend of both Sullivan and his lawyer, Richard Lubin. And why wouldn't he be? It was Lubin who had defended him in the embezzlement charges brought by Sales.

Don Samuels summed up for the defense on Friday, November 19. The government's case was entirely guesswork, he told the jury. They had not an iota of proof that James Sullivan hired someone to kill his wife. The case against his client hinged on the phone calls. "Yet for three of these calls, the government cannot show who was on the line, or what was said," he argued. "We don't know who was in the motel room, or even if the call reached the room. There is no direct evidence that

Sullivan was alone in the house, or even in the house, when the calls came in. And nobody knows who knocked on Lita's door at 6:00 A.M. on January 13. The only evidence that someone did knock is from a friend of Lita's.

"The government wants you to believe that the call [to the mansion on the day Lita was murdered] was from the hit man calling to say the job had been done," he said. It was pure speculation that Sullivan was on the phone with the murderer; they had no proof about what was actually said.

FOURTEEN
Dodging the Bullet

That Thanksgiving, James Sullivan truly had cause to get down on his knees and give praise. Three days earlier, on November 23, Judge Shoob had shot down all murder conspiracy charges against him, ruling that the prosecution simply had not made its case. But while he'd set Sullivan free, Shoob did not exonerate him.

"The defendant may have been involved in the murder of Lita Sullivan, but the government has failed to establish that a reasonable jury would find guilt beyond a reasonable doubt," he said. "The court has concluded there is no evidence from which a rational juror could find beyond a reasonable doubt, that the calls facilitated the murder, or related in some manner to the murder of Lita Sullivan." Turning to Sullivan he said, "Mr. Sullivan, you are discharged."

To the stunned McClintons he offered his regrets: "I understand your concern and involvement in this case. Your daughter was a very bright, attractive woman in the early stages of her life. It was a terrible crime. I hope the murderers will be apprehended." In explaining his position to the jury, he added, "It would not serve even the interests of Lita Sullivan's family to have a man convicted without regard to the rules of law."

But Judge Shoob plainly thought Sullivan was as guilty as sin. It had been one of the hardest decisions he had made in his long career. "Sometimes, as a judge, you have to bite the bullet and do what the law requires. It was a tough call."

Sullivan sat expressionless while the judge rendered his decision. Without a word, he scurried out through a side door. Detective Welcome Harris walked slowly out of the courtroom as if he had been hit by a bolt of lightning, muttering over and over again, "I feel sick, I feel sick, I feel sick."

Afterwards the statements came fast and furious. "I am absolutely innocent," Sullivan declared smugly. "I had nothing to do with Lita's death. Her death was a great tragedy." His crack defense team crowed.

"They [the prosecutors] tried to make the sun revolve around the earth . . . to reach a conclusion the evidence did not show," said a jubilant Ed Garland outside the courthouse. It was the media's fault; Mr. Sullivan had been tried in the press for nearly six years, he complained. Then, in what may have been a clue that he was not 100 percent convinced of his client's innocence, he added, "Mr. Sullivan said a prayer of thanksgiving for the fine judicial system we have." He also got in another dig at Suki who, he said, should have been impeached.

U.S. Attorney Joe Whitley said he was considering an appeal. "Despite Judge Shoob's ruling today directing a verdict of acquittal in the murder-for-hire case of

United States versus *James Sullivan*, it is our opinion that the government put forward more than adequate proof for the jury to return a verdict of guilty on all counts against the defendant. Suffice it to say this case is not closed."

But nobody felt worse about Sullivan's acquittal than Lita's parents. Given their belief that their former son-in-law had literally gotten away with murder, the judge's sympathy rang more than a little hollow. "I was not expecting this," said a tearful JoAnn, who had just been elected to the Georgia House of Representatives two weeks before. They gave immediate notice that this setback, however disheartening, would not deter them from pursuing Sullivan. "We will continue our fight. The murderer is still out there," vowed Emory, adding that the $25,000 reward for anyone who could put his daughter's killers behind bars, was still on the table.

The decision still rankles. "We went to court every day," says JoAnn. "We had very high hopes and they were dashed by the judge's ruling. To this day my husband curses every time he hears that judge's name. We were hurt and disappointed. We were not angry. It takes energy to be angry and we just didn't have the energy to be angry. I just felt this hurt, this heaviness in my chest, my head felt [like] it was about to explode." To make the decision even more painful, the police issued a warning, she added. "They said, 'Mr. McClinton, if anything happens to Mr. Sullivan, you'll be the first suspect.'"

In Palm Beach, a humiliated Suki licked her wounds and attacked the defense's portrayal of her as a money-grubbing and vengeful ex-wife who had concocted the story about Jim Sullivan's confession to punish him for cutting her off without a cent in their divorce. She was angry and puzzled at the accusation that she'd tried to extort $500,000 to keep quiet about her former husband's self-incriminating outburst.

"It is very embarrassing what they say about me," she told *The Palm Beach Post*. "It never happened like that. Never." She said she did not even grasp what Garland was implying when he questioned her about her alleged offer to keep Sullivan's secret—for a hefty price.

And she again denied that she was a serial predator who targeted wealthy older men for their money. "I feel bad. I wish I hadn't married so many times, but it happened. I did not plan it that way. Am I a gold-digger? These things they say about me? No."

She told the paper she lived on the proceeds of wise investments set up for her by her second husband, Leonard Rogers. She lived in the waterside condo he'd advised her to buy in West Palm Beach after their divorce, and tooled around in a small Japanese car. "I can live without working," she said. "But it's hard to go back. I have a certain way of living, I guess. I was spoiled."

Sullivan returned to the beachfront condominium in Boynton Beach where his life was not made any easier by the government's release of statements he had given to the agents who'd searched his home and interviewed him on September 6, 1991. Once again he found himself in banner headlines, his failed marriage to Lita, and his ugly insinuation that she had gotten what she deserved, under renewed scrutiny.

The documents revealed his response to FBI Agent Robert Ingram's question "Did you kill your wife?" Ingram's report said there had been a long pause while Sullivan gazed at the ceiling, then answered, "Unthinkable and inconceivable."

"Is there any reason you can think of that someone would name you as a suspect?"

"People point suspicion at me," replied Sullivan.

"Who do you think would have had the best opportunity to do this?" asked Ingram.

"No idea. I was frustrated. Lita had left me and I didn't know enough to answer that."

"Why do you think someone would kill Lita?"

"Involvement with drugs, other people with motives—but that's only conjecture," said Sullivan.

Sullivan again hunkered down with lawyers to plot a strategy for the two outstanding cases he still had to face: the charge of wrongful possession of firearms by a felon, and the civil suit being pressed by his former in-laws. The civil action was unaffected by his acquittal in Atlanta, and the burden of proof would be less onerous than in a criminal case. Although he could not be jailed even if he were found guilty, he knew that if this sweet, elderly, God-fearing couple was allowed to make their case to a jury, there was every chance that he would end up forking over way more than the damages "in excess of $10,000" they were seeking in compensation.

At the beginning of 1993, Sullivan's lawyer, Richard Lubin, filed a motion to dismiss the case, claiming that Florida's two-year statute of limitations had expired. It should date from January 16, 1987, the day Lita was murdered, he insisted.

The McClintons had filed nearly three years later, he said. He also claimed that Emory McClinton had no legal right to sue, having been removed as a temporary administrator of his daughter's estate in July 1992 by a judge who, given the hostility between Lita's father and her husband, had turned it over to the probate court.

Over the next few weeks, the McClintons' lawyers, Brad Moores and Richard Kupfer, argued that the statute of limitations did not apply because Sullivan had deliberately concealed his role in the murder-for-hire scheme. It was not until 1990, when Suki had made her sensational claim about his confession, that the true facts began to emerge. They also claimed the case fell under the RICO laws.

"The purpose of this murder, the reason it was carried out, was to derive property because of their impending divorce," said Kupfer. "This is not just because someone didn't like someone." On June 2, Palm Beach Circuit Judge Harold Cohen dismissed the RICO charges, but ruled that the wrongful death case could go ahead.

Two days later, Sullivan was back in court as the long-delayed firearms trial got under way. With no chance of talking his way out of the mess, he made a deal. He pled guilty to two weapons charges and was sentenced to a further 18 months' house arrest, to be followed by 42 weeks of probation. He would be allowed out to go to work, attend an exercise class and perform chores between the hours of 10:00 A.M. to 10:00 P.M., he would have to wear an electronic bracelet and he would not be allowed to attend movies or parties, or dine out. If he stayed out of trouble for three years, his probation time would be reduced.

Sullivan's desire to be "somebody" when he'd moved to Palm Beach twelve years before was granted in a way he had never planned when Court TV announced it was going to air the wrongful death trial, making him the first Palm Beach resident to be awarded such a dubious honor since the William Kennedy Smith rape trial saga had played out on national daytime television. His sole consolation was that the cable channel was not available locally.

As they waited for their chance to face their former son-in-law in court, the McClintons hoped it would shake loose new clues that would allow the Fulton County district attorney to go after Sullivan again. Brad Moores, knowing that he would have to overwhelm the jury with as much evidence as possible, albeit mostly circumstantial, to make their case, had Pat McKenna dig up any previously overlooked nuggets.

Moores' first job was to serve Suki with a subpoena. Actually, pressing the papers into her hand was the last thing the attorney wanted Pat to do. Moores gambled that Suki would play hide and seek. "Under the rules of court we can read [to a jury] a person's deposition if that person makes herself unavailable, and I had a feeling that Suki's deposition would be much better than her live testimony," he said. "I told Pat, 'Go over to her place at the Placido Mar Condominiums, stop at the gate, talk to security, tell them who you are.' McKenna went forty-eight times and Suki never came out once. As a result, I was able to put him on the witness stand during the trial to testify to going to her house forty-eight times, and because of that, I was able to use her deposition."

What Moores was looking for was Suki's testimony about the weapons Sullivan kept at the house. When she was questioned by Buzz Patterson from the state attorney's office in September 1991, he had shown her several photographs of guns.

"Do you see any weapons that you think you recognize, Suki?" he asked her.

"Yes, I recognize the first one and the third one."

"Where did you first see those guns, Suki?"

"Uh, the office, the house, his house."

"And when we speak of his office and his house, who are we speaking of?" asked Patterson.

"Oh," she said. "Jim Sullivan. 920 South Ocean Boulevard."

"Is that the home you lived in while you were married?"

"Yes."

"All right. When you say 'his office' at that residence, where was that office located, Ms. Sullivan?"

"Near the master bedroom."

"Was that upstairs or downstairs?"

"Upstairs."

"All right. And what else was in that office next to the master bedroom?"

"Umm, another gun," said Suki.

"What other kinds of guns were there?" Patterson persisted.

"Shotgun."

"Like a pistol there?"

"Pistol, yes," said Suki.

"What is different about the pistol that you saw than the one that is in the picture?" asked Patterson.

"In this picture is a wooden handle, but what I saw was silver," she said.

"Besides the other guns in the office next to the master bedroom, what else was in that room?" Patterson wanted to know.

"There's two knives, one like a machete, like big knife, and one knife you push—make it puff out like this," she demonstrated with her hands.

"Was there any furniture in the room?" he asked.

"In the office? The two knives, he kept that in his night table. In office he had bed in his office."

"Were there any filing cabinets in the office?" Patterson asked.

"Yes."

"All right. Did you ever see the contents of these filing cabinets? What was in them?"

"I saw the documents," said Suki.

"Okay. And that's where he kept his guns the entire time you resided there—in his office?" queried Patterson.

"Yes. Last time I saw his gun was there."

"Okay. Did you ever know of anybody, friends or relatives, business acquaintances, that might have ever kept guns there, stored guns at your home while you lived there?"

"No. I know one, this small, the silver gun. This person cleaned it for him," she said.

"Who was that person?"

"It was Bruce Forman, of Bruce Forman Motors," she said.

"Bruce Forman Motors?"

"Yes, there. Not Bruce Forman [himself]. His name is George, George Lewis cleaned his guns."

Suki's deposition made it clear that Sullivan had been lying through his teeth when he'd told the FBI agents that he knew nothing about the guns that were found in his house.

Next, Moores tried to question Sullivan. All he got was a wall of silence. "He was very cocky. It became the shortest deposition on record. He took the Fifth Amendment. I asked him his name and he gave me his name. I asked if he was the same James Sullivan that had been married to Lita McClinton and he took the Fifth Amendment on that. So I said, 'I just want to be clear what you're doing here. Are you going to refuse to answer any questions I ask you on the basis that the answer may incriminate you?' He said, 'Well, my lawyer has told me to do that.' And I said, 'Well, I just want to make sure—we have a record here. Is that true, that you are going to refuse to answer any questions at all because it could incriminate you?' And he says, 'Yes.' I said, 'Okay, thanks.' "

With the trial date set for February 1994, Sullivan's lawyers headed back to court to once again try to get the case dismissed. "This entire case has been a sham from the beginning," scoffed Richard Lubin. "Emory McClinton is not authorized to bring a wrongful death lawsuit. They could have appointed Humpty-Dumpty, but it doesn't make it right. It doesn't mean it should keep going."

Circuit Court Judge Harold Cohen looked at Brad Moores. "No problem, Your Honor," Moores assured him with a shrug. "The probate administrator will ratify the lawsuit." Cohen ruled that the trial would begin as planned.

It got under way on Monday, February 14, but without Sullivan's expensive legal eagle to lead the charge. In an eyebrow-raising turn of events, Sullivan fired Lubin and said he would defend himself. "It is not my wish that I not be represented," he told the court. "I do not have the funds to afford representation for an entire trial."

It was a catastrophic decision. Lubin had earned a

reputation for himself as a first-class criminal defense lawyer with winning strategies in several notorious trials, most notably in the case of Dora Chong, the mistress of a mega-rich Palm Beach denizen who was charged when her toddler drowned while she went shopping. It was also to the flamboyant Lubin that the legendary F. Lee Bailey would turn, when he was charged with contempt of court.

Once the champion of underdog—Lubin has been described as a "Woodstock Nation refugee," who wore his hair in an "Afro" in the sixties, and defended the poor. Now his clients were rich and he wore Armani suits. A familiar figure around Palm Beach on his turquoise Harley-Davidson bike, a fat cigar clamped between his teeth, he even posed astride the hog, a white dove perched on his hand, for the cover of *Palm Beach Life*. Ironically, the picture was snapped in front of the West Palm Beach office building he shares with, amongst others, Pat McKenna. McKenna knew how good a lawyer Lubin was: they had worked together to rescue a Delray Beach man from a lifetime behind bars by uncovering evidence that the cops had botched the inquiry. "He saved an innocent man from prison," McKenna says.

Lubin cemented his reputation in another murder-for-hire case when he bombarded a government snitch with so much evidence, that the man capitulated. "He just kept feeding him documents until he exploded on the witness stand," says McKenna.

Observing the melodrama from the sidelines was Lita's divorce lawyer, Richard Schiffman, who had been called as a witness. "My guess is, he figured if he got rid of his lawyer right before trial, he would get the case postponed, but the judge refused to do that and forced him to go forward. I don't think that was part of his plan," he says.

"He had a girlfriend who came with him every day. She was white and she did not fit with his usual taste in women, like Suki and obviously, Lita. I'd think, 'Lady, you are just not catching on. Wake up, you should be concerned.' It was hard for the McClintons, but they are impressive people, they've been determined, they are not going to let it drop."

Moores and David Boone, the Atlanta lawyer representing Lita's estate, were amazed when Sullivan showed up without his pit-bull attorney at his side. It was not as if he was penniless—he had to have millions still in the bank. Yet here he was, sitting all by himself at the defense table with a notebook in front of him.

"He played the part of being broke to the hilt," says journalist Malcolm Balfour, who covered the story. "Every day he would drive up to the courthouse in this little blue wreck of a car which looked like it was held together with bits of string. It was laughable."

"All classic Sullivan," says Brad Moores. "He tried to portray himself as a victim—that even though he and Lita were going through this acrimonious divorce, he still loved her, and when he found out she was murdered, it really tore him apart. But we had his diary for that day and the diary entry for January 16, 1987, read: 'Suki and I celebrate at Jo's with champagne and caviar,' Jo's is a very posh French restaurant, it's hardly the picture of the grieving, estranged husband."

Whether Sullivan thought that casting himself as the hapless victim against the power of the state would persuade the jury to cut him some slack; perhaps his tremendous ego could not resist the chance to outsmart some fancy trial lawyers with TV cameras trained upon him. Or maybe he thought he was untouchable, having already beaten the rap in Atlanta. Whatever his line of reasoning, it was a lousy move.

Judge Cohen explained court procedure to him and said several of the Atlanta witnesses would give video-taped testimony. "You mean people will make all kinds of assertions that I won't have a chance to rebut?" he asked. The judge told him his lawyer knew all about the depositions and could have chosen to be present.

He pleaded with Cohen to let him mention his acquittal in Atlanta. The judge told him he could not. "It strikes me as extremely important that the government mounted this attack on me and the judge threw it out before the defense put on its case," he groused. He griped some more when the judge put a gag order on both sides, cautioning them that he did not want the case being tried outside the courtroom. Sullivan acted hurt. "The last thing I would ever try to do is to try my life in the newspapers. Few people have been as victimized as I have by the newspapers," he huffed.

In his opener Brad Moores said the issue was plain: Sullivan killed Lita rather than part with a red cent. "He loved his money, he loved his mansion. And the mansion was Lita's bargaining chip in their pending divorce."

Sullivan bumbled and fumbled through his opening remarks. "Simply because I was getting a divorce in no way cancel my feelings for this woman. I beg your indulgence in as much as this is probably going to be a bit on the tedious side, but I'm sure you all appreciate this case is important.

"The loss of a child is the worst thing that can ever happen to a parent. But although I was only a mere husband, losing your wife violently is the worst thing that can ever happen to a husband. We all know the resources the government has—the FBI, the Atlanta Police Department, the GBI and the Palm Beach County State Attorney's Office. If there was any way I was truly responsible for Lita's death, I would not be standing before you."

Brad Moores remembers the grandstanding. "At one point we were having a conference up at the bench. He was very loud. He obviously wanted the jury to hear what he was saying, and so I asked the judge to tell him to shut up. The judge said, 'Mr. Sullivan, you are getting a bit loud.' We continue having this argument and he starts raising his voice again, so I said, 'Judge, would you please advise Mr. Sullivan to lower his voice?' I'm standing right next to him and he gives me this look of fury and I thought, 'Whoa!' And he's just a little wiry guy."

Sullivan's complete lack of expertise was a drawback from the start, but it was apparent that he had bitten off much more than he could chew when Todd Letcher took the stand on February 16. He told the jury he had been working on the murder investigation for three years. Sullivan was a man so obsessed with his third wife that he'd filled his diaries with accounts of her, he said. He had notes about her before they were married, when she was dating someone else. The journal showed how he had kept tabs on her every movement. Letcher read from one entry in which Sullivan had written that Suki turned down a date with him saying she had a headache, and had spent the night with another man. "In a sense, at one point he was stalking her," said Letcher, who surmised that it was this unhealthy infatuation for Suki, coupled with his mounting money troubles, that had led to Lita's death. When his financial outlook became bleak, Jim Sullivan doubted he could hang on to his expensive young lover.

When the authorities searched his home and talked to him, Sullivan showed no regret about Lita's murder, said Letcher. He had not gone to her funeral, sent flowers or called her bereft parents. Although they had been married for ten years, there was practically no mention of her in his diaries, not even of her birthday. Once again, and with devastating logic, Letcher walked the jury through the phone calls between the three hired guns in Atlanta and the mansion in Palm Beach, the botched first attempt to kill Lita and Sullivan's calls to Marvin Marable and Bob Christenson. He ended by referring to the diary entry Sullivan had made after celebrating his wife's death: it had been such joyous news, he had broken out the champagne.

For more than five hours, Sullivan tried in vain to rattle the veteran FBI man; he could not even get him to admit that the murder was unsolved, a line of questioning that backfired as Letcher shot back: "All other suspects have been eliminated after thorough investigation. *You* are still the prime suspect."

Sullivan again tried to blame the murder on drugs. Had the investigators checked to see if Lita's death had been caused by a drug deal gone awry or Mafia hit? Letcher confirmed that they'd followed up on both leads, which, he pointed out, had come from Sullivan himself. They had led nowhere, as had his suggestions that Lita had been killed in a robbery attempt or by the suitor who had slammed his car into her garage in a drunken rage. "I found nothing to indicate that he had any motive to kill Lita," Letcher told him drily.

More damage was inflicted by Robert Ingram, of the

Georgia Bureau of Investigation. He described the interview he'd conducted with Sullivan while Feds were crawling all over the oceanside mansion. Sullivan was nervous and afraid throughout and gave deceptive and evasive answers to his questions. When Sullivan had tried to put him on the spot by demanding where his wife's killers were in the two days before she was murdered, Ingram fired back, "You can answer that better than I."

The highlight of the trial came when, finally, Lita's parents got their chance to confront their former son-in-law. JoAnn wept throughout Bob Christenson's video-taped interview, in which he described the awful sight that had met his eyes when he pushed open Lita's door. Elegant in a dark suit and white blouse, with large pearl earrings peeping out from below her neatly groomed hair, a starfish pin on the shoulder of her jacket, JoAnn slowly took the stand. Gently, David Boone asked her to describe her daughter. Holding up baby pictures of Lita, she sobbed again as she talked of the vivacious young woman who had been her oldest child, of her compassion, her friendliness and her trusting nature. She told of the memorial service; everyone was there—except for the man she had loved.

"Did James Sullivan ever come to your house or to the memorial service?" asked Boone.

"No."

"Did he ever send flowers, JoAnn?"

"No."

"Did he send a card, JoAnn?"

"No. We never heard from James Sullivan during this period. We did hear from his former wife and his children. We heard from Catherine. She called, and his children called, they called almost every day. They sent flowers. One of his daughters sent us a poem she had written about Lita, but I have yet to hear from Lita's husband, James Sullivan," she testified.

JoAnn was followed by Emory, who painfully recalled the daughter who had been the apple of his eye. "I know this is difficult for all of us," Sullivan began as he rose to cross-examine him. Emory cut him short. "I don't think you do," he snapped.

He fought for control of his emotions when Sullivan then shifted his line of questioning, insinuating that Emory had profited from Lita's death. "Lita took out a two hundred and fifty thousand dollar life insurance policy and named you as a beneficiary. How much did you receive?" he asked. "I don't remember," replied Emory coldly. "She took out the insurance policy because she was traveling abroad, and since she was then separated from her husband, she named Mrs. McClinton and myself as the beneficiaries."

Lita's parents never got to hear James Sullivan grilled by their lawyers. Once again, he hid behind the Fifth Amendment.

Sullivan's defense was over in ten minutes. He portrayed himself as a victim, this time of lawyer Lubin, who had not subpoenaed any witnesses before he had been fired; moreover, the court had stymied his own efforts to produce people who would have testified on his behalf.

He read from two transcripts that he maintained proved his innocence. The first was a deposition of Suki, the other was the deposition given by a private investigator he had hired to dig up dirt on Lita. The statements backed his argument that he had nothing to fear from Lita, so why would he have her killed?

"I have been the prime suspect in her murder since it

happened, while the real killer goes undetected." He also knocked the McClintons' attorneys: "The lawsuit was filed because of greedy lawyers, and a jury award will not bring the dead back to life. Turning it into an exercise over money, pitting victim against victim, is to disfigure Lita's memory," he wound up sanctimoniously.

In closing, David Boone made it simple: "James Sullivan stood to make one million dollars the day he had his wife killed, by not going through with the divorce. He also wanted to marry Suki," said Boone. "He had a juvenile fixation about her, which was here in black and white, in little lines of tiny, tiny writing," he said as he waved the diaries at the jury box. "He had caviar and champagne with his mistress, ladies and gentlemen, six days after he had his wife killed."

In his summing up, Brad Moores pounded away at the "coincidental" phone calls. "The call that was made to the mansion some forty minutes after Lita was murdered. What are the chances of Mr. Sullivan getting this one call?" he asked. "How many phones do you think there are in Florida and Georgia?"

FIFTEEN

Where's the money?

Three hours after the jurors trooped out to begin their deliberations, they were back in the courtroom. As Judge Cohen asked the jury foreman to deliver the verdict, JoAnn clutched Emory's hand. They bowed their heads, then raised their eyes heavenward as they heard the foreman say that Jim Sullivan had done it. Citing clear and convincing evidence, the panel of six awarded Lita's estate $3 million for her life, $500,000 for her terror and $500,000 in punitive damages.

Her grateful parents smiled through their tears. It was seven years and thirty-eight days since Lita had died. They hugged Brad Moores, David Boone and Pat McKenna, who was also in the courtroom to see justice done. "The purpose of suing him was to deprive him of his resources," says JoAnn. "It was worth enduring the indignity of being questioned by him and facing his arrogance."

A grim-faced Sullivan gathered up his notebooks and immediately moaned that he did not know how he would pay the $4 million. David Boone shrugged off Sullivan's plea of poverty. "He's reckoned to be worth about five million. Where did the dough go?"

Boone says that Sullivan ignored what he considered was sound advice. "After the trial, I looked at Mr. Sullivan and I said, 'You ought to sit down'—and I told his lawyers this, too—'You ought to sit down and try to resolve this with us, because as long as this is an open file in our office, we will continue to stir the pot.' "

The McClintons may have won the battle, but they had not won the war. While it was reassuring to hear a jury pronounce against him, they vowed they would not rest until Sullivan was found guilty by a criminal court. "The jury spoke, and we hope the Fulton County District Attorney's Office is listening," JoAnn told *The Atlanta Journal-Constitution.* "I really believe in the Old Testament, an eye for an eye, a tooth for a tooth," she said. "The eye for an eye this time means Jim will go to jail. The system *must* put Jim away at some point."

"We hope it might persuade the Georgia authorities to reopen the case. We think there is a good chance of it with this jury's verdict," added Brad Moores. But the only word out of Atlanta was that the case was still under investigation.

Less than two weeks after being found responsible for Lita's death, and despite the great show he had made of representing himself at his trial, Sullivan was back in court begging for a new hearing. He had been denied proper representation, he bleated. His high-priced legal team had dropped the case against his wishes. Citing lawyer–client privilege, Richard Lubin and Thomas Gano said nothing. Judge Cohen ordered a hearing for May 25.

Sullivan's new self-created image as a cash-strapped victim did not sit well with Moores and Boone. His plea of poverty sent up red flags, and Pat McKenna began to track down Sullivan's assets. There were troubling hints that he had no intention of ever paying up and that he had taken steps to stash his fortune in some offshore account. Brad Moores feared that wringing the money out of Sullivan might not be easy.

A month later, the man who claimed he did not have a dime to pay his old lawyers was shopping for new counsel. He lit on Roderick McDonald of Gilbride, Heller, & Brown, who immediately asked for a delay so he could familiarize himself with his case. The McClintons' attorneys cried foul. This was just another delaying tactic by Sullivan to keep them from collecting the judgment. What really concerned them was that his house arrest would be completed by December. "After that point, Mr. Sullivan doesn't have any ties to the community and can leave the country," protested Richard Kupfer. He asked the judge to post a $4 million bond. But the judge ruled that Sullivan had had years to hide his assets, another month was going to make no difference. He set a new hearing date for June 29. Next day, he denied Sullivan's motion for a new trial.

During the summer the McClintons' lawyers made several attempts to question Sullivan about his wealth. Once again he ducked and dived; he failed to turn up at one court-ordered deposition, and arrived at the next with a lawyer in tow. Finally Brad Moores had him where he wanted him, across a table in his office.

But once again, Sullivan repeated his Fifth Amendment mantra like a broken record. After taking the oath, Sullivan reached into his shirt pocket and whipped out a card which read, "I assert my right to remain silent as granted by the Florida and the United States Constitution and respectfully refuse to answer the question." For thirty minutes, Brad Moores lobbed question after question at him. "Do you have a car? Do you have a telephone at home? How much money do you have with you today?" To each one, Sullivan took the Fifth. "It was like a game to him," says Moores.

McKenna remembers running into Sullivan that December. "It was after we got our verdict. I share office space in the same ugly orange building with his lawyer. Sullivan was a cheap bastard—he used to drop into Lubin's office and make free copies of everything. I used to ask Lubin, 'Why do you let him do that?' But I was civil with him. He knew I was on the other side. At one point Lubin had asked me to work on the case, but I told him, 'I can't. I'm with the McClintons.'

"We were at the office Christmas party and I had my sixteen-year-old daughter with me. I was sitting with her when I looked up and saw Sullivan standing in the doorway. He was as welcome as a turd in a bowl of fruit punch. I couldn't believe he had the cheek to come to the Christmas party.

"I thought of the McClintons, who didn't have their daughter with them, and how they must feel. This cheap bastard had her killed, and all to save money. He had enough to make a divorce settlement and move on with his life. He had plenty of money. Instead he had her killed and put her family through hell."

McKenna bumped into Sullivan again a few weeks later. "One morning I got into the elevator and he was standing there. He started jabbing his finger in my face. 'Why did you sic these guys [Moores and Boone] on me? You're the guy that did that.' He said it like he was half-joking. We got off on the second floor. There's a balcony on that floor, and I got him by his collar, jammed him up against the balcony wall and said, 'Don't ever fucking poke your finger in my face again. If you do, I'll drop you over this balcony.'"

No matter how much he stalled and hid, it was clear even to Sullivan that he was going to have to pay up. He was also sick and tired of court battles, especially since lately his luck had turned and judgments were no longer going his way. He had also soured on Florida, where socially, he had become a pariah. What he needed was another fresh start, miles away from the town where his name had become synonymous with murder. Since selling the Palm Beach mansion, Sullivan had led a life of downward-spiraling luxury. There were no opening nights to dress up for, no politicians lobbying for his support and no more council committees hankering for his input. He had first moved to The Sanctuary in Boca Raton; a year later he downsized again, into digs at another gated complex, Mariner Village in Boynton Beach, where homes started at a much more affordable $158,000. At Christmas 1995, he relocated to a small rented condo in Belamar House, where he settled into the anonymous routine of a middle-aged retiree, with Coco as his only companion.

The perky little dog was a constant reminder of Suki, and despite all that had happened in the years since their divorce, he could not get her out of his mind. Hyun Sun Moon remembers him seeking her out at the 45th Street

Flea Market in West Palm Beach where she had a stall. "One day Mr. Sullivan stopped by and said he was going to give me a Korean book that had belonged to Suki. He came by later with it and told me he missed Suki and that he still loved her. I think he really did love her. I think it was Suki who wanted to leave. When I knew her, she never talked about him to me."

His old neighbor in Palm Beach also felt that Sullivan had been badly burned by Suki. "One day he dropped in on me out of the blue. He sat in my kitchen and cried—he had had some brandy—there were six or seven people present and we were sitting [in] my kitchen and he was crying. He said, 'I really thought she loved me. I was so positive she loved me. I can't believe what's happened.' Maybe it was the booze, they say the truth comes out when you've had too much to drink, but I felt sorry for him, I really did. I think she gave him a real bad time."

For the next few years he lived quietly, blending in with the community, shopping at the Publix store in a nearby strip mall. But all the while, he was laying plans to beat a hasty retreat.

While the civil trial was still in progress, Sullivan had arranged to transfer $3.3 million to a secret bank account in Liechtenstein, the pocket-sized European principality squeezed between Switzerland and Austria. At 62 square miles in area, and with a population of just 28,000, it is no bigger than the average American suburb. But in banking circles, the tiny speck of land is a giant: it is the third richest country in the world and a tax haven for billionaires, especially those with something to hide.

Incredibly, Sullivan's legal luck held just one more time. On September 13, 1995, Florida's fourth District

Court of Appeals tossed out the wrongful death verdict: the McClintons had indeed filed their suit too late. The court said it made its ruling reluctantly and added that it was asking the Florida Supreme Court to consider extending the statue of limitations. Sullivan was triumphant. The decision brought howls of protest from civil law experts and victims' groups, who maintained it rewarded perpetrators who connived to delay and obsfucate their part in a crime.

The McCintons kept silent. At every bump on the long road to win justice for their slain daughter, they retained their dignity and never lost their faith that one day they would succeed. "They are just remarkable people, they truly believed in letting the system work," says Brad Moores. "During the federal indictment I had gone along to the court to watch some of the proceedings and I was sitting over in a corner of the courtroom. Emory was there and Sullivan was there. During one recess, Sullivan walked right by him and gave him a jab with his elbow. Sullivan is a wiry little guy and Emory is 6'3" or 6'4". He could have put Sullivan through that wall if he'd wanted to, but he just turned and looked at him. That was okay. That's Emory."

But with Sullivan keeping a low profile, the McClintons raised theirs. All they could do was to keep up the heat. In April 1998, along with Moores and David Boone, they appeared on the tabloid show *Extra*. Watching at her home in Texas was Belinda Trahan. She was not paying much attention until a picture of James Sullivan flashed across the screen. She listened as he was described as the millionaire who'd been accused of killing his wife on the eve of a costly divorce. It was not a new story to Belinda; she already knew all about it.

Then Lita's parents were right there on her TV set,

pleading for help in bringing their daughter's killer to justice. They looked so gentle, so dignified despite their grief, that guilt and remorse began to tug at Belinda's conscience. No matter the consequences, she knew she could not keep silent any longer. She had lived with this secret for more than a decade, keeping it from her husband and family, afraid that the information she harbored could harm her—or worse, hurt someone she loved—and worried that they would perhaps think less of her for the company she once kept. No longer, she told herself, as she picked up the phone and called her attorney, Ed Lieck.

"I have something to tell you," she began. Ten years before, she had been a waitress dating a long-distance trucker named Phillip Anthony (Tony) Harwood. One night they were driving on a North Florida highway when Tony had pulled off the road and into a parking lot in front of a diner. Belinda had complained; she was tired and ready to curl up in the bunk at the back of the driver's cab, but Tony said he had to meet someone.

She was sitting in a booth when a man she now recognized as James Sullivan slipped into the seat beside her. She described him as being short and wiry with graying reddish hair and he had a Yankee accent. His eyes burned with intensity. While the two men talked, she had sipped a soda, wishing they would hurry up and finish so she could go back to sleep. She remembered him talking about bumping off his wife and giving Tony a wad of rolled-up bills.

Ed Lieck called David Boone and recounted Belinda's story. Boone immediately called Brad Moores. "At the end of the *Extra* clip, either Brad or myself stood up and looked at the camera and said: 'There is a reward and there are some people out there who have knowledge, someone please come forward and speak the truth,'" remembers Boone. "And apparently, when Belinda saw that, she broke down and called. I think she was feeling terribly guilty—our purpose was to tell people that this was a real-live family who had this unresolved, horrible issue, and if anyone out there has knowledge, the right thing is to come forward."

"We got a call from a lawyer in Texas who said that he represented a woman who had information about Sullivan's involvement in the crime," says Boone. "Belinda was there when Tony Harwood was paid the money by Sullivan in a diner somewhere in the northern part of the state, but she was scared of Tony Harwood and scared of the ramifications on her current life, and you can't blame her for that. We tried to make it as pleasant as possible for her to come and tell the truth. We got the Georgia Bureau of Investigation involved, and its agents checked out her story every which way, and from that, they were able to get an indictment against Harwood."

Having gotten his money out of the country safely four years before, Sullivan decided he might also need a place to hide, away from the long arm of American justice. Early in 1998, he found what he was looking for in Costa Rica. Just before he slipped out of Florida, Malcolm and Ilona Balfour had bumped into him stocking up on supplies. "It was in April, just before he disappeared, and he was in the Costco store in Lantana. It was his cart that made me look at him twice," says Malcolm. "It was piled up with all sorts of stuff—cans of food and stuff for outside. Tents and things. I had never seen a shopping cart loaded with so much stuff in my life. It crossed my mind then that he must be going away, and for a long time."

Sullivan had found a hideaway in Herradura at the beach resort of Faro Escondido, where he had plunked $240,000 down on a simple home on a bluff high above an azure blue cove. The stucco house had a living/dining area, a small open-plan kitchen, a laundry room and a guest bathroom on the main floor, with three bedrooms, two baths upstairs, and a loft. The bedrooms all had balconies that faced the sea and there was a covered terrace at ground level overlooking a tiny garden. It was part of a complex built around a clubhouse with two pools, tennis courts, and an all-purpose sports court. Again he had chosen carefully. Faro Escondido is a community of beach homes occupied for a few weeks of the year. Few of the owners lived there year round.

While Sullivan was settling into his new tropical digs, the Georgia investigators went to Texas to meet with Belinda. According to *The Atlanta Journal-Constitution*, they persuaded her to reel in Tony Harwood. They coached her on what to say to him to make him implicate himself in the shooting, and put a bug on her home phone. Over the next few weeks, she and Harwood exchanged several calls during which she got him to talk about that night in the diner.

On April 19, Police Major Mickey Lloyd, Deputy D.A. John Cross and Inspector Bob Ingram of the GBI knocked on the door of Harwood's home in Albemarle, North Carolina. Local cops had already arrived at his house to make the arrest, but Harwood insisted he would only tell his story to the Feds. According to the paper, he calmly smoked and drank coffee as investigators from the various agencies, the APD, the GBI and the Fulton County District Attorney's Office, pressured him to turn state's evidence and rat out his accomplices, especially James Sullivan.

"First one on the bus gets a deal," he was reportedly told. "You have the opportunity to help yourself." For the next three hours, Harwood unburdened himself on video. He admitted to buying the flowers, but denied he was the shooter.

He said he had met Sullivan while working for the moving company that had carried his belongings from Macon to Palm Beach in 1983. Three years later, out of the blue, Sullivan had shown up and told him he wanted to get rid of his wife. Harwood said he had been paid $25,000 and described how he and an accomplice had gone to the flower shop, then picked up the gunman and driven to the Slaton Drive townhouse, where they'd circled the block while the shooter killed her. After picking up the triggerman, they headed to the rest stop, where Harwood called Sullivan. "I told him, 'Merry Christmas.' "

On April 20, after being charged with felony murder, the 52-year-old trucker was taken to Fulton County Jail. A look at his record puzzled investigators. He had a juvenile rap sheet and had done seven years for car theft, breaking and entering and larceny, according to the North Carolina Department of Corrections. Twice he had tried to escape from jail, in 1970 and 1971, and fell foul of prison rules twelve times during his stretch. But although he had been a petty criminal, he was, in the eyes of the Albemarle sheriff, "no desperado capable of murder."

In fact, since those early brushes with the law, Harwood had been straight for thirty years. He still lived in the small mill town forty miles north of Charlotte where he had been raised, worked as a handyman and drove trucks for a living. According to the *Journal*, in his spare time he puttered around his yard, restoring classic Fords. In 1990, he had married and found religion. With his wife, Donice, and their two kids, he was a regular at church.

Understandably, the McClintons were cautiously hopeful about this latest development.

What puzzled the investigators was that Harwood's name had never surfaced anywhere in the twelve years that had passed since Lita's murder. The police knew nothing about him until Belinda Trahan called her lawyer. A Georgia Bureau of Investigation spokesman said that further charges would soon be brought against others connected to the killing.

The statement that more arrests were imminent sent reporters scurrying back to Florida, but when they arrived at Sullivan's address in Boynton Beach, they discovered he was gone. And when the cops tried to pick him up, he had vanished into thin air. His escape was infuriating to Lita's family and friends, who believed that it might have been prevented if the Atlanta authorities had played their cards closer to their chests. "Fulton County District Attorney Paul Howard went public with the information before Sullivan was in custody," says Brad Moores. "He was allowed to get away." JoAnn thought of what she had been told years before, that Mr. Sullivan looks like such a nice man. "That's why when the warrant was put out for his arrest, the authorities called his attorney to have him turn himself in."

In fact, Howard might as well have sent Sullivan an airline pass. He held a press conference at which he revealed that Harwood was claiming that Sullivan had hired him to kill Lita. "We are asking Mr. Sullivan that he please turn himself in immediately to the Atlanta Police Department," he said. "He can either do that through his attorney, or he can come to us directly."

Sullivan declined the invitation. Two weeks after Harwood's arrest, the cops were no nearer to tracking him down. Howard admitted that he'd heard rumors that Sullivan had fled to Costa Rica, which, if true, would prove to be an enormous headache. The Central American country has no extradition agreement with the United States.

Quincy, Massachusetts, police paid a call on Sullivan's 83-year-old mother, Caroline, at her modest retirement home in Wollaston, Massachusetts. She said she had flown down to Costa Rica for a ten-day visit with her son at his latest seaside paradise, and spoke to him frequently by phone. He had given her address as his last U.S. residence. She admitted he had called her just days before the cops showed up on her doorstep, but refused to divulge his phone number.

On Saturday, April 25, Sullivan's lawyer, Don Samuels, said that Sullivan would turn himself in, probably the next day. "He's got an awful lot of faith in the legal process at this point." Samuel's partner, Ed Garland, issued a statement denying that he had tipped Sullivan off about his imminent arrest, adding that, despite what Samuels had said, "There has been no communication with Mr. Sullivan. And there is no information to indicate that Mr. Sullivan is aware of the warrant."

The following Wednesday, the FBI issued a warrant for unlawful flight to avoid prosecution. The Georgia bureau had called in the Feds to help expand the search outside their jurisdiction and abroad. Again, Samuels reportedly declared that his client would do the right thing. "I don't know exactly when, but I will probably be talking to him in the next day or so. Will he turn himself in? Absolutely, but that's a prediction, like the [Atlanta] Braves are going to win. He's been exonerated repeatedly, and he's looking forward to being exonerated again."

SIXTEEN
Wanted

The rules had changed. James Sullivan was no longer just a millionaire suspect hiding behind an army of highly paid lawyers who kept him one step ahead of justice by throwing so much muck around that it inevitably muddied the waters and engendered an atmosphere of reasonable doubt. He was now an accused murderer on the lam; his days of grinning smugly in *The Shiny Sheet* were over. Now the glowering mug shot on his FBI WANTED poster showed an aging, gaunt-looking felon in prison scrubs.

The FBI's bank robbery and fugitive squad promised to hunt Sullivan down to every last corner of the nation. Investigators were assured by their bosses in Atlanta that he would be extradited from any location in the United States, no matter the cost.

On May 26, 1998, a grand jury indicted Sullivan and Tony Harwood on charges of murder, felony murder, aggravated assault and burglary. Despite his protestations that his only role in the killing was to buy the roses, Harwood was named as the man who pulled the trigger. No mention was made of Thomas Henley, Clinton Botts or Marvin Marable.

"We know that there were three people involved, because three people checked into Howard Johnson's, two were at the florist's," says Brad Moores. "The police did profiles of the men at the flower shop and neither of them fit the profile of the shooter who Lita's neighbors saw running away. His composite looks a lot like Tony Harwood, by the way."

Meanwhile, Fulton County D.A., Paul Howard, confirmed sightings of Sullivan in Costa Rica and said he would attempt to have him repatriated. Instead, he found out that Sullivan was as slippery as he was wealthy. He had fled to Panama City where he blew his cover by getting in touch with his mother, then hopped on a flight to Caracas, Venezuela, before vanishing into thin air. At any rate, the investigators had no idea where he had gone. "He has now left Panama," Howard told *The Atlanta Journal-Constitution*, adding that he was now looking at Thailand as a possible destination for Sullivan. "We know he has a penchant for Asian women, considering his last wife was Asian," Howard said. "I think he would go to a country where some people might be influenced by the money he is able to throw around. He would stick out like a sore thumb."

The attorneys who were trying to recover the $4.6 million they had won for the McClintons were also keeping tabs on Sullivan's travels. "In Costa Rica he lived the life of Riley," said David Boone. "But whatever life he's been having, and regardless of his money, he has to have been living in fear."

In actual fact, far from being afraid, Sullivan had thrived amongst the friendly Costa Ricans. There was no doubt he meant this to be a permanent residence; he shipped boxes of files and antiques to his new hideaway, surrounding himself with favorite pieces including a tall dresser, an oval dining table and his desk. He claimed they were worth around $30,000, even though they had been damaged by the salty air. The rest he stored in a warehouse in San Jose, and, true to his anal nature, he kept a log of every item.

"My wife didn't think much of the antiques," says Mike Guinn, a retired policeman from Calgary, Alberta, in Canada, who spent winters in Costa Rica and who, with his wife, Lyse, knew Sullivan well. "I remember, Lyse coming back from his place one day and saying, 'Jim's so proud of that old stuff. I think it's worthless. I would sling the lot on the back of a truck and take it to the dump, if I were him.' But he did have an amazing wine collection. It was valued at $15,000, and I remember he had trouble getting it through customs. He built a climate-controlled room to keep the racks of bottles in peak condition.

"We had picnics on the beach and he would bring the wine. I remember on one occasion he opened a bottle saying, 'This cost $1,000.' He was usually alone, but occasionally he did have an Asian woman called Nana with him. Lyse thought he was a really nice fellow— like her, he drank all day. But I never liked him, he was a bullshitter and a braggart and a womanizer. One time he was over, we had Nana Mouskouri tapes playing on the stereo. Jim began spouting off about how he had spent a month in Greece and had an affair with her. I remember thinking, 'What a load of rubbish!' "

French Canadian Lyse shared Sullivan's appreciation of fine wine—too well, says Guinn. "Jim was in our house all the time. When he lived upon the hill, he couldn't have a phone. They tried putting lines in, but the jungle ate them up. He would come to our place to make calls. At the end of the month we would tote up what he owed, and he paid up. He talked about his wife Catherine, and about the Korean one, but he never mentioned Lita. I guess he wouldn't—he knew I was a cop. He also talked about his mother all the time, how he felt responsible for her, how he had to visit her, etc. I thought he was in love with his mother."

What offended Guinn even more than his plying the alcoholic Lyse with booze, was Sullivan's fixation on two young sisters who hung out at the same beach. "The older sister was fourteen or fifteen, and beautiful," he remembers. "Her younger sister was thirteen, and even prettier. She was well developed for her age, with a thirty-six or thirty-eight bust, and Sullivan chased her all the time. I didn't think much of that."

For months he blended in with the friendly beach community, says a former Faro Escondido resident who is too scared of retribution to reveal her identity. "The people are lovely, peaceful and kind, the country is unsophisticated and charming. One third of the nation is preserved as national parks; it is a beautiful place to live. There is no army, there is free health and education."

She remembers meeting Sullivan at a couple of parties. "But to be truthful, he didn't pique my interest. He talked about being Irish Catholic and going to school in Boston. He said he sold his wholesale liquor distributorship in Atlanta, and he had lived in Thailand for a period of time. But Jim did have a lovely wine collection and shared his libations with us that day. I saw him at several social events, but never with a woman, except for once, at the pool, when I did see an Asian woman accompanying him."

Contrary to what the investigators believe, it was probably not the scrutiny of the U.S. authorities that prompted Sullivan to take flight; he had done his homework and felt untouchable in a country that rarely extradites anyone. He was already gone when the Costa Rican police began asking questions about him in February after Lyse Guinn was found dead at her home with her head bashed in. She had often taken care of his dog when he was away, but on this occasion, at the last moment, Sullivan had called another couple he knew to ask if he could leave Coco with them. He was supposedly out of town when Lyse died.

When he returned, the dog sitters told him about Lyse adding that the police thought she had been murdered. It was as if they had never mentioned it. He totally ignored what they had just said. His reaction to his friend's tragic death left them dumbfounded.

The textbook first suspect was, of course, her husband, Mike Guinn. He had flown to Canada the day Lyse was found, but swore she was alive when he left, and he had a watertight alibi. He cried at her funeral, which the local cops doubtless took to be a further sign of his innocence.

When the results of the autopsy came back, she was said to have died of internal bleeding, from a tumor that had burst, no doubt as a result of her years of drinking, says her husband. The wound on her head had been put down to a fall. "I went to the house. Friends tried to stop me, but I told them, 'I've been a cop for twenty-five years and a homicide detective for eight of those, I can handle anything I might find.'" But even Guinn was unprepared for the amount of blood. "It was everywhere, all over the house," he remembers. "Lyse had a huge gash on her forehead. I looked around and for the life of me, I could not see what she hit her head on to have opened this huge wound, to lose so much blood and to cause it to be splattered all over the place."

He became increasingly suspicious when he learned that Sullivan had fled. "Lyse died on the fourteenth or fifteenth of February; on the sixteenth or seventeenth, Sullivan asked a young woman who occasionally worked for him, Patsiana Ulata, to drive him to Panama City. When he got there, he told Patsiana, and the girlfriend she brought along with her, that he was going to stay on for a few days and said they should take the car back to Costa Rica. He disappeared. I began to wonder, did Lyse overhear something when he was using our phone?" With Mike Guinn asking questions, Sullivan apparently decided not to wait for the local cops to take another look at the accused murderer in their midst.

Guinn knew nothing about Sullivan's past until the following December when he was at a New Year's party with friends. "We ran out of wine and I said, 'I'll just run over to Jim Sullivan's house and get a bottle.' There was this silence and everyone looked at me. 'Haven't you heard?' they asked.

"That's when I talked to the Atlanta cops and told them all I knew. I told them that they would find Sullivan in Thailand. I knew that's where he would go. He talked about the place all the time, going on about how beautiful the women were, how easy they were and how everything was so cheap."

According to Guinn, he also told investigators that Sullivan boasted about having a friend in the prosecutor's office in Atlanta. "I never understood how Sullivan knew they were coming for him," he says. "The guy I spoke with told me when he took out the arrest warrant, it was a sealed warrant. The only people who would have known about it were the prosecutor, the FBI and the judge. His lawyers wouldn't have known anything about it. Yet he was tipped off. He told me he was convinced Sullivan had not only killed his wife, but Uncle Frank and possibly others.

He also says he told the Atlanta investigator to check his phone records. "See who he called from my house. Maybe you will uncover who helped him with his financial transactions and who was the mole in the prosecutor's office."

Meanwhile, Lita's parents were celebrating a major victory. The Florida Supreme Court, which had reluctantly overthrown the wrongful death verdict on the grounds that the statute of limitations had expired, reversed itself on November 24, 1999, in a 5–1 decision. Brad Moores explains what caused the judges to change their minds.

"When we got our verdict in February of 1994, the Fourth District Court of Appeals said, 'Well, I think the plaintiff is wrong about the statute of limitations issue.' Ordinarily, we have a two-year statute of limitations. We used to have an exception to that in a wrongful death case; where the wrongdoer fraudulently concealed his involvement, the victim had until such times as they could reasonably find out about his involvement.

"Well, that's really not what that means, so we are going to throw out this verdict, but we think a great injustice is being performed here, and we are going to ask the Florida Supreme Court to take a look at it.' Our argument was, 'That *is* the law." You shouldn't let someone hide just because that person is clever. That means victims can't do anything about it.

"Our fallback position, which really should have been our primary position, was that it doesn't matter what Florida's wrongful death statute says, because the murder took place in Georgia, and Georgia has a provision for fraudulent concealment, and so you ought to make your decision based on Georgia law. They said, 'Oh, you're right. This is a Georgia law question, so we are reinstating the verdict.' "

By the time the Millennium arrived, Sullivan's mug shot was featured on the Georgia Bureau of Investigation's Web site along with fourteen other so-called felons, including Eric Rudolph, wanted for Atlanta's Centennial Olympic Park bombing. At the request of the U.S. Department of Justice, the Voice of America joined the search with an international radio appeal for information and also posted Sullivan's mug shot on its site. The V.O.A. broadcast said Sullivan was believed to be in Latin America or Thailand and asked anyone with information to call the nearest American Embassy or the Georgia police. It also reported that Tony Harwood had confessed to taking $25,000 from Sullivan to kill his wife. Harwood, who had been locked up without bail in Fulton County Jail since his arrest, had more on his mind than international notoriety. District Attorney Paul Howard announced he would be seeking the death penalty.

The investigators were looking at Asia, and Thailand in particular, since hearing that, despite the fact that he was wanted for murder, Sullivan had a new girlfriend, Thai-born Chongwattana Sricharoenmuang, the wife of retired Palm Beach basketball coach Howard Maxwell Reynolds, who she had married on January 12, 1994. Struggling with the spelling of her unusual name, the baffled clerk listed the new Mrs. Reynolds as the former

Chongwattan A. Chardensrimuang. Hyun and Hiro Sun Moon bumped into Sullivan and his new girlfriend shopping in a Lantana supermarket shortly before he fled the country.

While he was on the move, the "ham and cheese house" was sold again; the home Sullivan had sold for $3.2 million in 1991 had been bought by Michigan businessman Charles Becker for $13 million—in cash.

Every day, the McClintons waited for news. Every holiday that rolled around, and which they had to get through without Lita, was difficult for them. Not being able to put her unsolved murder to rest began to take its toll. "We are the last to know about any progress in the case," Emory griped as alleged sightings of their former son-in-law failed to lead to his arrest.

"We were determined to get Jim Sullivan," says JoAnn. "When we heard he had fled, we were very upset. We kept the case alive, we continually called the FBI, the GBI and the Fulton Country District Attorney's Office. The GBI have just been excellent. We have a long-standing record with these agencies, if we didn't hear from them for a while, Emory and I made regular trips to the office. The FBI don't tell you anything, but after you know a person for a while you can tell little things by their body language."

GBI agent Bob Ingram tried to console them. Yes, their former son-in-law was not behind bars, but his life was far from rosy. He told *The Atlanta Journal-Constitution*: "Every fugitive I have ever interviewed said they got tired of looking over their shoulder every time they got up and moved around. It's not a way to live; it's freedom without being free. When Sullivan is caught, I think he'll fold like an accordion."

January 2002 kicked off with two developments.

The first was the advertisement the FBI took out in the classified section of the January 14 edition of *USA Today*, two days short of the fifteenth anniversary of Lita's death. It showed a scowling Sullivan underneath the headline WANTED FOR MURDER. "This case is alive and well," said agent Mark Giuliano, adding that the paper had a healthy international circulation.

Hoping that a hefty payday might loosen a few more tongues, the McClintons announced that they would increase the reward money to $500,000 for anyone who could bring Sullivan in. The country was in a very different mood since the feel-good era when their former son-in-law had fled. America was reeling from the 9/11 attack on New York's World Trade Center and security was at a premium. David Boone, for one, hoped that the federal government's new focus on the financial maneuvers of terrorists and criminals might lead them to Sullivan's secret bank accounts.

While they were eyeing Thailand as being his next refuge, the investigators were tipped off that Sullivan was in Ireland, a development as troubling as it was confusing. He had applied for an Irish passport on August 8, 1994, six months after the McClintons prevailed in the wrongful death case. The lawyer who handled the paperwork reportedly urged the Irish Consulate in New York to hurry it up, since his client "would be traveling extensively in the near future."

It was no sudden burst of Celtic pride that had motivated Sullivan to seek citizenship of the Emerald Isle, even though he claimed an Irish chieftain as an ancestor, and his grandparents had emigrated from County Donegal. Like all European Union nations, Ireland has no death penalty and therefore, it would hardly be likely to extradite him if he were ever hunted down. Better to be sent to jail in Ireland than to face a needle in Georgia.

Reports then filtered out of London that Sullivan had spent time in a suburb of Belfast. A taxi driver told the Royal Ulster Constabulary that he had ferried Sullivan around on a guided tour of the city's trouble spots. The cabbie said he had picked him up and dropped him off at a house in the suburb of Jordanstown near the University of Ulster, but when the Irish police went to the address the hack had given, it seems that Sullivan had once again disappeared.

While Sullivan was supposedly visiting his roots, Harwood was being offered a deal by the Fulton County district attorney: they would take the death penalty off the table in exchange for his testimony against Sullivan, he was told. If he agreed, Harwood would receive a 20-year sentence. He turned it down.

The McClintons were in court as his lawyer, Tom West, asked for a speedy trial, claiming that his client was convinced he would be acquitted. Then, in a more realistic vein, he added that Harwood had refused to accept 20 years in return for his testimony because he hoped to wring out a better deal. JoAnn and Emory had steeled themselves to attend the hearing, hoping to send a message to the fiend cops said had killed Lita; they would see him burn in hell.

In July, the district attorney had another meeting with Tony Harwood, hoping to persuade him to testify against Sullivan. After six hours of fruitless wrangling, Harwood hung tough; he would not cop a plea. The following morning, a trial date was set by Superior Court Judge T. Jackson Bedford for February 5; it would be a capital case.

By the end of August, court papers filed by West claimed that Harwood was an accomplice, not the triggerman, in the death of Lita Sullivan. He said that Harwood had met with the actual hit man before the murder, drove the killer to and from Lita's Buckhead townhouse, and had called Sullivan at his Palm Beach mansion from the rest stop to tell him the job was done. It was bad, he agreed, but not bad enough to warrant the death penalty.

Investigators next turned their attention to what role, if any, Chongwattana Reynolds had played in helping her lover flee. They believed she was taking care of his financial affairs; they had discovered she had sent flowers to his elderly mother. Her marriage to Howard Reynolds was dissolved on September 14, 2000. The divorce was amicable, with neither party looking for alimony, since the two had come to an extraordinarily civil financial agreement. Yet oddly, there still seemed to be contact between her and her former husband. For one thing, Reynolds made trips to Thailand.

Despite Bob Ingram's dire prediction that living on the lam is a recipe for paranoia, for nearly four years, Sullivan enjoyed a life of enviable ease. He had landed in Thailand on June 16, 1998, using his new Irish passport to obtain a retiree residency visa, and grew so secure in his new hideaway, he put his name on his door.

He had bought a $128,000 oceanside hotel–condominium in the idyllic resort of Cha-am. He would have preferred the privacy of a detached house, but foreigners are prohibited from buying single-family homes. But since most of the complex was owned by people who worked in Bangkok and used their condos only on weekends or for vacations, it was a perfect place to lie low. Every month 50,000 to 60,000 bahts ($1,200 to $1,440) dropped into his Thai bank account. In a country where the monthly income of its most affluent citizens is 27,514 bahts, or $650, and the average income is Bt 13,418 ($320), his monthly stipend allowed him to live like a king.

Sprawled out on the balcony of his spacious second-floor apartment, Sullivan looked like any other wealthy ex-pat enjoying a self-imposed exile from his native country. Yet he rarely ate out at any of the wonderful restaurants that ring the seaside town, and holidays were spent holed up in his unit with his lover—Christmas was a dismal affair as they feasted alone on a turkey provided by the hotel chef. Apparently age had not mellowed his frugal streak. "He's stingy," Chongwattana was heard complaining to the hotel workers. Like all his other women, a life of penury was not what she had bargained for when she took up with the liquor millionaire.

Chongwattana had been working as a waitress at the King and I Thai restaurant in Lake Worth when she'd met Jim Sullivan, and lived with her husband in a West Palm Beach condo where neighbors knew her as Nana. When she quit her job, she reportedly told her boss that she was moving to Thailand with Howard Reynolds. She made frequent trips to America, but always alone. She claimed to have owned a restaurant back home, which she'd sold.

The manager of the complex, Sompob Prasrakee, said Sullivan kept to himself, befriended no one, and had a nasty temper. The only time he spoke up was to complain about noise. And Chongwattana was just as bad, given to barking at the help.

The resort consisted of one tower block and two three-story buildings. The couple lived in the low-rise block, which had three floors, twelve apartments in all. Sullivan's unit had two bedrooms with adjoining bathrooms, a large open-plan living and dining area and a separate kitchen with Thai/Chinese-style furniture. He had two reclining wooden chairs on the balcony where he and Nana sat in the evening sharing a cigar. "He would say that one of his luxuries was a fine cigar after dinner," remembers Jane Podd, a former British government worker who was his next-door neighbor.

Despite his wariness of strangers, Sullivan took a liking to Jane. They had bumped into each other at the lagoon-shaped swimming pool where Sullivan would bask daily, despite having told his probation supervisor in Palm Beach that he had skin cancer.

He had regular checks on his skin at a hospital in Bangkok," says Jane. With his coloring he was at extra risk, he was very freckly.

"He would turn up at the pool about 2:30 P.M. in a bathrobe and swimming trunks, with one plastic container of cashew nuts and another containing a mystery drink which I never did like to ask about. There we would sit for two or three hours, occasionally swimming and discussing world affairs. This was part of his routine every day and so became part of mine, too."

Sullivan confided details about his life to Jane. "He talked about his own upbringing," she says, "but he didn't say much about his children, which I always found strange. I just thought that they must have taken his wife's side when he divorced. He told me his daughter was blind, but a brilliant horsewoman. He said his wife was a doctor, but all the time I was under the impression that this was a recent divorce, and no other women were mentioned at all. He mentioned briefly that he had lived in Costa Rica. He said he had been vice-president or some other honcho at Seagram's and had interests in lots of big companies.

"He played tennis some afternoons. If he could get a doubles match going, he was delighted. Sometimes the chef at Springfield played with him and anyone else who he could muster. He loved to be in the company of anyone who he thought was important or wealthy. He was so impressed when he got to meet the mayor of Cha-am and talked about him as if they had become bosom pals.

"He was on his own almost every night and spent most of his time reading, from what I could gather. He followed the financial markets closely; he always talked about the stock market. He occasionally talked about films he'd watched on TV—we have a satellite TV station here in Thailand, U.B.C., that carries five or six movie channels, like HBO, Cinemax, etc., as well as CNN, the BBC and many sports channels. He watched a lot of CNN.

"I was curious about him even in the early days, because so many things did not add up," she says. "I used to ask him why he didn't go out in the evening, but the reply was always the same: Nana might ring, and he needed to be there. He didn't have a mobile phone, she did. He spoke about her constantly and appeared to be completely smitten with her. But she was around very infrequently; my boyfriend and I could not fathom out the relationship at all. It seemed that she was mostly either in Bangkok or America. Jim seemed to be quite okay about this, but I found it difficult to understand why she didn't spend more time with him.

"We actually thought that she must have another man tucked away and was just stringing Jim along, but now I know the circumstances, it all looks slightly different; it would explain why he didn't mind her being in the States for weeks at a time. He kept telling me she was trying to get American citizenship and some judge in Florida was helping her.

"On the rare occasions that she was around, she and Jim would appear at the pool in matching long white honeycomb cotton bathrobes they said they had bought at the hotel in Palm Beach where they met. In fact, I think they may have had a hotel logo sewn into them. He always introduced Nana as his fiancée and she wore a beautiful solitaire diamond on her engagement finger. She also was a fitness addict, very slim. I never knew how old she was, but I thought about forty and in pretty good shape. We always knew when she was back because our bedroom wall adjoined theirs, and the soundproofing was not good! I have to say that it all sounded very hot stuff—or else she was a very good actress!"

Jane says she never saw any visitors, apart from Nana's daughter, Tam, in the six months they were neighbors. Jim rarely accepted invitations to go anywhere. "We did ask him if he played golf and he said he had played at Augusta once and carded a seventy-five and, after that, he never had the enthusiasm to play the game again—too easy! We did have a laugh about that, and it was one more reason for us to believe that he was a bullshitter, but you get a lot of men over here like that. I think that a lot of the ex-pat population have escaped from something or someone, and, because no one knows them, they can make up any stories they like and there is no one to refute what they are saying."

Jane says the two couples socialized occasionally. "We went to dinner at their apartment once. Nana cooked. As I didn't have a proper kitchen in my unit, we took them to a restaurant in Hua Hin, and the evening was pleasant until we drove home. We were all drinking wine and Nana became very talkative. We got very embarrassed because she was threatening Jim that if ever she found out that he had visited any girlie bars in Cha-am or Hua Hin, she would leave him." According to Jane, he apologized several days later and told her that Nana had had a bad experience with another former husband.

"I can also remember thinking that night that I wouldn't like to get on his wrong side, because he showed an angry and nasty side that I had never seen. He was always so gentlemanly and quiet when I was with him."

It was not long before Jane got another look at Jim's hair-trigger temper after a night of loud fireworks. "The noise went on and on, and it was very late, so I went to the reception desk," says Jane. "Jim was already there complaining very loudly. He had obviously been drinking, I remember smelling it. He was very, very angry. Anyone losing their temper in Thailand is looked at very oddly, because you lose face when you lose your temper here."

According to Jane, Sullivan was a creature of habit, rising late, then walking over to the main building to "borrow" the *Bangkok Post* and *Nation* magazine. He also read the English papers Jane's daughter sent to her and gave her American financial and news magazines in exchange.

Next he worked out for an hour. "He was always on about his 'abs,' and he jogged on the walking machine every day," she says. "He looked fairly scruffy in the mornings, on his way to the gym in an old tee-shirt and tight Lycra shorts. He would reappear hot and sweaty. I have to say that when he did go out in the evening, he always looked nice in a navy blue blazer, nice shirt and expensive-looking light-colored trousers. But there was a thing I absolutely hated, every time I looked at him— his teeth! They were an awful brown color and I used to wonder why he didn't spend some money on having them done."

When she first met him, Sullivan had no car and Jane would drive him to the nearest supermarket, which was about thirty miles away. "He never came to the restaurant at Springfield resort, he used to cook for himself when Nana wasn't around." He was very health-conscious about his eating habits and was always looking for broccoli.

Their shopping trips ended after Nana persuaded him to buy her a BMW. "I saw a second-hand one, a silvery blue convertible, advertised in the *Bangkok Post* and told him about it," says Jane. "But I never saw her drive it, he said that she was very nervous. He told me that he had done a spot of motor racing in his time, and also could fly! I used to think to myself that there was very little that he could not do."

But mostly the car sat under a plastic cover while he and Nana caught the local bus to Bangkok. "The funny thing was that although she seemed to want the best of everything, they used the non–air-conditioned buses in Bangkok which are the cheap ones only hard-up Thais ride. He never took a taxi, but perhaps that was one of his little savings, not hers."

SEVENTEEN
"Photo is G"

As he luxuriated in his last couple of months of freedom, chomping on a cigar and longing for conjugal visits from Nana, Sullivan had no clue that some of the beachcombers he idly gazed down on from his perch on his balcony were watching him back. He was blissfully unaware that mingling with the sun worshippers were plainclothes officers from the Royal Thai Police. But the FBI knew where he was, and so did the authorities back in Atlanta.

The Feds had visited the house in Costa Rica that he had left in such a hurry. After he abandoned it, the owners of the resort were concerned that the once well-maintained property had become an eyesore: the patio furniture cushions were being used as nests by pizotes—tropical raccoons that grow to nearly four feet in length and weigh up to twenty pounds—the screens were torn and its shabby appearance was attracting squatters and other unwelcome elements. With the likelihood of Sullivan ever coming back pretty much nonexistent, number 16 Faro Escondido was rented out to an American family.

By the time the FBI showed up, the family who had leased it had moved out and the house had been looted. All Sullivan's belongings, including the desk that had contained his personal correspondence, his travel books on Thailand and files that might have revealed what he had done with his fortune, were gone. There was no clue as to whether the clear-out was done at Sullivan's behest or whether the house had been ransacked by thieves. But the possessions he had stored in San Jose also disappeared.

Although the Feds were stymied in Costa Rica, they caught a break in the spring of 2002 after the unsolved murder of Lita Sullivan was featured on a May 4 episode of *America's Most Wanted*. As the story unfolded, one of Sullivan's Cha-am neighbors was paying close attention. When Sullivan's face flashed onto the screen, he had leaped up and yelled: "That's him, the American who lives at the Springfield!"

Sullivan had not the faintest inkling that the tipster had picked up the phone to the American Embassy in Bangkok, or that within days of that first sighting, the FBI had received another call from a Thai Internet surfer who had clicked on to the agency's Web site and recognized his picture with "WANTED" stamped on it.

Robert Cahill, the legal attaché for the FBI at the American Embassy in Bangkok called the local authorities. One of the country's top cops agreed to help. "Police Colonel Chachvan went down to Cha-am and located him for us, then periodic checks were made on him," says Cahill. But his agents could not just barge into Sullivan's condo and haul him off in chains.

"The FBI does not have the authority to arrest outside

the United States," he says. "It required the issuance of a provisional arrest warrant from the U.S. Department of Justice, which sent it to the consular section where it was translated into Thai before being delivered by diplomatic note to Thailand's Ministry of Foreign Affairs. There were a number of other entities involved, including the attorney general's office. So it took about two months from the time he was located until they could go and get him. He had no idea that we had found him."

Police Colonel Chachvan has worked with Cahill often. "There are many American fugitives who hide in Thailand," he says. "This case was quite special because when Bob gave us the information, he had some details of where Sullivan was hiding because the person who called the American Embassy said, 'There's a guy that looks just like him in the Springfield apartments.'

"When we went to do the surveillance, we saw him in the morning and followed him home. In the afternoon, we walked along the beach and watched his condo. We saw him and his girlfriend on the balcony. He led a pretty quiet life, very protective of himself. He tried to avoid getting arrested because he would come out in the afternoon to use the hotel pool, but only on weekdays. On the weekends he would mostly stay in his room. When the resort was crowded, he wouldn't come out."

Chachvan also took note of Chongwattana. "She usually stays with him on weekdays driving up and down to Cha-am. She has an apartment in Bangkok where she has family, her daughters go to school there."

Once he had made a positive ID of Sullivan, Chachvan's undercover cops kept tabs on him until the paperwork between the two countries had been completed. On June 30, a Thai court issued an arrest warrant. In charge of the bust was Captain Utane Noui-pin. When he pounced, his quarry had just returned from his evening stroll.

Sullivan was caught totally off guard and put up no resistance. "The captain showed Sullivan a copy of his FBI WANTED poster with his mug shot on it and asked him if he was the man in the picture. Sullivan wrote "Photo is I," and signed his name. Chongwattana claimed to have no knowledge that her lover was wanted for the murder of his wife.

"Many American fugitives offer bribes when they are caught," says Chachvan. "We, of course, turn them down. But I didn't think Sullivan did. He and the woman were very quiet and just talked to each other. When we brought him down to the Crime Suppression Division, she followed. During the search we found a lot of financial investments. He invested in Germany or somewhere, Liechtenstein, that's right, and he would communicate back and forward with the manager of this fund to give instructions about his investments. The documents were handed over to the FBI. His money is definitely not in Thailand, but he asked [his fund manager] to transfer cash to Thailand from time to time."

For Sullivan, fifteen years of keeping one step ahead of the law, four of those spent leading veteran cops on a chase across three continents, came to an unclimactic end with a knock on the door. He was taken to the Crime Suppression Division station in Bangkok to be interrogated and photographed before being transferred to the prison, where he would wait out the extradition process.

According to Captain Noui-pin, when Sullivan was

nabbed, he said he wanted to go home and fight the charges.

Three days later, dressed in khaki pants and a striped tan-and-white shirt, Sullivan appeared at Bangkok Criminal Court. As he was being led into the building, he covered his face with a green towel.

Behind him was Chongwattana, who had chosen a body-skimming white sheath strewn with large emerald green flowers, for her fiancé's first court date. Her long black hair was pulled back in a ponytail, and she was carrying a large, very expensive Louis Vuitton duffel bag. It was the real thing, bets Jane Podd. "Most of us expatriates wear the fake watches and carry the fake bags, but I doubt if Nana ever did. The Thai 'pussies' like to have the real thing."

Sullivan's police escort included Noui-pin, who laughed at the idea that the prisoner might make a break for the door. "He's an old man," he scoffed to reporters. "If he runs, I can chase him. I can run faster."

Seated at the defendants' table, the towel removed, Sullivan kept his head bowed. The once-cocky Jim Sullivan, who had blustered, charmed and cheated his way in and out of trouble for most of his life, looked cowed and defeated. He made a play for sympathy from the stern-faced judge. "I was a thousand kilometers [620 miles] away in Palm Beach, Florida, when my wife was killed," he said. "The United States is now trying to extradite me on the same charges, which is not allowed under Thai law."

Robert Cahill said Sullivan had misrepresented the facts. "This is not an issue of double jeopardy. He is just trying to confuse the court," said Cahill. An extradition hearing was scheduled for September and while the process got under way, Sullivan was locked up in conditions Amnesty International has labeled "deplorable."

That same month, Catherine Sullivan died after a long bout with cancer. Despite the struggle she had had to raise her family, she had forged a good life for herself, putting her children through school without any help from their millionaire father. "She worked for a chain of nursing homes where she had an upper level position and made some good money, and she retired at the right time in the late nineties when the economy was going well," says her friend Ann Mulligan. "She bought a place on the Cape [Cod] and after the children were grown, had a few years for herself doing odd consulting jobs. So things ended up moving on nicely for her."

At the September 16 hearing, Sullivan tried to persuade the Thai authorities not to return him to Georgia. Tired-looking and gaunt in his prison garb, his hands holding the rope attached to ankle shackles, he told the court that even though he has faith in the U.S. judicial system, he had changed his mind about going home. He would, after all, fight extradition.

His arrest and the ongoing proceedings were being monitored closely by Brad Moores. It was eleven years since he had taken on Lita's case and he was watching with interest to see which of Sullivan's army of high-priced lawyers would rush to his defense. Sullivan had not paid a nickel of the $4.6 million, that he owed Lita's estate.

"How he pays for his legal representation has got my keen attention," Moores says. "You are talking about putting on a million-dollar defense. Unless you found a very good defense lawyer who has lots of money to spend just for the notoriety—and I don't know too many lawyers that would take on something like that—it's not going to happen.

"I would have thought that any arrangement he has with Ed Garland has already been made. Don Samuels [Garland's partner] went to see him in Thailand, and I am sure he wouldn't jump on an airplane and go there unless he had [been paid a retainer of] $50,000 at least. And so I assume that, since Sullivan is already incarcerated, somebody else is helping him. But knowing how Sullivan feels about money, I doubt he would relinquish control of his money, so I think he's made arrangements to defend himself," says Moores.

He believes that through a Florida lawyer, Sullivan had transferred two sums of $9,000 into an account in the U.S., the amount obviously aimed at circumventing federal laws that require transfers of $10,000 and over to be reported by banks. This way, Sullivan could slip funds intended to mount a defense through without attracting the attention of the authorities.

Moores put Sullivan's legal team on notice that he intended to go after every penny. "I've sent Ed Garland a letter indicating to him that those funds do not belong to Sullivan and that anybody who accepts funds, whether they are for attorneys' fees or otherwise, we're going to sue him," he says.

Moores' Atlanta colleague David Boone reinforced the message. "Brad wrote to Garland, and I took him to lunch," he says. "I told him, 'Eddie, I want to be straight up with you because we are friends, but we've recorded our judgment and domesticated it in Georgia and written letters about it, and we intend to divest you of whatever fees you are going to get.'"

While the lawyers got in each other's faces, the police and the McClintons had another legitimate worry.

"We were concerned he would bribe his way out of jail. We've had big concerns about that since last June," says Boone. Their fears are justified, says Jane Podd. "I heard that Nana was at the Springfield apartment at Christmas with a man whom she introduced as her husband, and his description matched Jim's. Money can buy almost everything out here and so, there's little doubt Jim can have just about all he wants."

At the final hearing on his extradition, Sullivan was bolstered by Don Samuels and an experienced local lawyer, Puttri Kuvanonda. Ed Garland had said that they would argue the Irish card in spite of the Irish government's lack of enthusiasm for helping his client. "Mr. Sullivan is an Irish citizen, and to send him back to America would be to deny him his rights as an Irish citizen. If he is to be extradited anywhere, it should be to Ireland," he claimed.

But the Irish citizenship never really did become an issue. Neither did the death penalty, says Robert Cahill. Sullivan's case hinged on his double jeopardy claim. "It's the same event, but completely different charges," said Cahill, adding that Sullivan had run out of time.

Back in Atlanta, Sullivan's arrest had been greeted with joy. "This a great day for the family and friends of Lita Sullivan," said Fulton County D.A., Paul Howard, who announced the capture of Sullivan at a press conference attended by Emory, JoAnn and their 15-year-old grandson, Harrison McClinton Wiener, Lita's nephew. Howard said he would seek the death penalty for Sullivan.

It was also good news for Tony Harwood, still languishing in a jail cell awaiting trial, gambling that his stonewalling would force the D.A. to either let him walk free, or give him a greatly reduced sentence in exchange for his testimony. "We've all been waiting for Sullivan to be captured," said Harwood's lawyer. "He's the main bad guy in this case."

On February 12, Harwood had a change of heart. He might be venal but he was not stupid; he feared that with Sullivan in custody, the D.A. would not stick to his offer of a 20-year sentence. Time was running out for him to make his version of events stick.

Seventeen years after Lita was shot, in orange prison scrubs, his hands cuffed behind his back, his head bowed, he stood before a judge and pled guilty to a reduced charge of voluntary manslaughter. He would testify against James Sullivan. Clinton Botts, who had been named as the triggerman, but never charged, had died of cirrhosis of the liver a year before.

For the McClintons, it was an emotional roller-coaster. JoAnn could not face her daughter's killer and stayed at home, but her statement was read in court before Harwood was sentenced to 20 years, less the four he had already served. Her daughter's death had left her with a recurring and terrifying nightmare, she said. "Lita and I are talking, and then she vanishes, and I am left reaching for her, screaming her name. I have panic attacks in the middle of the night, only to awaken my husband and we cry together." Emory steeled himself to be in court to see a measure of justice done. Standing ramrod-straight, he addressed Harwood directly: "You are the scum of the earth. The only person worse than you are, is the person who paid you twenty-five pieces of silver."

The plea left Sullivan with an uphill battle to save himself from being strapped to a gurney and having a lethal syringe stuck into his veins, says David Boone. "Harwood pleaded guilty and got twenty years, and now, for Sullivan to get off this murder charge, he is going to have to prove that Harwood is a liar, Suki's a liar, Belinda Trahan is a liar. And with his jail cell confession to Paul O'Brien, he'd have to call him a liar. How coincidental is it that Mr. Sullivan has surrounded himself for the last twenty years with nothing but liars? I am very optimistic about the future of the case."

Valentine's Day 2003 brought more relief to the McClintons when the Thai judge ordered Sullivan to be returned to Georgia. Again Sullivan sought to delay what was surely his fate, to stand trial in Atlanta for the murder of Lita seventeen years ago. His Bangkok attorney immediately announced he would appeal. He lodged papers late in March and his case would be considered by Thailand's highest court. It would not be a short process; the investigators and Lita's parents braced themselves for another long wait. But the McClintons never lost faith. "After I told her I felt like we were frozen in time," said Brad Moores. "JoAnn told me not to lose heart and said, 'We are so much further ahead than we were five years ago.'"

So sure was he that a jury in Georgia would find him guilty, Sullivan chose instead to remain in the overcrowded Lard Yao Men's prison where, earlier that same week, Thailand's Mental Health Department found that 63 percent of inmates suffered mental health problems for which few were given treatment and that in a couple of Thai hell holes, 11.4 percent of prisoners showed signs of being suicidal. Moreover, 14.7 percent of all those incarcerated had personality disorders, and the system was also rife with prisoners hooked on amphetamines and alcohol.

In August 2003, Brad Moores took a gigantic step

toward tracking down Sullivan's fortune when he uncovered evidence that Sullivan had deposited between $5 and $10 million in a prestigious Swiss bank. On behalf of the McClintons, he filed a lawsuit in U.S. District Court against the Florida arm of Bank Julius Baer of Zurich & Company Ltd. and its alleged international agent, Palm Beach lawyer Michael Blank, accusing them of knowingly funneling funds to a fugitive.

"What they did was to create a bogus corporation named Nicola Resources in the British Virgin Islands," says Moores. "Nicola Resources has no business, it's a fiction, but they used it to set up a trust in Liechtenstein with a lawyer named Andreas Schurti as trustee, and then he set up the accounts in Liechtenstein and in Julius Baer of Zurich. That's how they layered it."

Once again it was Sullivan's anal attention to bookkeeping that bolstered Moores' charges. "He is a very cheap individual," he says. "He complained to Schurti about all of his charges, and Schurti sent a five- or six-page-long invoice of calls between himself and Michael Blank. Sullivan was indicted in 1998 and fled. Suddenly there are these conference calls between Sullivan, Andreas Schurti and Michael Blank in May 1998. I believe they were setting up money to be available to him when he arrived in Thailand." Moores also believes that $300,000 was sent to an Atlanta bank to finance his pricey defense when he finally faces justice there.

While waiting behind bars for the final decision on his appeal against extradition, Sullivan continued to protest his innocence, his wizened face showing the wear and tear of life on the run and the effects of his harsh surroundings. After one fight with a fellow inmate, he spent weeks in solitary confinement. "He got into several scuffles and may have lost some of those brown teeth," says Pat McKenna. The contrast between him and his loyal girlfriend could not be starker. Ironically, for the man rotting behind bars as a result of a lifetime of being a tightwad, Nana's devotion came at a price—she was the only visitor to turn up at the stinking jail in Chanel suits, and with snacks tucked into her designer tote.

In September 2003, Don Samuels announced that the couple had married, but refused to give details of the jailhouse ceremony. On Valentine's Day, her jailbird husband managed to conjure up a card in the shape of a pink heart for her. But it was hardly love that motivated Sullivan to take wife number four; it was the bid of a desperate man hoping that his new status as the husband of a Thai citizen would sway the supremes to rule in his favor. On Friday, January 23, 2004, shackled and handcuffed and in his grubby orange scrubs, he was hauled into court to hear his worst nightmare become a rubber-stamped reality. The judges had dealt him a one-way ticket to Atlanta to answer for Lita's murder, and now the stake was his life. On the way out, as he shuffled past a stunned-looking Nana, he flashed a quick thumbs down.

David Boone shakes his head over the trail of lives destroyed by Sullivan's greed. "He is such a jerk. Truly, if he had sat down and tidied up loose ends and made amends, he wouldn't be in jail right now. I think he's a very scared, very hollow individual. I like to concern myself with the reasons that people are doing what they are doing, and I think his tremendous insecurity and his lack of any personal accomplishments in life has just been driving him nuts."

Sullivan's plight brings some comfort to the McClintons. Not a day goes by when Valencia doesn't think of her big sister. "It took me years to get over her death. I would hear some tune, or someone would say something and I'd tear up. Now there's not the sadness anymore, I just miss her. I wish she could have met her nephews, she would have loved them dearly, and they would have loved her. She is not here to share each event that happens in life. Christmas is really big in this family, and the first few Christmases after she died, even with Harrison there, were very tough. I think it was having Harrison there that got my parents through. It was like we closed one door and another one opened."

JoAnn will never forgive him. "I get asked what I feel towards him and I say, 'What am I supposed to feel about him?' There is absolutely nothing Jim Sullivan could say to me. I never want to hear his voice again," she says. "I just want his plane to land at Fulton County Airport, and him taken into custody. I am not comfortable with the thought of sitting through another trial, but I will. We will be there every day. I want him to be given the death penalty. I believe in the death penalty. Lita didn't believe in it. Emory wants him to go to jail so he can suffer for the rest of his life.

"But I am the mother who nurtured Lita, saw her through her good times and bad, her prom, going to school. And I had her taken away. We tend to beatify a dead child, to make her wonderful, and of course Lita was just like everyone else.

"But she was mine."